Recession Proofing Your B
© Copyright, 2006, Frank Vickers, A
ISBN 978-0-6151-357

I0071839

Table of Contents

About this book

Recessions are not mysterious. They're periods during which the economy gets smaller. Business activity goes down. People buy less and worry more. Everybody looks for ways to save money and conserve cash. The big fear is that you won't be able to pay your bills--and that, as a result, your company will fail.

To do well in such an environment, you have to turn the situation to your advantage. That means mobilizing your entire organization to focus on cash flow and then using the cash you have to maintain and expand your customer base. This book shows you how.

1. This book is written in a non-technical style and only a basic knowledge in spreadsheets and word processing is required.

2. The approach is that of a trusted management advisor on site and assisting you in analyzing your business in a systematic manner and gradually introducing you to tools for managing, monitoring, and improving your business.

3. ***At first, avoid skipping around the book***. The presentation is based on the step method, that is, the sequence of material is designed to train you as well as help you develop new and better management habits in a systematic approach.

4. When you finish the book, you will be privy to the best tools and methods used in American business. In fact, you can use the book and the accompanying Excel and Word templates for creating you own consulting firm.

5. The templates accompanying this book were created in Microsoft® Excel 2003 and Word 2003; you may open them in any productivity software that has the correct converters. You may encounter problems in third party suites with the Visual Basic modules.

Why this book?

As a small business owner, there are many things for you to give your attention to on a daily basis. You do everything you can as well as you can, but often, you are too busy to really think about the little things and if you are doing them as well as you could be, as easily as you could be. Now there is a way to find out and fix what you maybe did not even know was broken.

This book and **Dynamic Small Business Manager**™ (**The Manager**) Excel workbook and templates serve as a combination of tools for the small business owner that focuses on increasing profits and cash flow by improving productivity, efficiency and financial proficiency through programs like Microsoft Excel and Word. The book's practical messages are understandable and can be immediately applied in your own small business.

Find out how technology can help you:

- Determine your business health.
- Perform accounting operations.
- Create daily financial and other reports.
- Manage your cash flow.
- Create a Business Plan.
- Create a Strategic plan.

Written by Frank Vickers, a small business owner with over 35 years of small business ownership and consulting experience, **Recession Proofing Your Business** tells you like it is and helps you get — and keep — your business's health on track.

Benefits of this book

Hands-on Experience:

Most small business books are a rehash of the same old boring subjects. They do not invite the reader to participate in learning by using their own business as a laboratory. Business laboratory simulation is not new; however, I challenge you to find one publication that does what this book does. This book and the accompanying Microsoft® Excel workbook *The Dynamic Small Business Manager*™ (**The Manager**) and templates are your team of interactive management trainers.

Inside knowledge:

After completing the book, you will have a grasp of how small business consultants investigate and propose solutions to problems they uncover. In short, you will be your own in-house consultant with your own set of analysis tools for going forward with your firm's success.

Simple to operate:

The Manager is a collection of linked Excel spreadsheets to one central data entry form *(The Master Data Entry spreadsheet)*. Simple to operate, you enter your raw data once and it cross-pollinates 120 worksheets for a multitude of analysis reports.

Method:

This book and its Excel spreadsheet templates divide **The Manager** into manageable worksheets and deals with each separately so that at the end of this book you will be able to understand and use the whole system to monitor and improve your business.

Unique to **The Manager** is the ability to do real time What-if analysis. Based on your actual financial information, the program can be asked what if this or that happens and it will yield the information instantly.

IMPORTANT NOTICE

Please download the supplementary Excel and Word files at:

http://www.jaxworks.com/lulu/recessionproof.htm

Chapter 1 - About Recession Proofing your Business

Recession Proofing requires a new way of business thinking. You can no longer actively plan for prosperity without simultaneously planning for a recession. A recent survey revealed that only 24% of all US businesses in 2005 had a plan for coping with a recession.

Laying off employees is usually the first option when it should be the very last. The real solution is controlling wasted resources.

Wasted resources are not always easily seen. It often goes without notice, or when noticed, it is treated as a luxury or ignored as an acceptable excess.

At present day prices, these excesses have become too costly to tolerate. Competition won't stand for them.

Business's big problem has been sharply defined. It has to pin responsibility down. In the past, most of the blame for waste has been placed on the shoulders of everyone but the top executive. It is high time someone looked the issue straight in the eye and defined the obligation with respect to waste.

If this top executive is you, you had better get busy and do something about it, and don't pass the buck. Perhaps you don't know exactly how to proceed. Well, here's a simple method. Start with yourself. That's important. Otherwise, you won't have time to follow through the program.

Keep a detailed record of your own time for a period of two weeks. Note with whom time was spent and the subjects dealt with. If you analyze this record, you will probably arrive at the same conclusion as did one very capable executive, the president of a medium-sized company. She found that 95 percent of her time was being consumed by insignificant problems of the moment that could have been handled by her subordinates. She didn't have time for more important functions of far-sighted planning and overall direction.

The alert executive needs accurate instruments of measurement for overall planning and waste reduction. Installation of adequate administrative controls is the first step in meeting both objectives.

Administrative Controls

Five major divisions of administrative controls should be considered:

1. Organization.

On the whole, management has failed to realize the value of charting its organization. Too often it is considered mere "efficiency" clap-trap or theory. No instrument of business could be more practical in its intent and accomplishment. The organization chart is a graphic diagram specifying the authority and responsibility of each management function. Thus, the organization chart clears away the fogs of uncertainty. It straightens out the bypaths and circuitous routes in the flow of authority, eliminates overlapping and cross purposes. It rids management of the common causes of dissention and jealousy.

2. Policies, Procedures and Duties.

Once the organization plan is perfected and charted, complete manuals should detail the specific duties of those charged with each function or sub-function. Procedures and policies must be set forth clearly. Thus, repetitive matters of policy and procedures are properly channeled. Many problems, previously referred to top management, become a matter of routine, completely understood and properly controlled by subordinates.

3. Costs.

Substantial wastes remain hidden in many businesses because of the absence of accurate cost finding. Lacking the basis for knowing where costs are excessive and the mechanics for keeping them under constant observation, top management has no adequate means of controlling and fixing the responsibility for excesses. A modern cost system is one of the most important "musts" in business.

4. Budgets.

One of the most severe indictments against top management is its failure to institute an adequate system of budget control. As a result, "half-baked" decisions, whims, snap judgments and intuitions bring grievous wastes reflected in profit and loss statements. How can management hope to plan accurately without knowing what is a reasonable expectation for each phase of the business and without a measurement of accomplishment?

5. Operating Reports.

With a sound system of costs and budgets, management has the basis for effective operating reports. Foremost is the monthly summary of each department which shows actual direct labor cost compared to budget allotment.

Monthly and quarterly reports contrast estimated and actual performance pertaining to production, labor, expense, buildings and equipment. Other reports cover such phases as activity; production labor and burden; idle time; production, labor, materials and manufacturing costs; estimated vs. actual costs. Effective operating reports afford management a direct control of waste.

Production Control

With controls established over administrative phases, management is in a position to consider Production Control. This major business device reduces waste in actual production time. In scheduling work, it coordinates the movement of materials with the needs of the various work centers, thus providing a smooth, steady flow.

Production control is divided into two main phases:

(I) Elements of Planning, and

(2) Mechanics of Control.

---

1. Elements of Planning

Comprehensive information is required on product analysis in order to determine what material is required. Consideration is given to the record of material, quality standards, work center capacities, operating methods and standards, and sequence of operations and scheduling. Planning also takes into consideration floor layout, transportation of material, storage and issue of material, standardization of equipment, product and operations.

2. Mechanics of Control

Through control charts, dispatching and inspection and a system of records, continuous control is exercised over the release and progress of orders, overall material movement, delays and stoppages. With these mechanisms of control properly established, a constant check is available on actual progress as compared with the planned schedule. A lag immediately shows up and the factors responsible are quickly ascertained.

Job and Methods Standardization

In top management's drive to abolish wastes, no field offers greater possibility than job and methods standardization.

Job and methods standardization is distinctly not a task for the novice. It calls for the skilled techniques of a Vicon analyst. The preliminary approach analyzes and records overall arrangements, processes, equipment and material handling from the standpoint of worker efficiency. Motion and time study is conducted of the worker's movements and methods. Consideration is given to the convenient placement of tools and parts. All of these elements are then brought together into one harmonious whole and clearly recorded in a manual.

Productivity Incentives

With a complete installation of job and methods standardization, top management has the basis for establishment of an adequate incentive plan set according to sound standards. The possibilities are so great in the reduction of waste time and the lowering of labor costs that incentives should have a place of prime importance on all top management agenda for increased profits.

Typical Situations

Let us consider the case of a certain manufacturer with 200 employees. Here were conditions typical of almost every type of manufacturing enterprise, from the small machine shop to the big shipyard. Serious bottlenecks had developed. Without regard for delivery schedule or productive limitations, one department piled up cuttings considerably in excess of the next department's capacity. With overproduction here, underproduction there, the whole operation was in utter confusion.

To bring order out of chaos, proper capacities were determined for each operation and a true balance was effected between every productive unit. Then, definite control was established over material going into manufacture and schedules were set up for all operations. A smooth flow of work resulted. Output was balanced. Rejections were reduced to a minimum.

Floor Layout

Floor layout is always a major problem in the search for lower costs, particularly so because of changing and shifting conditions. Layout should be examined from the standpoints of orderly sequence of operations and the proper placement of desks, benches, machinery or equipment within work areas or departments.

Many concerns are still trying to get along with original floor layouts, entirely inadequate for present and future requirements. The waste of time alone in such cases may amount to many times more than revision costs.

Inefficient Layout is Waste

Simplicity-Flexibility

While complete waste elimination involves intricate analysis and scientific calculation, sometimes even the simplest readjustments may accomplish unbelievable time and cost savings.

For instance, a certain tool manufacturer continued to use facilities without considering present layout needs. Between two main operations, it was necessary to grind off the burrs resulting from a drilling operation. The parts were carted several feet away to the grinding and buffing department where a bottleneck developed. The parts waited hours at a time for this minor operation. A trained analyst suggested that a small bench grinder be put within easy reach of each operator. Important time was saved and the general manager was amazed that such a simple and obvious idea had never occurred to him. The company had been doing it the other way for 18 years.

We have thought too long in terms of grouping like machines by operation rather than an arrangement by product to be produced. The answer for many businessmen lies in layout of equipment for a new type of flexible operation, so that economical revisions can be accomplished when necessary to meet changing needs.

Waste Motions

High on the list for analysis is eliminating waste motions. Authorities state that the motions of the average business worker are at least 30 percent wasted.

Much misunderstanding exists regarding time and motion study. Scientific analysis is aimed not at making the worker labor harder and faster but at increasing his output without increasing energy expended. It seeks to eliminate needless, tiring motions. Excess lifting, moving, walking, reaching and bending are not only wasteful in cost but wasteful in energy.

What should all this mean to the individual businessperson? An alert executive might well say, "Competition is going to be much keener. I'll have to get my costs down or I won't get that next contract. Guess maybe I'd better look into the whole layout. I know we're doing a lot or crisscrossing back and forth. Wonder how many man-hours we actually lose?" (And are they going to get a jolt when they really find out!)

"While we're doing it, maybe now is the time to make our facilities more adaptable. Then we could probably take on that additional work we've been considering-yes, and put ourselves in shape now to make some real profits on those new products we're talking about."

This expression represents just a start in the right process of thinking, the type of thinking urgently needed in all businesses. Such thinking is not important from the standpoint of necessity alone. It is also important from the purely selfish viewpoint of keeping in step with fast-moving business. The laggard is dropped by the wayside. The forward-looking and aggressive businessperson rises to new heights of achievement.

With few exceptions, every business can improve its productivity from 25 to 50 percent. Many can improve a great deal more by the elimination of common waste factors.

Frankly, is your business an exception?

Management's Attitude

It is the hidden wastes of space, time and energy, existing throughout a company's entire operations, which management frequently fails to understand. Diagnosing and prescribing for business complexities is not magic, conjecture or guesswork.

It is definitely not a job for the novice. It is a science, a highly skilled profession. Presidents, production managers, foremen and supervisors, when they realize that fact, welcome the professional skills of the specialist on waste elimination. Progressive management has come to realize that an outside viewpoint on the subject of management is refreshing and stimulating to internal thinking.

One of the greatest problems is the attitude of management itself. Pointing out examples of inefficiency often has the same effect as challenging a business executive's ability, honor and integrity. Here is an impenetrable barrier as long as the executive persists in refusing to face the facts. No longer can any businessperson afford to have such a shortsighted, thin-skinned attitude. It must be realized that a detached, objective viewpoint is necessary.

Another common reaction is, "Well, we've always done it this way and our profit statement has always been pretty good." That is the type of self-satisfied management which will likely find itself lost in the shuffle of an economic recession.

Still another objection of management-and a more valid one-is the fear of lost time and cost in making internal adjustments. A company may be tremendously busy on existing contracts, with production up to schedule and prospects favorable. Why disturb what seems to be a satisfactory condition? That is a fair question and deserves a straightforward answer.

In most cases, the businessperson is simply penny-wise and pound-foolish if they don't make the changes. The reward is usually far greater than the cost of revision. However, a trained specialist on waste elimination considers all angles of such a problem. An accurate estimate of the cost of any recommended changes must be made and weighed carefully against the savings to be accomplished. The waste control specialist must figure out ways and means of making a smooth change with the least disruption of present facilities.

For example, in a battery company, 25 percent of the grids coming off the line were defective due to old equipment. Because of production pressure, the production managers felt the work could not be halted on any of the machines to have them repaired. This condition had persisted for along time. A specialist on waste elimination worked out a schedule whereby a sufficient bank was built up behind each machine to tide over the period of the machine's inactivity. One by one, the machines were repaired without the slightest disruption. With other factors corrected, production jumped at once from 320 to 400 batteries per day.

Management's Responsibilities

On every hand is seen startling evidence of management's failure to recognize and to take active measures in eliminating some of the most elementary sources of waste.

Frequently, management recognizes that flaws exist but attempts to correct them by decree. Such managers may know the operating end of the business only superficially. In some cases, they are simply getting out from under their own responsibilities and shifting the blame. At any rate, they overlook the importance of the human element. They fail to obtain the interested cooperation of intelligent personnel who are most familiar with the business and its practical problems. The active interest of managers, supervisors and foremen is of prime importance in any program of waste reduction.

For example, consider the case of the company with about 250 employees whose operations for forty years had been in the manufacture of hardware items and automotive equipment.

Analysis disclosed the typical condition emphasized in this article - the failure of management to live up to its responsibilities. Management had not adjusted to meet a changing situation.

In expanding, this company had vastly increased its personnel, but no thought had been given to reducing the work of others, or consolidating jobs and departments. Many employees were doing work needed 10 years ago but no longer necessary. Duties and functions were overlapping and conflicting. While management realized that corrections were necessary, it had lacked the necessary drive and knowledge to put scientific controls into effect.

Recession Proofing from Proper Controls

The first step in a waste elimination program is an analysis of the jobs of all employees, and the elimination of all unnecessary routines and duplication of effort. Nonproductive employees were transferred to productive jobs. Administrative controls were established, together with an organization chart and complete manuals fixing authorities and responsibilities. Budget and expense controls were developed with an adequate system of operating reports. Supervisory incentives were provided to reward department managers and key people who controlled properly the expenses for which they had been made responsible. Waste and expense leakage could be determined and responsibility quickly traced. The entire organization became thoroughly cost conscious.

Immediate results-production shot up 45 percent and profits increased 117 percent! The significant result of lasting importance is this fact: the company is now in a position to control and adjust its operations to meet fluctuations and rapidly changing conditions in an economic downturn.

Attitude About Computers

The age of computers is upon us in full swing, yet the management of many medium and small-sized companies are not taking full advantage of this technology. They don't have the right attitude.

Some managers have tried computers but became involved with inadequate systems. Some have bought larger systems than they need, but still aren't getting the kinds of reports they need to make the right decisions fast enough to generate optimum profits.

Many managers have computer systems that just do not work for them - various software programs do not interface with each other. Some reports management needs just cannot be produced or for one reason or another, the system seems always to be slow or bogged down.

Is your attitude about computers helping your company - or might it be another source of hidden waste?

Moral for Top Management

Because management has been blind to the instruments of scientific measurement and control, it is little wonder that 25 to 50 percent waste of productivity continues unrealized and unchecked in the average business.

So if business is going to successfully compete against waste, it is important that management start the necessary action to determine where wastes exist, measure them, then, establish proper controls for their elimination. The blueprint for action has been provided in a self-examination below.

An Audit to Track Down Unsuspected Wastes

Here are searching questions to help you and your associates track down and control unsuspected wastes in your entire company's operations. These queries strike comprehensively at the direct and indirect factors causing production wastes of from 25 to 50 percent in most businesses. A good suggestion: Have every person in executive or managerial capacity check this list and supply written reports on all questions pertaining to their functions. Then hold a series of staff meetings for microscopic consideration.

1. Administrative Controls Over Waste

Do you have an organization chart?

(a) Prepared how long ago?

(b) Is someone responsible for keeping it up to date?

(c) Is it up to date now?

Is there a straight flow of authority in your organization setup?

(a) Any conflict or overlapping of authority?

(b) In the case of each manager, does the attendant responsibility accompany the authority granted?

Do you have a written manual for each manager detailing specific duties and responsibilities?

(a) Do such manuals include a clear delineation of all company policies and procedures which can be set forth in definite terms?

(b) Who is responsible for keeping these manuals up to date?

(c) Are they up to date now?

Do you have a well-worked out plan of understudies?

(a) For major managers?

(b) For minor managers?

(c) Any system of promotion from the ranks?

(d) Any methods of study and tests to determine eligibility for promotion?

Do you have HR records?

(a) Are they kept up to date?

(b) Are they complete enough as to quality and quantity of performance?

Do you have a complete, modern cost and accounting system?

(a) Are costs broken down for each department?

(b) For each operation or assembly?

(c) Are department heads held responsible for costs in their departments?

(d) How long since your cost and accounting system has been scientifically analyzed and brought up to date?

Are costs estimated for each department and operating unit?

(a) Is responsibility fixed for keeping actual costs within estimated costs, by each department or operating unit?

Do you have adequate operating reports to enable you to plan on a sound basis and quickly observe and check excessive costs?

(a) Monthly budget comparison covering expense, production, labor, facilities and equipment?

(b) Reports of weekly results?

(c) Reports of production activity?

(d) Production labor and burden?

(e) Reports of inventory?

(f) Do you know the costs of production; manufacturing; labor-both direct and indirect; raw materials, supplies, and small tools; inspection; departments; stores?

(g) Are you aware of dollars lost through idle machines, idle employees, machine repairs, and spoilage?

(h) Do you know the actual costs vs. estimated costs?

How long since all records and forms were checked for simplification and avoidance of duplication?

Has office arrangement been checked recently for best flow?

Do you have supervisory incentives for managers and key employees based on proper individual performance?

Is your research department adequate?

(a) For present needs?

(b) For future planning?

Have you checked employment procedure recently?

(a) Adequate tests to determine employee's best capabilities?

(b) Have you a definite training program for new employees?

(c) Are vacancies supplied by upgrading as much as possible, so as to fill lowest positions with new employees?

Any systematic record kept showing tabulated causes of employees leaving, discharged or laid off?

(a) Have you analyzed as to causes under your control?

(b) Before discharging, is any effort made to test employee's ability for other work?

Have you analyzed temporary shutdowns as to how adequate controls might have prevented them?

(a) Labor trouble (Wage Incentives)?

(b) Unbalanced production (Production and Materials Control)?

(c) Breakdowns (Preventive Maintenance)?

(d) Lack of planning (Administrative Controls)?

What was labor turnover for last year?

(a) How does it compare with comparable industries in your area?

(b) What percentage of new employees make good?

(c) Have you studied effect of labor turnover on production and cost?

Have you a wage incentive plan based on fair and sound standards?

How much waste in productive time during last year due to strikes and lockouts?

How many accidents during last year?

(a) What was the cost per year as a result of such accidents (Compensation insurance and damages awarded, wages paid during incapacity)?

(b) What percentage might have been prevented by adequate safety measures?

(c) Anyone specifically responsible for safety control? OSHA Compliances?

How adequate is the company's welfare work?

(a) Locker facilities, conveniently placed?

(b) Toilet facilities, conveniently placed?

(c) Convenient restaurant or lunch facilities?

(d) Rest rooms?

(e) Rest periods?

(f) Recreation facilities?

(g) Transportation facilities?

(h) Housing conditions?

Do you have a planned method of encouraging workers to make suggestions and rewards for adopted suggestions?

Do you have tabulated record of time lost by employees due to ill health?

(a) Cost of such lost time?

(b) Analysis of unhealthy conditions?

Are authority and responsibility placed in one person for all purchases?

(a) Maximum and minimum stocks properly determined?

(b) Closely coordinated with production schedule and accurate estimate data?

(c) Quality and grade of material properly controlled by adequate specifications?

(d) Material adequately inspected and tested on receipt?

(e) Methods of coordination and control between purchasing and planning heads as to sufficient time for obtaining materials needed?

(f) Proper follow-up on time delivery?

(g) Sufficient turnover in material?

(h) Comparative loss in "dead stock" over period of last three years?

What methods do you have for enlisting active interest and encouraging suggestions from department heads, superintendents and foremen?

2. Waste of Space

Are you utilizing facility space to best advantage?

Have you had a production layout made?

(a) How recently?

(b) Does it show in detail all departments, machines and work areas?

(c) Any backtracking or crisscrossing in flow of work?

(d) Is material storage located most strategically?

(e) Is space going to waste on pillars and upper air area which could be utilized for space-saving arrangements?

(f) What responsibility is delegated for continuing study of production layout?

(g) Have you held any staff meetings for suggestions of better production layout?

(h) How recently?

Who is responsible for production housekeeping?

(a) Are aisles kept clear?

(b) Could you use blank side of machines for banks of material, thus better utilizing space to gain accessibility and eliminating excess handling?

3. Wastes of Productive Time

Are skilled workmen required to do jobs which could be performed by less expensive labor?

(a) Grinding and sharpening of tools?

(b) Machine setups?

Are tables and charts posted conveniently for quick reference?

Is time lost deciphering poorly prepared and/or incomplete instructions?

How much productive time is lost due to:

(a) Waiting for materials?

(b) Waiting for parts?

(c) Waiting for tools?

What is the cost of idle time due to inconvenient lockers, toilets, drinking fountains, eating facilities?

Have you had a scientific time and motion study made of workers' operations?

(a) How recently?

(b) Have you increased production per man-hour this year over last?

Have individual and department performance standards been determined?

(a) On scientific and equitable basis?

Is productive time properly controlled?

Have machine capacities been determined and recorded?

(a) Are machines being worked to capacity?

(b) Could capacities of any individual machines be increased by minor adjustments or alterations?

Have you had an analysis made of grouping machines for the needs of the product to cut time between operations?

Have you charts and sheets detailing operations, sequence of operations and specifying equipment to be used?

> (a) Are alternatives indicated?

> (b) Standard instructions for each operator?

How is machine or work place capacity controlled?

Have you a well-systematized method of continuously scheduling and recording work ahead of department, work area and worker, to prevent idle time and coordinate needs in material, tools and facilities?

Is downtime of machines excessive?

Do you have a continuous recording of wasted machine time?

> (a) Any effort to sell waste machine time?

Could wasted time between operations be cut down by better transportation within production?

Have you analyzed material storage conditions, raw materials, processed material, finished parts and products which may cause wastes of time?

> (a) Better location, nearer production?

> (b) Excess handling?

> (c) Easily moved?

> (d) Properly indexed for ease of finding?

> (e) Authority fixed for issue of material?

> (f) Movement of material to work place properly timed and controlled?

Any waste of time caused by lack of inspection?

> (a) Inspection after every operation where salvage could be effected and processing time saved?

> (b) Have you adequate methods of reporting wastes of machine and man-hours applied to parts or assemblies later rejected?

Do you have adequate system of preventive maintenance?

> (a) Responsibility fixed?

> (b) Periodic inspection and repair?

> (c) Properly reported? (d) Machine and man-hours lost by breakdowns and repairs?

Adequate tool control?

> (a) Responsibility fixed?
>
> (b) Analysis for possible time loss through inadequate tool control?
>
> (c) Tool room equipped properly?
>
> (d) Tool room kept neat and orderly?
>
> (e) Tools kept properly sharpened?
>
> (f) Tools standardized?
>
> (g) Department for making tools and jigs?
>
> (h) Tools assigned to work areas properly?
>
> (I) Record of tools available?

Adequate designing and engineering department?

> (a) Are company secrets, plans and specifications of product well recorded?
>
> (b) Complete drawings of all products?
>
> (c) Complete material lists of all products?
>
> (d) Could parts going into manufacture be better standardized?
>
> (e) Could odd shapes and sizes be eliminated?
>
> (f) Products of slight variation which could be standardized as to materials and processing?
>
> (g) Better interchangeability of manufactured parts?

Could various operations be better standardized?

> (a) As to work methods?
>
> (b) Arrangement of work areas?
>
> (c) Motion sequences?

Have you analyzed new timesaving technological developments for feasible application to your manufacturing operations? -e.g., infrared lamps for drying of paint and other purposes.

What is your total estimated waste due to:

> (a) Idle time of workers?
>
> (b) Idle time of machines?
>
> (c) Deliberate curtailment of production?

(d) Other factors enumerated in this section?

4. Waste of Productive Energy

Have you had a scientific study made of workers' methods:

(a) To eliminate unnecessarily tiring motions and fatiguing routine?

(b) To provide adequate facilities to save workers' energy?

(c) To prevent excess bending and motion due to poor arrangement of material and parts boxes?

(d) To determine whether traveling belts or automatic conveyances save workers' energy?

Adequate tests for physical condition to stand tiring and fatiguing operations?

(a) To determine emotional adjustment to requirements of job?

Any dust or fumes which sap workers' energy?

Inadequate light causing strain?

Inadequate ventilation?

Insufficient rest periods?

Inharmonious working conditions?

(a) Thoughtless actions and attitudes of foremen?

Badly functioning machines or tools?

False economy in poor material?

Unnecessary noise?

Undue accident hazard?

Needless monotony?

Waste of energy on line shafts?

Are motors of right capacity for load assigned?

5. Waste of Materials

Adequate reports of scrap and rejects?

(a) Fullest possible salvage?

(b) Determination of causes?

(c) Responsibility properly fixed?

Waste in material due to improper storage?

Waste due to excessive cuts?

    (a) Oversize stock used?

Waste caused by poor workmanship?

Waste due to poor handling methods?

Waste resulting from poor condition of machines, tools and equipment?

Waste caused by overloading of machines?

Waste due to working to unnecessarily close limits and tolerances?

Waste resulting from poor training methods?

Waste due to poor inspection?

    (a) Inspectors capable?

    (b) Inspection of raw material?

    (c) Proper inspection standards?

    (d) Specifications of limits and tolerances?

Centralization of authority and responsibility over quality and workmanship?

6. Waste of Technology

Has computerization brought economies to your business which outweigh its cost?

Does your management information system deliver data you need, when you need it, to make crucial business decisions, or does it give you so much detailed information that you fail to see the problem clearly?

How many times is the same information repetitively entered into your computer for different purposes?

How much productive time is wasted by your management people avoiding a cumbersome system they do not understand?

How much productivity have you lost by failure to move forward into computerization, by "over shopping" for the right management information system?

What have you done to educate yourself about your company's information needs, analyzing the effectiveness of your management controls?

What facility has been installed to ensure your ability to track the progress of your business and measure achievement against your goals?

Are you sure that your management information system is effective at helping you control costs, eliminate waste, and increase profit performance, or is it just another waste factor in your operation?

Summary

When businesses rise above the common notion that waste is an acceptable folly, when buck-passing stops and top managers are willing to put themselves, as well as their organizations, under critical examination, the potentials for business improvement are infinite. There is almost certainly a 25 percent increase in productivity forthcoming.

It is this increased productivity that creates a Recession Proof organization that is capable of withstanding and surviving general economic downturns without resorting to quick fixes such as employee layoffs.

Potentials are not easily realized, the real problems are seldom obvious, goals are not easily set and the obstacles that lie in the way of fulfillment are formidable.

Management's self-examination is distracted by the daily drive for business. But more than that, management's view of itself is subjective, and therefore, likely to be distorted, prejudiced and inhibited in many ways.

Even if management could rise above such barriers, a concerted, professional self-appraisal is nearly impossible because few businesses have the time or the necessary specialized talents on their regular staff. Why should they?

There is no continuing need for such people in the normal running of a business. It is more economically sound to turn to a highly trained staff of professionals whose talents are complementary and whose view from outside the business can be purely objective.

Chapter 2 – The Essentials

Financial Reporting Demystified

To use financial reports most effectively, you should:

1. Look at the highlights.

2. Examine in depth those items which indicate that they require the greatest attention.

Proper analysis of a report is to a large extent a matter of comparison:

1. Comparing the elements of a report with each other,

2. Comparing elements of a report with the same elements in reports of other periods.

3. Comparing elements of a report with the same elements in reports of other businesses that are similar in size, kind of business, and general method of operation.

By these comparisons, you can determine performance, trends, and the relative position of your business. On the following pages, we are going to examine financial reports, first looking at the primary points, then following up with a detailed examination of selected specific items that warrant examination. We will, in other words, use the "exception principle" and examine those items that obviously need the greatest amount of attention.

As you read this discussion, please refer to the sample reports. If you will follow the examples shown in these sample reports, the information concerning these reports will be more meaningful to you. You should study your reports very carefully. It would be helpful to follow through with a detailed evaluation of your reports based on the material presented here. Once you are familiar with the reports, you will be able to interpret them quickly and use them efficiently. They will become an essential part of your operation, making possible higher profits and a stronger business generally.

Essential Financial Statements

In the final analysis, the performance or success of all businesses is reflected in basic financial statements, namely the *Income Statement* and *Balance Sheet*, and *Statement of Cash Flows*.

The Income Statement (sometimes called a Profit and Loss Statement or an Earnings Statement) can be thought of as a "moving picture" of your business over a specific

---

period. It shows the basic relationship between "sales" and "costs" of doing business, which are typically broken down into two additional categories-cost of merchandise and operating expenses.

The Balance Sheet may be thought of as a "snapshot" of your business at a given moment in time. It shows the relationship between "assets" in the business and "liabilities" plus "net worth." The liabilities and net worth together provide the sources of money that are needed to provide for the assets. This explains the basic equation:

$$\text{Assets} = \text{Liabilities} + \text{Net Worth.}$$

The Income Statement

Every small business should receive an Income Statement of the business for:

1) The month just ended

2) The year to date

By showing the information in this manner, it is possible to see performance in the most recent period and over a longer period so that a trend can be established.

Go to the template folder and open *Income Statement.xls.*

This figure shows the Income Statement template designed specifically for analyzing your business financial health both current and year-to-date.

Income Statement

Your Company, Inc.
For Period Ending June 30, 2005
(all numbers in $000)

	Current Month		Year to Date	
	Amount	% of Sales	Amount	% of Sales
REVENUE				
Gross Sales	$9,970	100%	$29,910	100%
COST OF SALES				
Beginning inventory	$22,950		$22,930	
Plus goods purchased / manufactured	6,355		19,065	
Total Goods Available	$29,305		$42,015	
Less ending inventory	22,698		22,698	
Other costs	106		330	
Total Cost of Goods Sold	$6,713	67.3%	$19,647	65.7%
Gross Profit (Loss)	$3,257	32.7%	$10,263	34.3%
OPERATING EXPENSES				
General/Administrative				
Salaries and wages	$1,254	12.6%	$3,762	12.6%
Employee benefits	215	2.2%	646	2.2%
Payroll taxes	3	0.0%	9	0.0%
Insurance	2	0.0%	6	0.0%
Rent	225	2.3%	675	2.3%
Utilities	108	1.1%	324	1.1%
Depreciation & amortization	125	1.3%	375	1.3%
Office supplies	1	0.0%	3	0.0%
Travel & entertainment	4	0.0%	12	0.0%
Postage	1	0.0%	3	0.0%
Equipment maintenance & rental	4	0.0%	12	0.0%
Interest	2	0.0%	6	0.0%
Furniture & equipment	1	0.0%	3	0.0%
Total General/Administrative Expenses	$1,945	19.5%	$5,836	19.5%
Total Operating Expenses	$2,319	23.3%	$7,171	24.0%
Other income	0	0.0%	0	0.0%
Net Income Before Taxes	$938	9.4%	$3,092	10.3%
Taxes on income	290	2.9%	66	0.2%
Net Income After Taxes	$678	6.8%	$2,241	7.5%
Extraordinary gain or loss	$0	0.0%	$0	0.0%
Income tax on extraordinary gain	0	0.0%	0	0.0%
NET INCOME (LOSS)	$677.60	6.8%	$2,241.09	7.5%

An Income Statement is a "moving picture" of your business over a period of time. The most basic relationship is "sales" minus all "costs."

If sales are greater than costs then there is a "profit." The simplest possible Income Statement, therefore, is as follows :

Sales	$10,000
Less: Costs	9,000
Profit	$1,000

While it would be technically possible to utilize the above format for an Income Statement, a more common format would separate two distinctly different kinds of "costs," namely "cost of goods sold" and "operating expenses." When this is done it is possible to establish a sub- total, which is known as "gross margin of profit." A more typical Income Statement, therefore, would appear as follows:

Sales	$10,000
Less: Cost of goods sold	$6,000
Gross Margin of Profit	$4,000
Less: All Operating Expenses	$3,000
Profit	$ 1,000

The reason why cost of goods sold is separated from operating expenses is that this provides an important further indicator of where profits are coming from. For example, gross margin of profit shows the way in which prices, volume, and merchandise cost come together. (Sales being, of course, the combination of prices charged on individual items of merchandise times the number of items actually sold.)

Suppose that you are dissatisfied with your level of profits. By examining performance in businesses similar to yours, you find that other businesses have about the same level of expenses. On the other hand, you find that your gross margin of profit is lower than what is typically the case. You further look at cost of goods sold and find that it is in line with similar-size businesses. This provides you with a perspective with which to analyze sales. It is possible that prices are too low on certain items, causing you to lose adequate gross margin where it is important. On the other hand, it could be the reverse, in that prices on certain items are too high, causing you to lose important volume (and consequently sales) on certain lines. These factors show how important the Income Statement is to a business.

The Income Statement is far more than a historical record. It is a vital tool that provides the basis for corrective action and profit planning. This is why a monthly Income Statement is so important.

The Income Statement example facilitates direct comparisons. Immediately you will be able to identify the basic categories of the Income Statement as mentioned above. They are presented in more detail, however, showing the components of cost of goods and of operating expenses. Note also the category "other income," which is set forth separately to show the amount of cash discounts earned on purchases and any other income that the business may derive from investments or from other sources.

When making comparisons with other businesses, you should be careful to remember that such information is reported as average or typical performance. Therefore, it is only a guide to assist in decision making. Such average data should not be regarded as "best" performance by any means. Also, when comparing to other businesses, make certain that the information is truly comparable, that is, that comparisons are made between businesses in similar lines of trade, operating essentially in the same way, and approximately the same size.

It is not realistic, for example, to compare a drug store with a jewelry store, for these businesses by nature operate with different markups, different stock turnover rates and different expense structures. Likewise, a drug store doing $100,000 a year in volume will likely have a cost of merchandise and expense structure somewhat different from one doing $500,000 a year.

An analysis of the sample Income Statement reveals a drop in net income from 7.5% year to date to 6.8% for the month. While this is a signal, it does not necessarily mean that something is wrong. Perhaps the current month is unusually slow in sales. Fixed expenses, of course, go on regardless of the level of sales, and in a low sales month such expenses would cause lower profits.

A better perspective on this situation would be revealed by looking at similar performance for the same period (both the month and the year to date) last year. Such an analysis may show that the above figures are typical for reasons such as explained above. On the other hand, if last year's figures do not show this to be the case, further analysis should be made to uncover the difficulty.

Even if net income is determined to be satisfactory, it is important to examine the Income Statement in greater detail. There are several reasons for this:

1. There may be items in either sales or expense that are peculiar to this period, and without which the profit this period would be far different. An unusually large sale to an institution or a non-recurring drop in sales, such as a freak blizzard lasting several weeks, are examples of non-recurring factors affecting net income.

2. There may be an unsatisfactory condition or trend that will not affect net profit this period but will reduce profits later. An example of this would be a build-up in inventory out of relation to sales. This could cause excessive later markdowns, which would reduce profits considerably.

Note that each element of information provided by the Income Statement is shown as a dollar amount and as a percentage of sales. The percentage figure shows the relative importance of an item and allows it to be compared to the year-to-date percentage and to an average percentage for similar businesses to determine whether it is in line.

We will now analyze the sample Income Statement to see where we stand and indicate areas for watching or improvement:

First, let's look at Net Income - both for the month at hand and year to date. We see that our net income for the month is $677.60 or 6.8% of sales. For the year to date, our net income is $2,241.09 and 7.5% of net sales. This data can be compared with

1) our own past performance for a similar period and/or

2) other similar business as revealed by published reports by trade associations or financial institutions like Dun & Bradstreet.

As mentioned earlier, net income may be in line, and still there may be unseen difficulties in the business. This is because many different variables affect profits. Unusually good performance in one category, such as low expenses, could offset poor performance in obtaining a satisfactory gross margin of profit. The result is a business not reaching its potential, for with good performance in both categories profits would be much higher still.

This is why an Income Statement needs to be analyzed in detail - to see if each of the factors that make up profit is contributing its share. In our sample Income Statement, we see that our gross profit for the month is considerably lower than the year to date figure -down to 32.7% from 34.3%. Here we have an indicator that something may be wrong. Further examination reveals that Cost of Sales is up to 67.3% for the month from 65.7% for the year to date. It may be that we have not been careful enough in our buying. An increase in cost of merchandise sold, other factors remaining the same, will always reduce gross margin of profit.

The problem could sometimes be in the "Freight In" category. It looks all right in this case; however, as "Freight In" is constant at 1.1% for the year to date and for this month. When freight does get out of line, a good hard look needs to be taken to determine what is going on. Are ship- ments being sent the wrong way, on the wrong type of carrier, or is there some other explanation?

In this case, however, merchandise cost is higher for the month than for the year to date period (66.3% versus 64.6%). It would be wise to take a look at purchase invoices to see if we are paying more for some items than is war- ranted.

A word of caution is in order at this point, however. Cost of Merchandise Sold and Cost of Sales (the former adjusted for freight in) are expressed as a percent of sales. Hence, the problem may not be one of cost of merchandise sold but one of pricing or of volume. Sales, it will be re- called. is composed of two different elements:

1) The price charged on an individual item of merchandise

2) The volume sold.

We will assume, for the moment, that the attached Income Statement represents a hypothetical retail appliance business with Sales composed of the following:

1. Sale of 10 Brand X washing machines at$175each	1.750.00
2. Sale of 10 Brand y washing machines at $225 each	2,250.00
3. Sale of 20 Brand X clothes dryers at $125 each	2,500.00
4. Sale of 5 Brand y clothes dryers at$175each	875.00
5. Sale of 20 Brand Z refrigerators at$110each	2,200.00
6. Sale of 5 Brand Z humidifiers at $79 each.	395.00
Total Sales for the Month.	$9.970.00

The above serves to illustrate sales as a function of price times volume. A change upward in price or volume will increase sales. In our example, we will assume for the moment that a close examination of our pricing reveals that our markup on Item 3, the sale of 20 Brand X clothes dryers at $125, was in error and that the price should have been $135 each. Had this error not been made, sales would have been $200 higher (20 dryers x $10 additional per dryer) and since an increase in price in this case did not affect cost of merchandise sold or cost of sales, these percentages would automatically decrease as a percent of sales. The figures would have been 64.9% for cost of merchandise sold ($6,607 ÷ $10,170 = 64.9%) and 66.0% for cost of sales ($6,713 ÷ $10,170 = 66.0%).

A change in volume would also affect sales. Let us suppose for a moment that instead of selling 10 Brand X washing machines for $175 we sold 15 units. This, of course, would increase sales by $875 ($175 x 5). In this case, however, note that the increase in sales brought about by the increase in "volume" always brings about an increase in cost of sales. This stands to reason, for you obviously can't sell something that you don't have. Assuming no change in cost of sales per unit as a result of the added volume, the percentage figures would remain the same in this latter case. Increases in volume can contribute significantly to increased profits, nevertheless. This is because the higher sales volume generates more gross margin dollars, which in turn can cover fixed expenses more advantageously and thus yield higher total profits.

This illustrates the importance of looking beyond percentage in evaluating financial statements and merchandising reports. Percentages are useful, but they don't tell the whole story. A greater appreciation of the significance of this will be apparent as you become more familiar with the reports.

In analyzing the "gross margin of profit factors" in your business, you will also find merchandise management reports to be invaluable. The Income Statement presents an overall picture of your sales, cost of sales, and inventory position. Merchandise management reports provide you with this information in detail by individual merchandise classification. There is no need, therefore, merely to guess and hope that you are right in an individual merchandise line. You now have available the data to make factual decisions - which will increase sales, increase turnover, and generate additional profits.

Before leaving the Income Statement, we must talk briefly about "operating expenses." You will note that operating expenses are itemized in detail and that each category of expense is presented in dollars and as a percent of sales. The technique with which to use this information is the same as above. tt is wise to examine each expense item, look at the dollar amount, and determine its relative importance as a percent of sales. Compare these figures with the "year-to-date" figures as a check on how things are going. In our example, note that expenses for the month are slightly lower than for the period to date and that each individual expense item is much in line. On the surface, this looks like a very healthy situation. Vigilance is necessary, however, to keep expenses in line on a month-to-month basis. If they get out of control, the results can be disastrous.

Pending the availability of figures, expenses should be compared with prior periods to ascertain any long-run trend in expenses. If a trend upward is found, corrective action can be taken at once to bring about a more favorable situation.

Do not, however, form the ironclad opinion that all expenses are bad and should be reduced. Your object in business is still to make the most dollars of profit. It may be that an increase in certain expenses, which may make your store more attractive (such as lighting) or which may promote additional sales (such as advertising), might substantially increase your volume of sales and as a result increase your net profit.

Careful records of expenses and trends provide the basis for expense budgeting. By having an accurate knowledge of each type of expense and knowing its relative percentage to sales, you can plan your expense outlays in advance based on anticipated sales. The most effective expense control is that which starts at the first of the period, not after it is too late to be effective. If sales are not up to plan, certain expenses may be adjusted accordingly.

The Balance Sheet

The Balance Sheet, as mentioned earlier, can be thought of as a "snapshot" of the financial position of your business at a given moment of time. This "snapshot" is usually taken at the end of each month.

The significance of the Balance Sheet and the financial picture that it portrays may not seem important at first glance. However, significant items, and trends in the balance sheet items, may indicate future profits or losses or serious financial problems that may be developing in your business, but which are not yet apparent by an examination of the Income Statement alone.

Balance Sheet

ASSETS					
Current Assets					
Cash	$349.02			$2,047.06	
Bank	$1,124.00			$6,116.56	
Accounts receivable	$24.99			$8,480.97	
(less doubtful accounts)	($3.00)			($412.00)	
Inventory	($252.00)			$22,698.00	
Total Current Assets		$1,243.01			$38,930.59
Prepaid insurance	($52.00)			$494.00	
Prepaid supplies	($107.00)			$909.00	
Total Prepaid expenses		($159.00)			$1,403.00
Fixed Assets					
Buildings	$0.00			$3,500.00	
(less accumulated depreciation)	($17.00)			($1,251.00)	
Plant & equipment	$118.00			$17,117.00	
(less accumulated depreciation)	($67.00)			($11,184.00)	
Furniture & fixtures	$0.00			$2,200.00	
(less accumulated depreciation)	($35.00)			($905.00)	
Total Net Fixed Assets		($1.00)			$9,477.00
TOTAL ASSETS			**$1,083.01**		**$49,810.59**
LIABILITIES					
Current Liabilities					
Accounts payable	$237.00			$3,005.00	
Short-term notes	$123.00			$2,913.00	
Current portion of long-term notes	$114.00			$2,425.27	
Interest payable	$5.00			$15.00	
Taxes payable	$10.41			$31.23	
Accrued payroll	$111.00			$333.00	
Total Current Liabilities		$600.41			$8,722.50
Long-term Liabilities					
Mortgage	($150.00)			$9,050.00	
Other long-term liabilities	($45.00)			$315.00	
Total Long-term Liabilities		($195.00)			$9,365.00
Total Liabilities			$405.41		$18,087.50
Shareholders' Equity					
Capital stock	$300.00			$300.00	
Retained earnings	$377.60			$31,423.09	
Total Shareholders' Equity		$677.60			$31,723.09
TOTAL LIABILITIES & EQUITY			**$1,083.01**		**$49,810.59**

It is for these reasons that you should familiarize yourself with the significance of items in the Balance Sheet. Recognizing the fundamental importance of the relation- ships of each of the balance sheet items will be of value in recognizing significant conditions in your business.

Recession Proofing Your Business

It is important that you understand the Balance Sheet, not only from the standpoint of interpreting it properly for your own guidance, but also because bankers and credit managers of wholesalers and manufacturers use such statements to evaluate your financial status for credit purposes. The Balance Sheet, therefore, may not only signify an unsatisfactory condition to you, but it may also have a significant effect if you are seeking additional credit.

The Balance Sheet is designed to help you detect immediately whether your financial position is improving or worsening by showing the change each month in each balance sheet item. The increases or decreases in the items in the balance sheet that you know to be significant will tell you whether you are making the progress, on which you had planned.

The Balance Sheet is divided into three major sections: "Assets," "Liabilities" and "Net Worth." Assets are what the business "owns." Liabilities are what the business "owes" to outsiders. Net worth is the net amount the business "owes," so to speak, to investors.

Assets are those things (items of wealth) that the business needs in order to be in business. In retailing, one of the most important assets is always the merchandise inventory. In many retailing businesses, another very important asset is accounts receivable, as it is customary in many lines of trade to sell a considerable amount of merchandise on credit. This means that instead of receiving cash, another asset item, the merchant receives a customer's promise to pay at a later date. Since this becomes a legal obligation by the customer, such accounts receivable items are regarded as assets.

Liabilities, as mentioned above, are the financial obligations that the business has to others. Among merchandising firms, accounts payable is typically an important item, as a large amount of merchandise is purchased from suppliers on some type of trade credit.

The Net Worth (Equity) section of the Balance Sheet portrays that portion of the business that is financed with ownership (as opposed to creditor) funds. Care should be taken not to confuse personal ownership in a business (regardless of whether the business is a corporation, partnership or proprietorship) with what the business itself owns in the form of assets. There is a considerable difference and it is particularly important to understand this in connection with double entry bookkeeping. An increase in an asset account, for example, is a "debit"; an increase is a liability or net worth account is a "credit."

Both assets and liabilities are classified as to "Current" and "Fixed." The criteria for such classifications are as follows:

- **Current Assets** are usually thought of as "cash and those assets which are reasonably expected to be realized in cash or sold or consumed during the normal operating cycle of the business." A "Normal operating cycle" in most businesses is a year or less.

- ***Current Liabilities*** are short-term obligations generally due and payable in less than one year. To liquidate current liabilities will normally require the use of current assets or the creation of other current liabilities.

- ***Fixed Assets*** are those assets which are usually not sold or liquidated in the normal business cycle, and are usually not readily converted to cash.

- ***Fixed or Long-Term Liabilities*** are those obligations due more than a year from the date of the balance sheet.

- ***The Net Worth (Equity)*** section is comprised of the capital invested in the business plus or minus the net earned surplus (or deficit), which is the sum of the profits and/or losses of the business.

With these preliminaries in mind, let us now turn to the sample balance sheet. Note that Assets are shown at the top of the page, then the Liabilities and then the Net Worth. Keeping in mind the balance sheet equation: Assets = Liabilities + Net Worth. Note that total assets are $49,810.59 which equals $49,810.59 for liabilities and net worth ($18,087.50 + $31,723.09 = $49,810.59).

Note that in addition to an itemization of all asset, liability and net worth items, the Balance Sheet shows the amount of change-increase or decrease -of each item from the preceding period. This is a particularly important feature, for with only a quick examination you can note favorable and unfavorable changes that you feel are of special interest.

An analysis of the sample balance sheet reveals that current assets have increased by $1,243.01 since the balance sheet of the prior period, for a new total of $38,930.59. Actually, the business is more "liquid" now than before, because the cash accounts are up, the accounts receivable is about the same (only an increase of $24.99 for the period), and merchandise inventory is down $252.

On the surface this looks quite favorable, at least insofar as it indicates that no violent changes took place. Of course, this assumes that significant changes were not called for. For example, if the business were going into its heavy selling season, it would be advantageous to increase inventories in order to support the higher anticipated sales.

The Prepaid Assets require just brief mention. Actually, these could be classified under current or fixed assets, depending upon accounting interpretation. In this case they are separate, however, just to show that they are of a special character. We note only a slight change downward ($159) in the prepaid asset accounts, reflecting that portion of the prepaid insurance and supplies, which were used during the period.

Turning to fixed assets, we see that no significant changes were made here. New store fixtures were purchased for $118, but this addition to fixed assets was just about cancelled out by the various depreciation allowances on office equipment, store fixtures, and delivery equipment.

An examination of the Liabilities of this business reveals that current liabilities increased altogether by $600.41. Most of this took the form of "accruals," that is, various tax obligations due to the government. Some net increase was found in accounts payable, however.

The ability of the business to meet these various current obligations can be appreciated by looking at the "current ratio" of the business. The current ratio is merely the relationship between all current assets of the business and all current liabilities. In our example, this may be expressed as follows:

Current Ratio = Total Current Assets ÷ Total Current Liabilities

= $38,930.59 ÷ $8,722.50 = 4.46

What this means is that for every dollar of current debt, the business has 4.46 dollars of current assets. In most retail businesses, a current ratio of 4.46 would be considered good indeed. In fact, it may be "too good" particularly if the company has idle cash that it is not using to any good purpose. That is not true in our example, however, as total cash on hand and in the bank is only $8, 163.62.

An examination of the Long-Term Debt in the business (sometimes referred to as fixed liabilities) shows a decrease for the period of $195 for a total of $9,365. The big item here is "notes payable to the bank." To determine the impact of this item on the balance sheet, we would have to know more about the conditions under which these notes are to be paid back. They are not "current debt:" but perhaps they are due next year. If so, this would place a severe strain on the financial structure of this business, for there does not appear to be the necessary cash to make such a payment. On the other hand, the notes may be due over a longer period of time, so that only a portion of the obligation needs to be paid at once. If this is the case, retirement of this debt does not appear to be a problem.

An examination of the Net Worth section of the balance sheet reveals an increase from the last period of $677.60. Note that this corresponds to the "net income" shown on the Income Statement, as net income has the effect of increasing net worth (unless, of course, net income is paid out to owners in the form of dividends or other distribution payments).

Relative to the specific period under consideration, the business looks highly profitable. Profits for the last three months are $2,241.09. If this is representative of the other periods in the business, net income for the year would be approximately $9,000.00 ($2,241.09 times 4.)

Compared to invested capital at the end of last year this looks favorable indeed:

$9,000.00 net income ÷ $29,482.00 invested capital = 30.5%

One word of caution relative to profitability analysis in smaller companies. Net income, remember, is what is left after cost of goods sold and all operating expenses are subtracted from sales.

Care must be taken to make certain that net income is not distorted, upward or downward, by the owner's salary as an expense item. Salaries should be commensurate with the size of the business.

Obviously, if owners pay themselves very high salaries, the net income of the business will be understated. Likewise, if very low salaries are paid, net income will be exaggerated.

Chapter 3 – The Recession Savvy Small Business Owner

When it comes to having a handle on their firm, the profile of the recession immune small business owner goes something like this:

1. They know each morning their sales and gross margins (that is, gross profit as a percentage of sales) of all of their products or services by category from the preceding day.

2. At the end of each week, they can tell you their sales and gross margin for the preceding week by product or service by type from the preceding week.

3. At the end of each month, they know the sales, cost of goods, gross profit, and gross margin on every type of product or service by category, both for that month and for the year to date.

4. They are eager to know the key historical summary information developed by their accountant each month as a check against their own tracking information, which they accumulate daily.

5. They have all of the internal and external information needed to make fast expenditure decisions on a daily basis. They simply do not feel secure at delaying decisions that might improve their business or cost them profit.

Remember, your accountant's information is historical. Even your own computerized internal accounting system can have information that is outdated, unchecked, and sluggish to retrieve for those quick, critical decisions.

Here is a eye-opener, you can do all of the steps listed above with two printed forms, a pencil, and a hand calculator. The next section explains how.

Please perform the steps in order and avoid taking short cuts.

From the template folder please open the following form templates and print them.

1. *Daily Profit Tracking and Weekly Summary.doc* and

2. *Weekly Profit Tracking and Year-to-Date Totals.doc*

Daily Profit Tracking Form

This figure shows the Daily Profit Tracking and Weekly Summary form. It is designed to give you a concrete understanding of your gross margins and their accumulated effect on your bottom line.

Daily Profit Tracking and Weekly Summary
Today's Date _____

Product Description	Sales $	Cost of Goods $	Gross Profit $	Gross Margin %
Totals				

This form is straightforward. You enter the date at the top. Then you post each item sold and the unit cost (This information should be readily available, if not; this is a good time get a handle on cost controls and vendor prices).

Using your calculator, subtract the total cost from the total sale transaction. For quantities sold of an item just multiply the number times both the sale price and the cost per item. This result is called *Gross Profit*.

Finally, divide Gross Profit by Sales. This will give you the *Gross Margin* as a percentage of sales.

Recession Proofing Your Business

Your gross margins may be doing fine with some products and customers, but the others could be dragging the average down. There are four ways to deal with this type of situation:

1. You can raise your prices.
2. You can reduce your manufacturing and/or vendor costs.
3. You can say no to low-margin business.
4. or you can find other products that you can sell at higher margins.

However, before you can make any of these decisions you must have controls in place and you cannot develop controls until you have detail financial knowledge of your business.

Tracking gross margins is the answer. Why? Because high gross margins translate into high gross profit and gross profit is the main source of the cash you will need to support yourself and build the business.

What may first appear as an exercise in futility will make all of the sense in the world after you work these forms for 90 days.

Now let us look at the second part of the Daily Profit Tracking and Weekly Summary form. This section, Weekly Summary, is for accruing your results from the daily postings. There are seven lines for posting the totals for each business day.

Profit Tracking Weekly Summary Form

This figure shows the form for accruing your results from the daily postings. Here you have seven lines to post the totals for each business day of the week.

Weekly Summary Days by Date	Sales $	Cost of Goods $	Gross Profit $	Gross Margin %
Summary Totals				

It is the totals from this summary that you will enter in the **Weekly Profit Tracking and Year-to-Date Totals.doc** form.

Weekly Profit Tracking and Year-to-Date Totals Form

This figure shows the form for posting the weekly summary numbers. This form condenses daily data into weekly data into year-to-date data.

Weekly Profit Tracking and Year-to-Date Totals
Beginning Date _____

Weeks	Dates	Sales	Cost of Goods	Gross Profit	Gross Margin
Start Week 1					
Week 2					
Week 3					
Week 4					
Week 5					
Week 6					
Week 7					
Week 8					
Week 9					
Week 10					
Week 11					
Week 12					
Week 13					
So forth to Week 52					
Year-To-Date Totals		$0.00	$0.00	$0.00	0.00%

You will see at the bottom of this form Year-to-Date totals. It is very important to keep these items up to date since it shows you the rolling gross margin percentage number.

The rolling gross margin percentage number is computed by dividing the gross margin total dollars by the sales total dollars.

> Beware that if you skip at least 90 days of doing it by hand you will lose something when you let a computer do the work.
>
> The numbers become indistinct and abstract. You lose focus of their impact and you stop absorbing them. You don't get to know them as well as you must if you're really going to be in control of your business.
>
> **There are thousands of small businesses owners that still do this process daily by hand, even though their firms do millions of dollars annually.**

If you choose to use a spreadsheet program, we have included an Excel workbook template with the two manual entry forms converted into spreadsheets.

Go to the template folder and open *DailyProfitTracking.xls.*

Daily Profit Tracking and Weekly Summary Spreadsheet

This figure shows the worksheet Daily Profit Tracking. This is where you enter your data into the cells for daily transactions. The worksheet automatically computes the weekly summary.

Workbook *DailyProfitTracking.xls* opens with the Daily Profit Tracking and Weekly Summary worksheet in view. The second worksheet Weekly Profit Tracking can be selected by the tab at the bottom of the program window. These are the spreadsheet representations of the manually entered forms explained earlier.

Instructions:

> 1. Entering data in these worksheets is straightforward. All entries in Bold Blue are replaced by your data.
>
> 2. Specific instructions are presented in comments by placing your mouse pointer over the red triangles.
>
> 3. To avoid overwriting formulae, both worksheets have simple protection, which can be easily removed: From the Standard Menu click on Tools > Protection > Unprotect sheet.

Weekly Profit Tracking and Year to Date Totals Spreadsheet

This figure is the second worksheet Weekly Profit Tracking. This is where you enter your data into the appropriate cells from the summary section on the Daily Profit Tracking worksheet.

The Weekly Profit Tracking worksheet requires you to copy each week's totals on the Daily Profit Tracking sheet and paste them to the appropriate week.

In Excel, to copy and paste numbers from one worksheet to another follow these steps:

1) Select the appropriate cell or block of cells with your mouse.
2) Press the CTRL key and tap once on the C key.
3) Go to the receiving worksheet in any workbook and click on the corresponding first cell in the destination sheet. Click on Edit > Paste Special > Click on the Values radio button > finally, click on the OK button.

The reason for choosing the Values button is that the values will be pasted without bringing forward formulas and formatting. You only need the values and not any additional information.

Alternatively, you may print the summary and manually enter the numbers at the appropriate week in the Weekly Profit Tracking worksheet.

Do this procedure at the end of each week to keep the year-to-date information current on the Weekly Profit Tracking worksheet.

Help your accountant

The dynamic business owner understands accounting and is very conversant with their accountant in all aspects of the statements received each accounting period.

Unfortunately, many small businesses rely too much on their accountant for critical information that is, by the nature of the accounting cycle, too late. It is too late because the information is historical and outdated by the time it is compiled and issued each month or quarter.

Accountants are very busy professionals and they simply cannot oversee all of their business clients in the role of a small business financial manager.

It is obligatory that you should make every effort to understand the basic ingredients of accounting. It will make the accountant's job more efficient and your financial understanding greater. The next chapter should help you understand this culture and their tools.

Chapter 4 - Kick Start the Analysis Engines

This chapter lets you hit the ground running. It is designed to introduce you to analyzing and correcting your business with a proven tool created by the author and installed in over 3,500 U.S. small businesses since 1970.

The Dynamic Small Business Manager© is the tool and it is included ***exclusively*** with this book.

But wait! Let us not get ahead of ourselves. There is only one sensible way for you to learn its use and that is step-by-step. This chapter deals with some key components treated as standalone worksheets.

Get a handle on your payroll expense

A good first step is getting a handle on your payroll expense. Go to the template folder and open *PayrollAnalysis.xls.*

This figure shows the template designed specifically for performing a payroll analysis.

Payroll Analysis

NOTE: Replace numbers that are in Bold Blue with your numbers.

Input descriptions	Results
Current Number of employees	24
Current sales annualized (weekly X 52 weeks)	$1,007,074
Prior years sales	$967,818
Current payroll annualized (weekly X 52 weeks)	$300,040
Prior year payroll	$251,849
Sales volume required	$1,153,009
Sales deficiency is	($145,935)
Gross payroll allowable	$262,064
Gross payroll burden	($37,976)
Gross payroll burden %	-15.1%
The number of excess employees on the payroll	-3.6

The logic of this analysis is simple. It has one of three results:

> 1. If your current year's sales are projected downward over last year then you will have too many employees on the payroll to generate last year's profit.
>
> In other words, the worksheet states that using the current number of employees (24) with an impending small increase in sales there will be an

excess of 3.7 employees to equal the profits earned under last year's sales at the new projected payroll.

2. If your current year's sales are projected upward over last year then you will have too few employees on the payroll to generate last year's profit.

3. If projected sales are static then no change in employee requirements will be necessary.

In this example, you will note that sales have been projected to increase from $967,818 to $1,007,074. To accommodate this sales increase additional employees will be required. Although stated in negative numbers, the last row in the template indicates a shortfall of almost 4 employees required to equal the previous year profit.

> Please note that this tool is designed to give you an indication of excess or deficiency in employee numbers based on normal business conditions. There are unique instances where an excess or deficiency in employee numbers is justified regardless of sales, i.e., plant expansions or closings respectively.

The steps for using this template are simple. First, from your financial statements capture the following information:

1. Current number of employees on the payroll,

2. Current Weekly Sales Annualized. This can be calculated by extracting from the internal accounting records,

3. Gross Sales Annualized. Add the weeks together and divided by the number weeks extracted times 52 weeks,

4. Prior Year Sales. This is taken directly from your income statement.

5. Current Payroll Annualized. This number should be all employees including total management compensation. This can be calculated by extracting each week of gross payroll. Add the weeks together and divided by the number weeks extracted. Take that number times 52 weeks.

6. Prior Year Payroll. This is taken directly from your income statement. Your accountant can guide you through extracting this information.

Finally, enter the numbers into the template at the appropriate cells.

> If the last line indicates either a positive or negative number then immediate corrective actions should be considered. Continued overstaffing will eat away at profits. The opposite is true as well – understaffing will reduce productivity thereby having a negative effect on profits.

A more comprehensive version of this tool is in *The Dynamic Small Business Manager.*

Reduce Your Employee Turnover

The dynamic small business has low employee turnover coupled with high employee morale. The contrary is also true. Therefore, it is logical to conclude that a business with generally low employee morale will have higher than normal employee turnover. Employment turnover is expensive and should be constantly monitored by management.

Go to the template folder and open *EmployeeTurnoverAnalysis.xls.*

This figure shows the Employee Turnover Analysis template designed specifically for performing the employee turnover analysis.

Employee Turnover Analysis
A serious buried cost

NOTE: Replace numbers that are in Bold Blue with your numbers.

Total present employees			25		
Less permanent employees			18		
New employees			7		
Total employed in a given year			43		
Less permanent employees			18		
New and transient employees			25		
25	people hired to fill	7	jobs.		
25	divided by	7	equals	357.14%	
Therefore the turnover rate is			36	to 1	
Training cost each employee =			$1,000		
Total employed in a given year =			43		
Total training cost =			$43,000		
Less training investment =			$18,000		
Wasted training cost =			$25,000		

© Copyright, 2005, JaxWorks, All Rights Reserved.

One of the first indications that productivity is suffering in any small business is a high velocity of new hires combined with the same pace in resignations, layoffs, and terminations.

A specialty parts manufacturer was involved in producing parts for a major manufacturer and could not understand why they were struggling to come in on budget and consequently short of the profit margin expected from the contract.

This is a warning sign to investigate the employee turnover rate. High turnover is known as a "Buried Cost". It is one of the concealed profit thieves. Unfortunately, it is often ignored and disguised as an "usual cost of doing business".

This analysis tells us several things about this business. The first red flag is the high number associated with "Total Employed in a Given Year" compared to the "Total Present Employees". If you divide the former by the latter, you get a whopping 58% ratio. Not good!

Second, the fact that 25 people had to be hired to fill 7 positions indicates a real problem in hiring practices and a deep-rooted morale problem.

The mechanics of using this template is straightforward. Using the most recently completed fiscal year; research your human resource files for the following information:

  1. Total number of present employees

  2. Total number of permanent employees

  3. Extract from your W-4 records, the total number on file

  4. Determine the average cost of training a new employee

Enter these numbers into the template at the appropriate cells.

If the last line indicates unreasonable wasted costs then immediate corrective actions should be considered. The next section entitled "Increase Employee Productivity Now!" introduces a dynamic, interactive analysis and solutions tool. It is specifically designed for performing an in-depth, in-house investigation into low productivity and high employee turnover causes.

If this very serious problem continues then you might consider help from an outside professional resource.

Increase Your Employee Productivity Now!

One of the most effective tools at your disposal is the Confidential Employee Questionnaire form and the accompanying Employee Productivity Analysis spreadsheet template.

These two tools are powerful for discovering, defining, and correcting a hefty and mostly hidden siphon of profits – low employee productivity.

1. Confidential Employee Questionnaire Form

To maintain objectivity, ask an outside person to conduct the survey, i.e., your accountant, friend, etc. Print the necessary number of forms retaining one copy to tally the results from the distributed copies. The form is completed by ownership, key people, and all permanent employees.

There are only 10 questions on the questionnaire form as shown below. They have been refined over the years and you will be amazed at the results they yield.

Go to the template folder and open *Questionnaire.doc.*

This figure shows the Employee Questionnaire Form. This form is handed out to all employees for completion and collection.

Employee Questionnaire

Please circle YES or NO to each question.
Please do not enter your name on this form.

1. Do you feel your employer is organized?	YES	NO
2. Are basic policy manuals available for review?	YES	NO
3. Are duties and responsibilities spelled out in detail?	YES	NO
4. Are personal characteristics an important factor?	YES	NO
5. Are standard operating procedures in writing?	YES	NO
6. Do you have just one boss?	YES	NO
7. Is there an organization chart posted?	YES	NO
8. Is the organization chart accurate?	YES	NO
9. Does your boss follow the organization framework?	YES	NO
10. Is the organization reviewed periodically?	YES	NO

It is important to understand the gravity of each NO answer to each of the questions. For the impact of the sample assessment, let us look at each NO answer and its consequences.

1. Do you feel your employer is organized?

A NO to this question indicates that management has failed to establish a spirit of teamwork and coordinated effort. Too much reliance has been placed upon cooperation that involves emotion rather than developing a functional and effective organization.

2. Are basic policy manuals available for review?

A NO to this question indicates that company policies are not understood by most of the employees. As a result, policies are likely to be ignored or misinterpreted, the consequences being confusion and diminished morale. Basic policies should be stated clearly and all employees notified when revisions are made.

---

3. Are duties and responsibilities spelled out in detail?

A NO to this question indicates employees, in most cases, do not have a detailed and clear understanding of the duties that have been assigned to them. The responsibilities of most job functions are not clearly defined and documented to the degree that they can be completely understood by the employees filling those job functions.

4. Are personal characteristics an important factor?

Organizational functions should be designed and executed with emphasis on the function and its relationship to other job functions. It is, at the same time, important that management consider the personal characteristics of the employee filling each job function. A NO to this question indicates that most employees feel that the "human side" of the organization has been neglected.

5. Are standard operating procedures in writing?

Standard procedures are necessary to insure that operations are executed in a controlled, consistent manner that is in accordance with the wishes of management. A NO to this question indicates standard procedures have not been thoroughly designed, installed, and documented.

Standards manuals often gather dust. One way to make sure employees trust and USE them more is when they see the Boss go to the shelf and look something up in front of them when he needs help recalling a certain way of dealing with something. This does not show weakness, it shows the importance of the manuals and it develops good habits in the workforce that the manual is there to be used as a guide.

6. Do you have just one boss?

Employees perform better when they are directed by only one supervisor. A NO to this question indicates this condition is lacking in the organization at the present. The cost of this problem cannot be ignored, as the company is vulnerable to severe losses in productivity. Morale also suffers when employees are subject to instructions, often conflicting, from two or more supervisors.

7. Is there an organization chart posted?

The relationships between job functions have not been properly defined and documented. A NO to this question indicates employees have no reference to show them how their work relates to the work of others. As a result, losses occur in both quantity and quality of work performed. These losses show up not only in employee satisfaction, but also in profits.

8. Is the organization chart accurate?

A NO to this question indicates management has failed to provide an organization chart that recognizes the actual company conditions and reflects them realistically. Communications, the chain of command, and performance all suffer. This and other symptoms of a weak organization indicate a severe limitation on the company's ability to attain its maximum potential and its maximum profits.

9. Does your boss follow the organization framework?

Most employees feel that the executives of the company display a "Do as I say, not as I do" attitude in their actions. A NO to this question indicates the executives too often show too little regard for the organization and fail to operate within its structure. This practice has profoundly negative effect on bottom line profits.

10. Is the organization reviewed periodically?

A NO to this question indicates this company has failed to make adequate periodic reviews. All companies change with time, some get better, some get worse, but all companies change. Many factors, growth, personnel executives, etc. cause changes. These changes demand that the organization be reviewed periodically and revised accordingly. Consequently, the company has become vulnerable to being put in the position of operating with an outdated and ineffective organization structure, reducing its ability to realize maximum profitability.

Go to the template folder and open

EmployeeProductivityAnalysis.xls.

This figure shows the data entry section of the spreadsheet template designed specifically for performing an Employee Productivity Analysis.

Employee Productivity Analysis

NOTE: Replace numbers that are in Bold Blue with your numbers.

Overall average of "YES" answers	73%	Enter
Enter total distributed	10	number of
Enter total returned	10	"YES"
Percent responding	100%	answers

1. Do you feel your employer is organized?	8
2. Are basic policy manuals available for review?	6
3. Are duties and responsibilities spelled out in detail?	8
4. Are personal characteristics an important factor?	7
5. Are standard operating procedures in writing?	6
6. Do you have just one boss?	7
7. Is there an organization chart posted?	8
8. Is the organization chart accurate?	8
9. Does your boss follow the organization framework?	7
10. Is the organization reviewed periodically?	8

You will be entering 12 numbers in this template.

1. Total Questionnaire Forms Distributed (Number Distributed)

2. Total Questionnaire Forms Returned (Number Returned)

---

3. The 10 numerical YES totals for each form returned.

It is imperative that the "Total Distributed" number equal the "Total Returned" number.

If this number is less than those distributed, then worksheet will shut down with error messages.

This carries a heavy penalty since it may be a reflection of serious general discontent.

This figure illustrates the spreadsheet template designed specifically for performing an Employee Productivity Analysis based on the questionnaire tabulations. This template yields an overall rating percentage. The inverse of that number will be the negative effects occurring in your workforce.

Questionnaire Results

Number distributed			10
Number returned			10

		Number	Percent
Total distributed	10	of	of
Total returned	10	YES	YES
Percent responding	100%		

	Number of YES	Percent of YES
1. Do you feel your employer is organized?	8	80%
2. Are basic policy manuals available for review?	6	60%
3. Are duties and responsibilities spelled out in detail?	8	80%
4. Are personal characteristics an important factor?	7	70%
5. Are standard operating procedures in writing?	6	60%
6. Do you have just one boss?	7	70%
7. Is there an organization chart posted?	8	80%
8. Is the organization chart accurate?	8	80%
9. Does your boss follow the organization framework?	7	70%
10. Is the organization reviewed periodically?	8	80%

OVERALL RATING............................ 73%

Your BOTTOMLINE is being affected by an employee "Negative Attitude Factor" of.............................. 27%
This factor should never be over 18%.

The results of this analysis will be utilized in the next section to further illustrate the discovery of the hidden thieves of profit.

Bring out the best in your employees

You can sense a firm's energy. The dynamics are at work in every department. Managers and employees are eager to talk about their job, the company and its prosperous future.

It is almost certain that productivity is at a high mark in an organization that has an energetic atmosphere.

Another sign that you are bringing out the best in your people: Are your customers greeted with a smile and a sense that the front-line employee is genuinely happy to be there?

A good tip here would be to add that sending friends of yours into your business periodically, if they are unknown to the employees, and get a complete report from the friend afterwards as to how the experience went from the moment he or she walked in the door until leave after making a purchase.

Make productivity a priority

Volumes have been written about productivity; however, it is not within the scope of this book to go beyond key concepts.

Productivity is a simple concept. It is the amount of output produced per unit of input.

The impact of less-than-optimal productivity can be significant. The spreadsheet template Workforce Productivity Analysis demonstrates how 30 minutes of wasted "water cooler" time can impact profit.

Your role in high productivity

The key to high productivity in a small business rests squarely on the back of Management. The accountability for both positive and negative employee behavior ultimately resides in managerial style.

Research indicates that there is no one best managerial style; instead, leadership style is a function of the situation.

Motivation is influenced by the equity an employee perceives in the reward system. An employee who believes their ratio of inputs to outcomes is different from that of their co-workers will be motivated to reduce that inequity by changing inputs or outcomes.

Managers should strive to create an organizational climate that boosts employee morale and seeks to achieve job satisfaction. Management actions speak louder than words, and those actions should encourage mature behavior among employees.

Managers must deal directly with the sources of conflict in order to reduce or eliminate its negative effects on employees and team performance.

A business that suffers from low morale manifests itself with lower-than-potential profit.

Using the example in the preceding section, let us use 73% in the next Productivity Analysis.

Workforce Productivity Analysis

Go to the template folder and open ***WorkforceProductivity.xls.***

This figure illustrates the spreadsheet template designed to analyze an additional Employee Productivity problem.

Workforce Productivity Analysis

NOTE: Replace numbers that are in **Bold Blue** with your numbers.

Date entry descriptions					Data
Your direct labor cost is….	$300,000	times	100%	=	$300,000
If we apply the productivity % from the "Employee Productivity Analysis" worksheet to your direct labor cost we get…..	$300,000	times	**73.00%**	=	$219,000
The result can be startling as to the amount of waste that is directly attributed to low productivity					$81,000
In the final analysis, an increase in productivity from the estimate to 100% would increase labor efficiency by					$81,000
This would be a direct new contribution to profit which would be………..					
Current operating profit of…………………………….					$346,647
and new operating profit of………………………….					$427,647
with an increase in profit of………………………….					$81,000
by reducing labor waste…………………………….					27.00%

This analysis tells us the business is having problems and corrective steps must be performed at once. This analysis is really an extension of the preceding section to demonstrate in profit loss the effect of lower-than-maximum productivity capacity.

You will be entering 3 numbers in this template.

  1. Direct Labor Cost.

  2. The productivity % from the "Employee Productivity Analysis" worksheet.

  3. Current operating profit.

It becomes more and more obvious that the long reaching rippling effect of low productivity factors can rob you without even feeling its affect until it is too late.

The next thief is more obvious and you see it every day. However, up until now you have not been able to measure it.

It is the cost of a one wasted and minute each day. It is the accumulation effect over a year that makes it so stealthy.

Buried Costs Analysis

Numbers do not lie! The Buried Costs Analysis is good example of exposing another small, hidden profit thief.

How many times have you observed idle employees, employees on excessive breaks, employees late for work and so forth? Nagging your mind may be the question, "I wonder what it's costing me for this unproductive time?" If you suspect this is a problem, then The Buried Costs Analysis is the tool for you.

Go to the template folder and open ***BuriedCostAnalysis.xls.***

This figure shows the spreadsheet template designed for performing a buried costs analysis.

Buried Costs Analysis

NOTE: Replace numbers that are in **Bold Blue** with your numbers.

Description	Data
Wasted time per day per employee...	30 minutes
Number of employees..	37 employees
Total wasted time in one day...	1,110 minutes
There are 36.83 productive hours per 5 day work week.	
This translates into 2210 minutes per week.	
There are 260 available work days per year.	
Current sales..	$2,010,000
Therefore the formula is: Using current payroll of.........................	$350,064
Current payroll divided by work minutes per year............................	$3.05
Wasted time per day in minutes...	1,110
Cost of wasted time per work week..	$3,381.23
Cost of wasted time per year..	$175,824
As a percent of current payroll...	50.23%
As a percent of current sales...	8.75%
If one half of the minutes were recovered and added to profit, the new profit would be......	$568,280
Instead of the current profit of..	$480,368
or an increase in profit of..	$87,912

© Copyright, 2005, JaxWorks, All Rights Reserved.

You will be entering 4 numbers:

1. The number of employees.

2. The current sales

3. The current payroll

4. The current profit

Notice the minute spinner at cell F5 that moves the minutes up or down for quick changes and experimentation. You can also directly enter minutes in the cell.

Its default setting is 30 minutes and may be excessive for your operation, however, drop the number to 10 minutes and see the impact. 10 minutes translates into $29,000 in wasted profit.

> This is a great spreadsheet to share with employees in a "team" way. Approaching them with "here is a problem that's costing us more than any of us realized, what can WE do to help reduce this?"

Internal and industry comparisons.

Previous sections have dealt with the draining of profit. We now endeavor on a more positive approach with tools that help you analyze and improve your profit while increasing your *Return on Ownership.*

> Your Return on Ownership is the sum total of all benefits you derive from the business by being the owner.

Compute your firm's optimal performance

The Optimal Performance Analysis has almost magical powers when used on a regular basis. It is a popular tool for determining the real potential of a small business. It has the ability to look with an analytical eye across 4 financial periods, preferably Years, and capture the best financial performances and then automatically create your optimal model.

The optimal model represents how your firm would appear financially if you could make everything fall into place over one magical year.

Additionally, the Optimal Performance Analysis has the ability to present an unlimited number of experimental situations to help you target problem areas and create corrective plans.

Why is this tool so popular? Above all, it is a learning tool. By gathering the necessary information and entering it into the spreadsheet, you will gain a clearer understanding of your firm's actual and potential financial health.

And, actually interacting with your Income Statements and their information will naturally amplify their importance to you and your business. In short, the perceptive small business owner/manager is always driven to control their firm's internal operating systems using all sound tools available.

> To get started using this tool you may need assistance from your accountant or bookkeeper. You will need Income Statement data from 4 financial periods, preferably Quarters or Years.

Go to the template folder and open ***OptimalPerformanceAnalysis.xls.***

This figure illustrates the large potential increase in the Return on Ownership when the best business performances of the previous 4 years are applied.

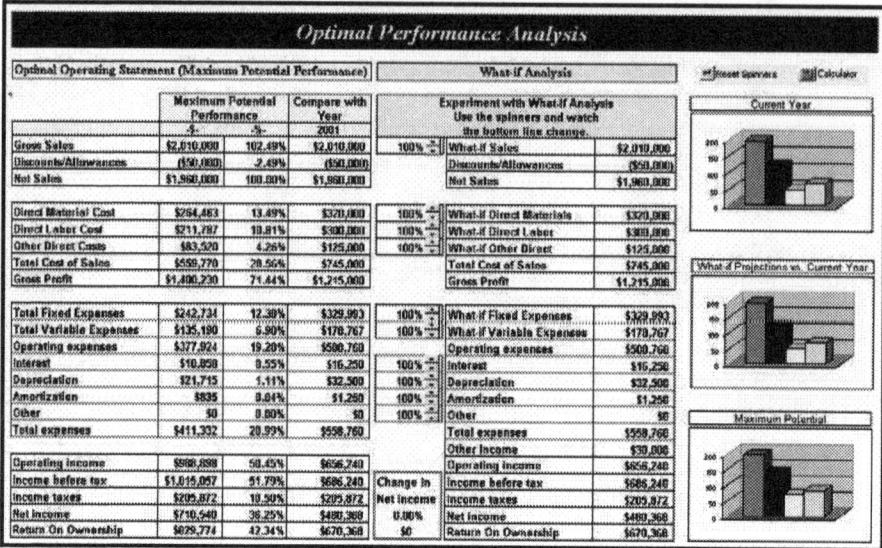

Optimal Performance Analysis

Optimal Operating Statement (Maximum Potential Performance)	Maximum Potential Performance $	%	Compare with Year 2001		What-if Analysis (Experiment with What-if Analysis — Use the spinners and watch the bottom line change.)		
Gross Sales	$2,010,000	102.49%	$2,010,000	100%	What-if Sales	$2,010,000
Discounts/Allowances	($50,000)	-2.49%	($50,000)		Discounts/Allowances	($50,000)
Net Sales	$1,960,000	100.00%	$1,960,000		Net Sales	$1,960,000
Direct Material Cost	$264,483	13.49%	$320,000	100%	What-if Direct Materials	$320,000
Direct Labor Cost	$211,787	10.81%	$300,000	100%	What-if Direct Labor	$300,000
Other Direct Costs	$83,520	4.26%	$125,000	100%	What-if Other Direct	$125,000
Total Cost of Sales	$559,770	28.56%	$745,000		Total Cost of Sales	$745,000
Gross Profit	$1,400,230	71.44%	$1,215,000		Gross Profit	$1,215,000
Total Fixed Expenses	$242,734	12.38%	$329,993	100%	What-if Fixed Expenses	$329,993
Total Variable Expenses	$135,190	6.90%	$178,767	100%	What-if Variable Expenses	$178,767
Operating expenses	$377,924	19.28%	$508,760		Operating expenses	$508,760
Interest	$10,858	0.55%	$16,250	100%	Interest	$16,250
Depreciation	$21,715	1.11%	$32,500	100%	Depreciation	$32,500
Amortization	$835	0.04%	$1,250	100%	Amortization	$1,250
Other	$0	0.00%	$0	100%	Other	$0
Total expenses	$411,332	20.99%	$558,760		Total expenses	$558,760
					Other Income	$30,000
Operating income	$988,898	50.45%	$656,240		Operating income	$656,240
Income before tax	$1,015,057	51.79%	$686,240	Change in	Income before tax	$686,240
Income taxes	$205,872	10.50%	$205,872	Net income	Income taxes	$205,872
Net income	$710,540	36.25%	$480,368	0.00%	Net income	$480,368
Return On Ownership	$829,774	42.34%	$670,368	$0	Return On Ownership	$670,368

Charts: Current Year; What-if Projections vs. Current Year; Maximum Potential.

Go to the template folder and open ***OptimalPerformanceAnalysisDetail.xls.***

This figure shows with callouts the Optimal Performance worksheet and explanations as to its operation.

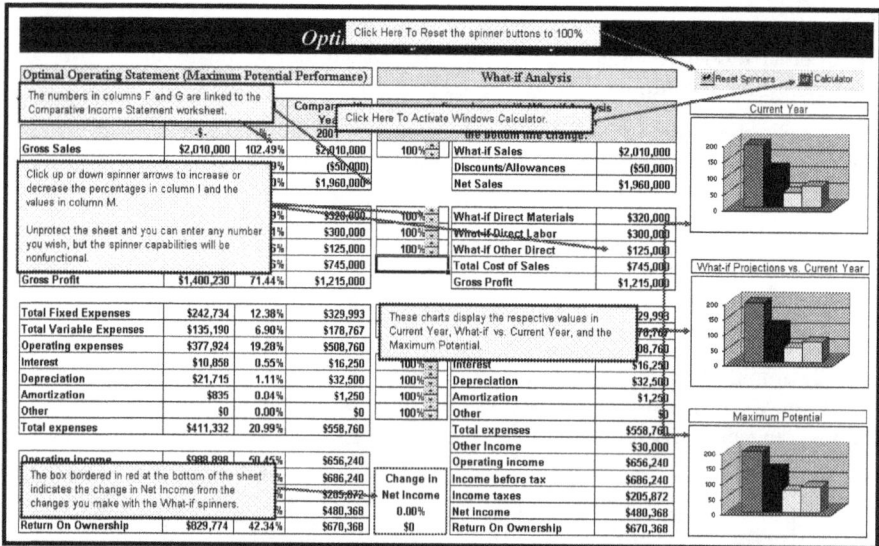

Callouts in the detail figure:
- Click Here To Reset the spinner buttons to 100%
- Click Here To Activate Windows Calculator.
- The numbers in columns F and G are linked to the Comparative Income Statement worksheet.
- Click up or down spinner arrows to increase or decrease the percentages in column I and the values in column M.
- Unprotect the sheet and you can enter any number you wish, but the spinner capabilities will be nonfunctional.
- These charts display the respective values in Current Year, What-if vs. Current Year, and the Maximum Potential.
- The box bordered in red at the bottom of the sheet indicates the change in Net Income from the changes you make with the What-if spinners.

There are 2 worksheets in this workbook:

1. Comparative Income Statement

2. Optimal Performance

Go to the Comparative Income worksheet (first tab) and replace the data that has been entered in Bold Blue with your data. You will notice red arrows by selected line items. These signify key values that must be entered.

> The data you enter in the Comparative Income sheet is instantly linked to the formulas in the Optimal Performance worksheet. This insures accuracy and reduces the data posting time for both worksheets.

The magic of this workbook takes place on the Optimal Performance worksheet.

After completing the Comparative Income Statement sheet, click the tab entitled "Optimal Performance".

> The Optimal Performance worksheet has been protected to insure key cells are not accidentally altered. To unprotect in Excel, click on Tools, Protection, and Unprotect Sheet.

On the left side of Optimal Performance worksheet is a section entitled "Potential Maximum Performance". Look down the rows on the left at the line item descriptions and values. This data is linked to the Comparative Income worksheet and has been consolidated for easier viewing and analysis.

Each line item represents the best performance, by dollar and percentage, over the 4 periods entered on the Comparative Income worksheet. The lowest expense and the highest income producing percentages have been extracted and applied.

For example, the best Operating Income percentage occurred in year 4. This percentage is then applied to the year 1 to show how much more income was available if the expense controls of year 4 had been applied.

To the immediate right of this section is the "Compare with Year" section. This section allows you a quick view your optimal potential status versus your current status.

Continuing to the right of the sheet you will see a special section for performing line item "What-if" experimentation with the percentage spinners.

A red outlined box at bottom of the sheet will instantly indicate the changes to Net Income as you experiment with the percentage spinners.

Comparative Industry Analysis

It is important for you to perform comparative analysis with your colleagues in the same business in a similar economic market. The Optimal Performance Analysis gave you a snapshot of your firm's efficiency compared to internal best performances over time. We now shift to comparing you business to outside best performances.

For example, if you are a grocery & beverage store in a town of 11,213 people, how does your business compare financially to those in a similar locale with the same demographic profile? Where do you find this information?

Almost every type of business is represented by a national trade association, which publishes detailed financial data compiled from its membership. In this instance, you would contact the National Association of Retail Grocers for comparative financial data.

Where do you stand in your industry?

Go to the template folder and open *ComparativeIndustryAnalysis.xls*.

This figure shows a spreadsheet tool that has a data base containing key financial data from 81 business types. It can with a single mouse click, instantly apply values to compare with your data.

Services - Other Business Services / Services - Publishing Services / Services - Real Estate Agents, Brokers & Managers	*Comparative Industry Analysis*						
Category	**Actual**		**Industry**		**Variance**		**Your Business vs.**
Services - Publishing Services	$	%	$	%	$	%	**Your Industry**
Total Revenue (Sales)	$2,010,000	100.00%	$2,010,000	100.00%	$0.00	0.00%	N/A
Total Expenses as % of Revenue	$1,889,400	94.00%	$1,388,910	69.10%	$500,490	24.90%	Negative Trend
Net Income to Owner as % of Revenue	$116,600	5.80%	$621,090	30.90%	($504,490)	-25.10%	Negative Trend
Detail of Expenses (as % of Revenue)							
Cost of Goods Sold	$1,995,440	99.28%	$404,010	20.10%	$1,591,430	79.18%	Negative Trend
Salaries & Wages	$108,490	5.40%	$90,450	4.50%	$18,040	0.90%	Negative Trend
Advertising	$8,040	0.40%	$30,150	1.50%	($22,110)	-1.10%	Positive Trend
Auto & Truck Expenses	$10,050	0.50%	$110,550	5.50%	($100,500)	-5.00%	Positive Trend
Depreciation	$20,100	1.00%	$54,270	2.70%	($34,170)	-1.70%	Positive Trend
Employee Benefits	$2,010	0.10%	$6,030	0.30%	($4,020)	-0.20%	Positive Trend
Home Office Business Expenses	$0	0.00%	$18,090	0.90%	$0	0.00%	Positive Trend
Insurance	$16,070	0.80%	$12,060	0.60%	$4,010	0.20%	Negative Trend
Interest Expense	$10,050	0.50%	$18,090	0.90%	($8,040)	-0.40%	Positive Trend
Legal & Professional Services	$6,030	0.30%	$16,080	0.80%	($10,050)	-0.50%	Positive Trend
Meals & Entertainment	$0	0.00%	$12,060	0.60%	$0	0.00%	Positive Trend
Office Expense	$2,010	0.10%	$44,220	2.20%	($42,210)	-2.10%	Positive Trend
Retirement Plans	$0	0.00%	$2,010	0.10%	$0	0.00%	Positive Trend
Rent - Equipment	$10,050	0.50%	$18,090	0.90%	($8,040)	-0.40%	Positive Trend
Rent - Office & Business Property	$72,310	3.60%	$36,180	1.80%	$36,130	1.80%	Negative Trend
Repairs	$12,060	0.60%	$4,020	0.20%	$8,040	0.40%	Negative Trend
Supplies	$12,060	0.60%	$30,150	1.50%	($18,090)	-0.90%	Positive Trend
Taxes - Business & Payroll	$30,150	1.50%	$16,080	0.80%	$14,070	0.70%	Negative Trend
Travel	$0	0.00%	$36,180	1.80%	$0	0.00%	Positive Trend
Utilities	$40,200	2.00%	$34,170	1.70%	$6,030	0.30%	Negative Trend
Other Expenses	$54,270	2.70%	$397,980	19.80%	($343,710)	-17.10%	Positive Trend
Total Expenses as % of Revenue	$2,409,390	119.87%	$1,388,910	69.10%	$1,020,480	50.77%	Negative Trend
					Number of Positives		14
					Number of Negatives		10

This file opens with the Comparative Industry Analysis worksheet in view. There only 2 steps required for utilizing this worksheet:

1. Enter your financial data in the cells with bold blue values.

2. In the box in the upper left hand corner, scroll to your business classification or one that is similar and click on the description.

Instantly a comparative analysis executes and you can view the results in column G. In column K is a brief rating statement for each line item.

This tool is designed for you to observe that comparing external data is important. For example, if your total expenses are much larger than the industry average then immediate action should be taken to find out why.

Standard Industrial Classification (SIC)

Go to the template folder and open *SIC.xls.*

This file opens with the SIC Comparative RMA Analysis worksheet in view.

This figure shows a spreadsheet tool that contains key financial data from 460 Standard Industrial Classification (SIC) codes. Partially automated, you can quickly rate your business using RMA Annual Statement Studies data.

SIC Comparison

	2731	Financials For	
SIC			
DESCRIPTION	PUBLISHING, OR PUBLISHING & PRINTING	The XYZ Company	Analysis
SALES	100.00	100.00	
GROSS PROFIT	52.30	61.99	Positive
OPERATING EXPENSES	46.50	28.51	Positive
OPERATING PROFIT	5.80	33.48	Positive
ALL OTHER EXPENSES	1.10	1.53	Needs Attention
EARNINGS BEFORE TAXES	4.70	35.01	Positive
CASH	7.70	10.82	Positive
ACCOUNTS RECEIVABLE	27.80	8.40	Positive
INVENTORY	31.80	9.60	Positive
ALL OTHER CURRENT ASSETS	3.40	0.02	Needs Attention
FIXED ASSETS	14.80	69.59	Positive
ALL OTHER NON-CURRENT ASSETS	14.50	0.60	Needs Attention
ACCOUNTS PAYABLE TRADE	15.80	14.40	Positive
ALL OTHER CURRENT LIABILITIES	28.30	0.38	Positive
LONG TERM DEBT	12.50	14.43	Needs Attention
ALL OTHER NON-CURRENT LIABILITIES	6.60	1.20	Positive
NETWORTH	36.70	58.79	Positive
CURRENT RATIO	2.50	1.30	Needs Attention
DEBT/WORTH	1.00	0.70	Positive
PROFIT BEFORE TAXES/TANGIBLE	0.42	0.28	Needs Attention
SALES/ASSETS	2.30	0.47	Needs Attention

First, A word about RMA and SIC codes and their use in benchmarking. The RMA Annual Statement Studies is compiled from more than 150,000 statements of commercial bank borrowers and prospects. These financial statements come directly to Risk Management Association (RMA) from member institutions, which get their data straight from the customer. This information is free for research purposes at most public libraries.

Most customers are, according to the RMA, small and medium size businesses. The data is presented by SIC (Standard Industrial Classification Code), with more recent volumes providing access via the NAICS. The Annual Statement Studies have been published for more than 80 years, making timeline analysis possible.

By becoming familiar with the RMA ratios, you can improve the financial measures of your business - before it is time to apply for a loan.

The SIC Comparative RMA Analysis worksheet is the summary analysis that compares your business against averages of 150,000 statements of commercial bank borrowers and prospects in the same SIC code.

The best way to learn about RMA ratios is to visit your local public library and read about the ratios and methodology. Most librarians are familiar with the RMA and have several back issues. If you do not know your SIC code number go to http://www.osha.gov and click on SIC Search.

Now, let us click on the Standard Industrial Codes tab and follow these instructions:

> 1) Click the "down arrow" buttons in the "SIC Codes" or "Description" headings to find your firm's SIC Code or nearest description.

> 2) Click on the appropriate selection.

> 3) With your mouse, select across the row to the last column, then click on the "Process Data" button.

> 4) You are then taken to the "SIC Comparative RMA Analysis" worksheet.

> 5) On this sheet you need to post your numbers in the cells with **Bold Blue** numbers. You may need assistance from your accountant or bookkeeper to ascertain these numbers.

> 6) When you return to the "Standard Industrial Codes" worksheet you will see that it has been automatically reset to repeat the process for the next SIC.

Cash Flow Primer

Why is cash flow important? I bet you know!

The dynamic small business is never short of cash. When a bill is due, with a discount for paying it early, the cash is there to pay it. Saved last for its importance, the Cash Flow statement template enables you to monitor this important financial element with regularity.

> The importance of Cash Flow analysis cannot be overemphasized. You must keep an eye on it constantly. Do not rely on your accountant or bookkeeper to monitor it – do it yourself! You will be glad you do.

> Cash flow is covered at length in a later chapter, however, it is very important that a brief introduction is necessary in this chapter, and we have included a spreadsheet template tool for monitoring it.

What is cash?

Cash is money in the bank for paying your firm's expenses. Profit does not mean more cash.

What is profit?

Profit is the amount of money you expect to make if all accounts are current and your sales exceed your expenses.

What is cash flow?

Cash flow refers to the flow of cash into and out of a business.

Go to the template folder and open *BasicCashFlow.xls.*

This figure shows a spreadsheet tool that demonstrates a typical cash flow statement.

CASH FLOW STATEMENT

	Week 1	Week 2	Week 3	Week 4
Cash from operations				
Net cash from operations	$514,118	$787,797	$834,845	$1,198,922
Cash provided (used) by operating activities				
Net cash used by operations	$1,621,000	$1,969,630	$2,619,719	$3,256,237
Investment transactions Increases (decreases)				
Net cash from investments	$0	$0	$0	$0
Financing transactions Increases (decreases)				
Net cash from financing	$1,831,200	$1,591,100	$2,795,727	$3,443,982
Net increase (decrease) in cash	$724,318	$409,267	$1,010,853	$1,386,667
Cash at beginning of period	$451,000	$464,530	$478,466	$492,820
Cash at the end of period	$1,175,318	$873,797	$1,489,319	$1,879,487

This file opens with the Cash Flow worksheet in view. In the left margin you will see plus (+) icons. Clicking on each will expand that section for detail viewing and data entry in the cells with bold blue numbers.

The worksheet is grouped into the 4 essential components: Net cash from operations, Net cash used by operations, Net cash from investments , and Net cash from financing.

Initially, the time periods are set at weeks, however, you can set them as you wish. We strongly suggest that shorter periods will give you greater control.

You might consider having your bookkeeper or accountant help you get started with the data entry. Once this is done you'll find that periodic posting will get easier until it becomes routine.

The "Triple Header" of cash management
What are they?

> 1. Accounts Receivable
>
> 2. Accounts Payable
>
> 3. Inventory Control

The one attribute that seems prevalent with dynamic small business owners is *focus*. They are able to naturally zero in on the tasks that make them more money.

It is simply impossible to track every dollar that flows through a business. The dynamic owner knows instinctively how to quickly get the cash in the door, hold on to it as long as possible, and not store it in inventory. Their focus is on these 3 dynamics of good cash flow management.

1. Accounts Receivable

- In the ideal cash world you sell a product and receive payment in cash at the point of sale.

- In the ideal credit world you sell a product on credit and the customer sends you a check in 10 days to receive a 2% discount.

The real world of granting credit, selling on credit, and receiving payment is a world of constant stress. However, the dynamic small business owner suffers little stress from accounts receivable. How can they be so lucky?

It is not luck! They follow the fundamental rules of good credit management and they are:

> 1. Require the completion of a credit application. This is as normal as breathing and is understood by everyone as required to acquire credit.

Go to the template folder and open *CreditApplication.xls.*

The workbook opens with the spreadsheet *Credit Application* in view.

This figure shows the Commercial Credit Application worksheet.

Commercial Credit Application

T O
Name _____
Address _____
City/State/Zip _____
Credit Mgr _____
Phone _____

F R O M
Name _____
Address _____
City/State/Zip _____
E-Mail _____
Phone _____

Business Type: ☐ Sole Proprietor ☐ Partnership ☐ Corporation: State _____

How long in business: _____   D&B Number: _____

Names/Addresses of Individuals or Partners   -or-   Name/Title/Phone Number of Corporate Officers

Name of Person to Contact Regarding Purchase Orders and Invoices, Title, Address, and Phone

2. Always, without exception, run a credit check on the applicant. I know! I know! She is the wife of the largest furniture dealer in the state and I don't want to insult her. Do it anyway! You will not insult her if you are up front with it being a routine practice in your business.

3. You must have a solid written credit policy so the applicant knows up front your credit terms. Rather than list paragraphs of credit policy content here, **you should consult with your attorney and accountant**. Every business is different and your credit policy must be customized to your to business, local market, customer profile, and comply with state and federal regulations.

Terms and Conditions of Sale

These are typical headings used in many Terms of Sale with credit policy documents:

- ACCEPTANCE OF ORDERS

- PRICES

- TERMS OF PAYMENT

- DELIVERY

- TITLE AND RISK OF LOSS; SECURITY INTEREST

- RETURNS

- LIMITED WARRANTY; SPECIFICATIONS

- LIMITATION OF REMEDY

- NO RECOVERY OF CONSEQUENTIAL OR SPECIAL DAMAGES

- DEFAULT

- SEVERABILITY

- MODIFICATION OR TERMINATION

- GOVERNING LAW; JURISDICTION

- INTERNATIONAL SALES

4. The dynamic small business owner has an eagerness for tracking their accounts receivables and uses tools other than historical accounting data to do so.

Go to the template folder and open *AccountsReceivableAging.xls.*

The workbook opens with the spreadsheet *Accounts Receivable Aging* in view.

Use this template to organize a company's current and past due accounts according to how long they have been outstanding. It can be used on paper or filled in electronically. Because many businesses maintain their accounts receivable in a database, you may wish to use file-linking formulas to reference the appropriate figures from another file.

This figure shows the Accounts Receivable Aging worksheet. Properly and regularly used, you will be on top of your accounts receivables and prevent them aging too much.

Accounts Receivable Aging
July 1, 2005

CUSTOMER	Last Payment Date	Amount	Current 0-30	31-60	61-90	Past Due 91-119	120-150	150+	Total Due
Customer	September 12, 2003	$1,000		$2,140	$2,450		$20,800		$33,390
Customer	October 7, 2003	$5,300		$1,010	$1,300	$2,140		$4,450	$8,900
Customer	October 23, 2003	$7,600	$950	$2,790		$1,310			$5,050
Customer	December 3, 2003	$4,600	$2,040		$1,160				$4,000
TOTALS			$3,790	$5,940	$4,910	$3,450	$28,800	$4,450	$51,340

1. Entering data in this worksheet is straightforward. All entries in **Bold Blue** are replaced by your data.

2. Specific instructions are presented in comments by placing your mouse pointer over the red triangles.

3. To avoid overwriting formulae, both worksheets have simple protection which can be easily removed: From the Standard Menu click on Tools > Protection > Unprotect sheet.

Not all small businesses sell on credit. For those that do, the ***Accounts Receivable Aging*** digests into a small template the condition of credit sales. As you can see there is substantial amount due that is over 30 days. That is your money in the hands of others that constrains your cash flow.

2. Accounts Payable

Go to the template folder and open *AccountsPayableAging.xls.*

This figure shows the Accounts Payable worksheet. Properly and regularly used, you will be on top of your accounts payable and prevent them aging too much.

Accounts Payable Aging
June 24, 2005

Creditor	Last Payment		Current			Past Due			Total Due
	Date	Amount	0-30	31-60	61-90	91-119	120-150	150+	
Customer	September 12, 2005	$1,000		$1,140	$1,450		$8,800		$11,390
Customer	October 7, 2005	$3,300		$1,010	$1,300	$2,140		$4,450	$8,900
Customer	October 23, 2005	$3,600	$950	$2,790		$1,310			$5,050
Customer	December 3, 2005	$2,600	$2,840		$1,160				$4,000
Totals			$3,790	$4,940	$3,910	$3,450	$8,800	$4,450	$29,340

Use this template to organize a company's current and past due payable accounts according to how long they have been outstanding. Such an analysis can help your company maintain a good credit rating and give *cash flow* priority to older payables.

> 1. Entering data in this worksheet is straightforward. All entries in Bold Blue are replaced by your data.
>
> 2. Specific instructions are presented in comments by placing your mouse pointer over the red triangles.
>
> 3. To avoid overwriting formulae, both worksheets have simple protection which can be easily removed: From the Standard Menu click on Tools > Protection > Unprotect sheet.

3. Inventory Control

The dynamic small business owner will focus on the techniques available to control the inventory investment. For many small companies, especially wholesalers and retailers, the investment in inventory is the firm's largest outlay, and the owner must take active steps to protect this valuable asset. In addition to the direct costs of purchasing inventory, the small business incurs several other types of inventory expenses. Depending on the nature of the materials, the owner must protect them from the elements, secure them from theft and damage, categorize them for easy access, and maintain timely, accurate records of them.

The business incurs an interest expense if it must borrow the funds to purchase inventory. In addition, the owner must recognize the opportunity costs of tying up working capital in merchandise and materials.

The small business owner's goal must be to balance the costs involved in holding and maintaining inventory with customer requirements for merchandise. The business should strive to keep a minimum level of inventory on hand to reduce costs while maintaining enough stock to meet customer demand.

It is vital to have proper inventory control and the overwhelming choice is perpetual inventory control.

Perpetual Inventory Control

Go to the template folder and open *PerpetualInventoryControl.xls.*

This figure shows the Perpetual Inventory Control worksheet. Properly and regularly used, you will be on top of your inventory and prevent tying up too much cash.

Use this template to record the inventory status of a given part or item. Because there are relatively few formulas, this template can be used on paper as well as electronically.

Although this template may an initial start at perpetual inventory control, I strongly suggest the purchase of software that will be more productive as your business grows.

Summary

Why are we doing this? Why do we need these tools? The purpose is twofold:

1) Be a Winner! In the finals of the Miss America beauty contest all of the girls are beautiful. They could all win! However, only one must be chosen. The tool applied is Comparative Analysis. One contestant is compared against the other by a set criterion, and by the process of elimination, yields the winner.

The same principle applies to you and your business. For you to be the winner you must have or develop winning characteristics. Among these characteristics is the intense curiosity of what the competition is doing. These tools help give you that skill.

2) Develop Good (Profitable) Habits: When a professional golfer starts to persistently hook or slice the ball, you can bet they will seek help. They have developed a bad habit in their swing.

A bad habit must be replaced with a good habit. Good habits perpetuate themselves by repetition. They literally push the bad habits into obscurity. These tools are designed to be used repetitively. They are good habits and the enthusiastic small business owner/manager uses these tools continuously to monitor their business.

This chapter has covered tools for rating your firm's dynamics and taking corrective actions to better manage your small business.

We addressed how to identify employee surplus headcount and lower employee turnover with the Payroll Analysis and Employee Turnover Analysis tools.

The Confidential Employee Questionnaire and Employee Productivity Analysis tools continued the process by identifying and dealing with employee morale problems.

The key to high productivity in a small business rests squarely on the back of management. Displaying an energetic attitude will bring out the best in your people. The Workforce Productivity and Buried Costs analyses tools revealed for you the impact of lost productivity in your business. Use them in team situations to ask what WE can do to improve the productivity numbers.

With proper productivity in place, we ventured into the first stage of strategic planning. The realm of making a profit can be narrow in scope and confined to your own situation. To break out into the open we used the Comparative Income Statement and Optimal Performance worksheets. The one compared our actual performance and the other showed "what we could do" if we got everything right for just one year.

Next, we used 2 tools to compare your business with those in the same or similar business. The Comparative Industry and the SIC Comparative RMA analysis worksheets launched you into the world of wide area comparison.

The Cash Flow statement template enables you to monitor this important financial element with regularity.

Last, but definitely not the least, the triple header of Accounts Receivable, Accounts Payable, and Inventory Control.

We learned that if you do not adopt an accurate and timely cash flow monitoring system you will be concentrating "IN" your business rather than "ON" your business. Concentrating "IN" your business will stunt your firm's growth.

The Dynamic Small Business Manager contains all of the foregoing templates and much, much more. Let us explore.

Chapter 5 - The Dynamic Small Business Manager

he Dynamic Small Business Manager© (**The Manager**) has been used worldwide in one form or another for over 34 years. Created by this book's author, it was originally printed for a loose-leaf notebook. Each small business was analyzed by manually entering data in over 100 forms. Calculations were done with a hand calculator. The process took over 50 hours to complete.

The advent of the computer plus the introduction of a miracle program called VisiCalc in 1979 changed everything. It was the first computer spreadsheet program as we know them today. Co-created by Dan Bricklin and Bob Frankston, it became the standard for early "spread-sheeting" and was included on the first IBM PC in 1981.

Much of the Manager's arithmetical analysis was transferred to VisiCalc in an IBM PC in 1982. In 1989 the Manager was converted to Microsoft Excel Version 2 and has been improved continually since then.

Once you have entered all of the necessary information in one data entry worksheet the Manager automatically creates over 100 separate analysis worksheets for your business. It compresses over 50 hours into 1 hour or less.

For those of you who read, study, analyze, and manage your business with financial spreadsheets, this chapter and **The Manager** will be good news, for everyone else – learn by doing!

The key to successfully operating a business is having the right information to make your decisions. This concept may appear elementary, but it can be one of the greatest strategic and operational obstacles your company faces. As any person who reads or analyzes financial statements knows, there are more financial indicators available than are needed. The trick is to choose the indicators that have the greatest relevance to your financial goals.

A dynamic small business owner concerns themselves with the internal operations and drivers of their firm's performance. *Two primary tools are Comparative Analysis and What-if Scenarios.*

The Manager explores the relationships among key variables. It shows you how to use What-if analysis to identify which actions you can modify to meet your goals.

There are two assumptions for the efficient use of *The Manager:*

- First, let us assume that you receive from your accountant monthly or quarterly financial statements that include the Income Statement, Balance Sheet, and the Statement of Cash Flows.

- Second, you compare line-by-line each item on each document to determine trends. This is commonly called trend analysis and it is doing this that flags problem areas. *The Manager* does this for you <u>automatically</u> in its analysis worksheets.

Please go to the c:\Manager folder and open *Manager.xls* workbook.

The workbook opens with The Manager's Summary Analysis worksheet in view.

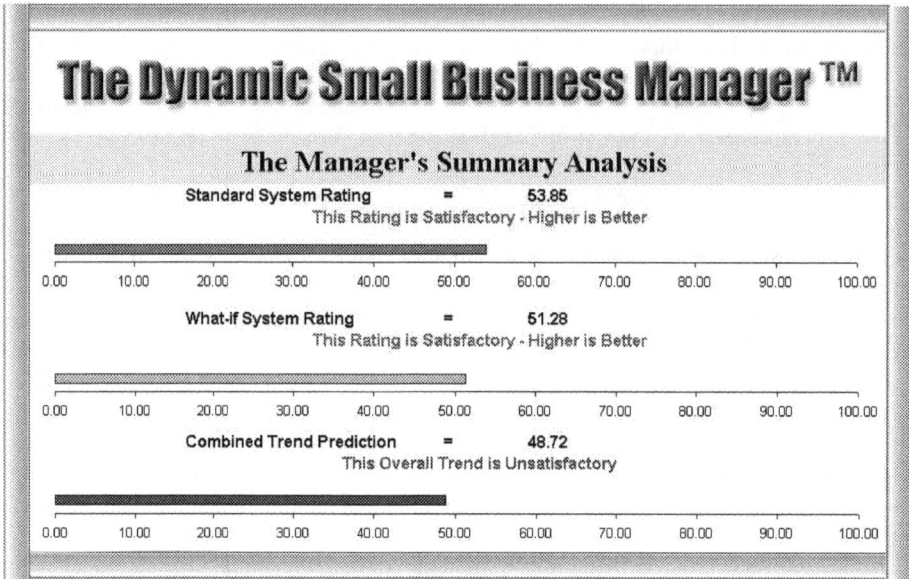

The Dynamic Small Business Manager ™

The Manager's Summary Analysis

Standard System Rating   =   53.85

This Rating is Satisfactory - Higher is Better

| 0.00 | 10.00 | 20.00 | 30.00 | 40.00 | 50.00 | 60.00 | 70.00 | 80.00 | 90.00 | 100.00 |

What-if System Rating   =   51.28

This Rating is Satisfactory - Higher is Better

| 0.00 | 10.00 | 20.00 | 30.00 | 40.00 | 50.00 | 60.00 | 70.00 | 80.00 | 90.00 | 100.00 |

Combined Trend Prediction   =   48.72

This Overall Trend is Unsatisfactory

| 0.00 | 10.00 | 20.00 | 30.00 | 40.00 | 50.00 | 60.00 | 70.00 | 80.00 | 90.00 | 100.00 |

The Summary Analysis

How do they work?

The Manager is 3 very powerful integrated analysis systems running simultaneously as one:

1. The Standard System:

The Standard System analyzes data entered on the Master Data Entry Worksheet and broadcasts these numbers over the analysis system and funnels one rating number back to this worksheet.

2. The What-if System:

The What-if System is directly linked to the Master Data Worksheet. It also broadcasts the what-if numbers across its own separate system and funnels one rating number back to this worksheet.

3. Trend Prediction:

Using regression analysis we predicted the trend based on the two scores. Since only two entries are used the predicted 3rd regression will appear exaggerated, however, it immediately indicates how proposed positive operating controls can improve the overall performance.

The Summary Analysis worksheet

The Manager's Summary Analysis worksheet shows in horizontal bars a rating from 0 to 100 of each criteria. These charts are driven from summary analysis of key measurements fed in from across the Manager's multiple analysis worksheets to the Rating details worksheet.

The Analysis Details worksheet

The Manager uses "Data Funneling" to arrive at the one number rating. All of the worksheets in the Manager contribute objective analyses. These results funnel to the Analysis Details worksheet where they are further analyzed and assigned individual scores. The total of all scores are common sized at 100%. The final score reflects the sum of positive scores.

The Manager's Analysis Details

FINANCIAL INDICATORS	Year 2001	Year 2002	Year 2003	Year 2004	Trend 2005	Comments
Z Score: If Publicly Held (Higher is Better)	2.40	2.94	3.04	3.51	3.83	Trend is Upward
	If Z is less than 1.8 then the firm is classified as Failed.					
Springate Analysis (Higher is Better)	1.25	1.93	1.82	2.42	2.71	Trend is Upward
	If Z is less than 0.862 then the firm is classified as Failed.					
Logit Analysis (Lower is Better)	58.42%	46.56%	20.78%	8.28%	-10.54%	Trend is Downward
	If percentage is higher than 50% and trending higher-Not Good!					
Fulmer H-Factor Analysis (Higher is Better)	2.62	2.98	3.28	3.82	4.15	Trend is Upward
	If H is less than 0 then the firm is classified as "failed"					
Breakeven Dollars	$636,455	$593,738	$668,999	$618,603	$634,875	Trend is Downward
Acid Test (Quick Ratio)	0.87	0.97	1.37	1.88	2.13	Trend is Upward
Current Ratio	1.30	1.61	2.20	2.81	3.26	Trend is Upward

This worksheet is a consolidated analysis of the following data:

Altman's Z-Score Analysis

Routinely used by Stockbrokers trying to determine if a company is a good investment, Bankers to determine loan risk, and internally, by anyone who wants to take close look at their own company's financial health.

Data Needed:

• Earnings before taxes
• Total assets
• Net Sales
• Market Value of Equity

- Total Liabilities
- Working Capital
- Retained Earnings

The worksheet will indicate:

The short-term potential for financial problems at your company.

The Expert

Edward I. Altman, Professor and Vice-Director of New York University's Salomon Center, Leonard N. Stern School of Business.

Dr. Altman is known as the founding father of using statistical techniques to predict company failure. He developed the Z-Score analysis almost 30 years ago, and is the author of several books, including The Z-Score Bankruptcy Model: Past, Present, and Future (New York: John Wiley & Sons, 1977), and Corporate Financial Distress and Bankruptcy, 2nd edition (New York: John Wiley & Sons, 1993).

The Analysis

The original data sample consisted of 66 firms, half of which had filed for bankruptcy under Chapter 7. All businesses in the database were manufacturers, and small firms with assets of less than $1 million were eliminated.

Altman's Z-score calculates five ratios:

1. return on total assets,
2. sales to total assets,
3. equity to debt,
4. working capital to total assets, and
5. retained earnings to total assets.

Ratio	Formula
Return on Total Assets	$\dfrac{\text{Earnings Before Interest and Taxes}}{\text{Total Assets}}$
Sales to Total Assets	$\dfrac{\text{Net Sales}}{\text{Total Assets}}$
Equity to Debt	$\dfrac{\text{Market Value of Equity}}{\text{Total Liabilities}}$
Working Capital to Total Assets	$\dfrac{\text{Working Capital}}{\text{Total Assets}}$
Retained Earnings to Total Assets	$\dfrac{\text{Retained Earnings}}{\text{Total Assets}}$

These ratios are then multiplied by a predetermined weight factor, and the results are added together. The final number--the Z-score--yields a number between -4 and +8. Financially-sound companies show Z-scores above 2.99, while those scoring below 1.81 are in fiscal danger, maybe even heading toward bankruptcy. Scores that fall between these ends indicate potential trouble. In Altman's initial study of 66 bankrupt companies, Z-scores for 95 % of these companies pointed to trouble or imminent bankruptcy.

Although the numbers that go into calculating the Z-score (and a company's financial soundness) are sometimes influenced by external factors, it provides a good quick analysis of where your company stands compared to the competition, and a good tool for analyzing the ups and downs of your company's financial stability over time.

The Z Score is an overall indicator of a company's risk of failing due to financial weakness. It consists of five combined calculations. The resulting score is compared to the following scale:

Z Score	Probability of Business Failure
1.8 or less	Very high
1.81 to 2.99	Not Able to Determine
3.0 or more	Very low

Although these formulae are current, Dr. Altman is always updating his criteria. It would be wise to check his web site regularly at:

http://pages.stern.nyu.edu/~ealtman/

---

1. Altman's Z Score - Publicly Held   Publicly Held

Altman's model is probably the classic of this genre. The original data sample consisted of 66 firms, half of which had filed for bankruptcy under Chapter 7. All businesses in the database were manufacturers, and small firms with assets of less than $1 million were eliminated.

The Z-Score formula is as follows:

$$Z = 1.2X.sub.1 + 1.4X.sub.2 + 3.3X.sub.3 + 0.6X.sub.4 + 1.0X.sub.5$$

Where X.sub.1 = Working Capital/Total Assets.

Where X.sub.2 = Retained Earnings/Total Assets. This is a measure of cumulative profitability that reflects the firm's age as well as earning power. Many studies have shown failure rates to be closely related to the age of the business.

Where X.sub.3 = Earnings Before Income Taxes/Total Assets. This is a measure of operating efficiency separated from any leverage effects. It recognizes operating earnings as a key to long-run viability.

Where X.sub.4 = Market Value of Equity/Book Value of Debt. This ratio adds a market dimension. Academic studies of stock markets suggest that security price changes may foreshadow upcoming problems.

Where X.sub.5 = Sales/Total Assets. This is a standard turnover measure. Unfortunately, it varies greatly from one industry to another.

2. Altman's Z Score-Privately Held Firms

Privately Held

If a firm's stock is not publicly traded, the X4 term (Market Value of Equity/Book Value of Debt) cannot be calculated. To correct for this problem, the Z score can be re-estimated using book values of equity. This provides the following score:

Z.sub.1 = .717X.sub.1 + .847X.sub.2 + 3.107X.sub.3 + .420X.sub.4 + .998X.sub.5

3. Altman's Z Score - Non-manufacturing

Non-Manufacturing

The X.sub.5 (Sales/Total Assets) ratio is believed to vary significantly by industry. It is likely to be higher for merchandising and service firms than for manufacturers, since the former are typically less capital intensive. Consequently, non-manufacturers would have significantly higher asset turnover and Z scores. The model is thus likely to under predict certain sorts of bankruptcy. To correct for this potential defect, Altman recommends the following correction that eliminates the X.sub.5 ratio:

Z.sub.11 = 6.56X.sub.1 + 3.26X.sub.2 + 6.72X.sub.3 + 1.05X.sub.4

Springate Analysis

This model was developed in 1978 at S.F.U. by Gordon L.V. Springate, following procedures developed by Altman in the U.S. Springate used step-wise multiple discriminate analysis to select four out of 19 popular financial ratios that best distinguished between sound business and those that actually failed.

The Springate model takes the following form:

$$Z = 1.03A + 3.07B + 0.66C + 0.4D$$
$$Z < 0.862; \text{ then the firm is classified as "failed"}$$

WHERE A = Working Capital/Total Assets

B = Net Profit before Interest and Taxes/Total Assets

C = Net Profit before Taxes/Current Liabilities

D = Sales/Total Assets

This model achieved an accuracy rate of 92.5% using the 40 companies tested by Springate. Botheras tested the Springate Model on 50 companies with an average asset size of $2.5 million and found an 88.0% accuracy rate. Sands tested the Springate Model on 24 companies with an average asset size of $63.4 million and found an accuracy rate of 83.3%.

This figure illustrates an actual example of the Springate Analysis taken from the Manager.

	Year 2001	Year 2002	Year 2003	Year 2004
Working Capital	276,200	586,450	1,194,748	1,818,973
Net Profit before interest and Taxes	656,240	1,044,863	1,109,658	1,617,279
Total Assets	4,167,200	4,094,180	5,467,899	6,172,246
Net Profit before Taxes	686,240	1,075,763	1,141,485	1,660,061
Current Liabilities	936,000	964,080	993,002	1,007,719
Sales	1,960,000	2,500,000	2,651,800	3,205,454

Analysis

	Year 2001	Year 2002	Year 2003	Year 2004
Working Capital/Total Assets	0.07	0.14	0.22	0.29
Net Profit before interest and Taxes/Total Assets	0.16	0.26	0.21	0.27
Net Profit before Taxes/Current Liabilities	0.73	1.12	1.15	1.65
Sales/Total Assets	0.47	0.61	0.48	0.52
Z =	1.25	1.93	1.82	2.42

If Z is less than 2.675 then the firm is classified as Failed.

The Fulmer H-Factor Model

Fulmer, John G. Jr., Moon, James E., Gavin, Thomas A., Erwin, Michael J., "A Bankruptcy Classification Model For Small Firms". Journal of Commercial Bank Lending (July 1984): pp. 25-37.

Fulmer used step-wise multiple discriminate analysis to evaluate 40 financial ratios applied to a sample of 60 companies -30 failed and 30 successful. The average asset size of these firms was $455,000.

Fulmer reported a 98% accuracy rate in classifying the test companies one year prior to failure and an 81% accuracy rate more than one year prior to bankruptcy.

The model takes the following form:

$$H = 5.528 (V1) + 0.212 (V2) + 0.073 (V3) + 1.270 (V4) - 0.120 (V5) + 2.335 (V6) + 0.575 (V7) + 1.083 (V8) + 0.894 (V9) - 6.075$$

Fulmer H-Factor Analysis		Year 2001	Year 2002	Year 2003	Year 2004
Retained Earnings/Total Assets	V1	0.335957	0.376632	0.308210	0.280257
Sales/Total Assets	V2	0.470340	0.610623	0.484976	0.519333
EBIT/Equity	V3	0.280098	0.463591	0.313741	0.386103
Cash Flow/Total Debt	V4	0.684439	0.492646	0.814016	1.003614
Total Debt/Total Assets	V5	0.412075	0.433220	0.334606	0.303410
Current Liabilities/Total Assets	V6	0.224611	0.235476	0.181606	0.163266
Log Tangible Total Assets	V7	6.518514	6.462248	6.561836	6.570840
Working Capital/Total Debt	V8	0.160843	0.330640	0.653012	0.971301
Log EBIT/Interest	V9	1.625623	1.808026	1.820942	1.970759
		1.86	2.08	1.70	1.55
		0.10	0.13	0.10	0.11
		0.02	0.03	0.02	0.03
		0.87	0.63	1.03	1.27
		-0.05	-0.05	-0.04	-0.04
		0.52	0.55	0.42	0.38
		3.75	3.72	3.77	3.78
		0.17	0.36	0.71	1.05
		1.45	1.62	1.63	1.76
	Sum	8.70	9.06	9.36	9.90
	Less	-6.075	-6.075	-6.075	-6.075
	H =	2.62	2.98	3.28	3.82

If H is less than 0 then the firm is classified as "failed"

The Prediction of Corporate Failure: The Logit Analysis

Bankruptcy prediction models are more generally known as measures of financial distress. The best-known, and most-widely used, multiple discriminant analysis method is the one proposed by Edward Altman, Professor of Finance at the Stern School of Business, New York University, The Z-Score Analysis or Zeta Model. Despite the positive results of his study, Altman's model had a key weakness: it assumed variables in the sample data to be normally distributed. "If all variables are not normally distributed, the methods employed may result in selection of an inappropriate set of predictors". Chistine Zavgren developed a model that corrected for this problem. Her model used logit analysis to predict bankruptcy. Due to its use of logit analysis, her model is considered "more robust".

Logit Analysis developed by Christine Zavgren-Bankruptcy Predictor

Zavgren, C. 1983, The Prediction of Corporate Failure: The State of the Art, Journal of Accounting Literature

This figure illustrates an actual example of the Logit Analysis taken from the Manager.

	Year 2001	Year 2002	Year 2003	Year 2004
Cash	$451,000	$464,530	$478,466	$492,820
Marketable Securities	$10,000	$10,300	$10,609	$10,927
Accounts Receivable	$350,000	$460,500	$871,315	$1,382,454
Inventory	$400,000	$612,000	$824,360	$937,091
Fixed Assets	$2,900,000	$2,487,000	$3,221,800	$3,285,454
Total Assets	$4,167,200	$4,094,180	$5,467,899	$6,172,246
Current Liabilities	$936,000	$964,080	$993,002	$1,007,719
Long Term Debt	$601,200	$624,200	$645,630	$668,308
Sales	$1,960,000	$2,500,000	$2,651,800	$3,205,454
Income from Continuing Operations	$656,240	$1,044,863	$1,109,658	$1,617,279

Logit Analysis

	Year 2001	Year 2002	Year 2003	$2,004 2004
Constant	0.23883	0.23883	0.23883	0.23883
Inventories/Sales	-0.022	-0.026	-0.034	-0.032
Receivables/Inventory	-1.385	-1.191	-1.673	-2.335
Cash+Marketable Securities/Total Assets	-1.193	-1.250	-0.964	-0.880
Quick Assets/Current Liabilities	2.663	2.982	4.211	5.754
Income from CO/(Total Assets-Current Liab)	0.099	0.162	0.121	0.152
Long-Term Debt/(Total Assets-Current Liab)	-0.809	-0.867	-0.628	-0.563
Sales/(Net Working Capital+Fixed Assets)	0.068	0.090	0.066	0.069
Sum of Coefficients * Ratios	-0.340	0.138	1.338	2.404
Probability of Bankruptcy	58.42%	46.56%	20.78%	8.28%

The remaining items in the Rating Details worksheet are discussed in later chapters. Please refer to the Table of Contents for their locations.

The Master Data Entry Worksheet

Go to the *Manager's Index* worksheet and click on the ***Master Data Entry*** hyperlink.

This key spreadsheet is linked to over 100 worksheets and sends information to all of them, therefore you only have to fill it in one time.

We will now take closer look at the Master Data Entry worksheet and see how it works

This figure shows the top portion of the Master Data Entry worksheet. The automated button selections are on the left with callout explanations of their functions.

Step 1
Please Read First
Step 2
Clear Sheet
Two Periods
Three Periods
Troubled Firm
Prosperous Firm
Step 3
Publicly Held
Privately Held
Non-Manufacturing
Step 4
Manufacturer
Service
Retailer
Wholesaler
Job Shop

Click this button for worksheet instructions.

Click on the "Clear Sheet" button to clear the entire worksheet and set up for posting four periods.

Click on the "Two Periods" button to clear and set up regression analysis for periods three and four.

Click on the "Three Periods" button to clear and set up regression analysis for period four.

The "Troubled Firm Demo" button returns the demo numbers to view a completed posting operation of a business that is in trouble and headed toward bankruptcy.

The "Prosperous Firm Demo" button returns the demo numbers to view a completed posting operation of a business that is in excellent condition.

These buttons tell the system whether your business is public, private, or non-manufacturing.

Click on a business category that best represents your firm's type: Manufacturing, Service, Retail, Wholesale, or Job Shop.

Breakeven Dollars $636,45

This worksheet is where the rubber meets the road. It drives all of the analysis sheets with links in hundreds of locations. It is suggested to leave links and formulae undisturbed.

General instructions

The setup buttons on the top left perform the following functions:

1. Click on the "Clear Sheet" button to clear the entire worksheet and set up for posting four periods.

Clear Sheet

2. Click on the "Two Periods" button to clear and set up regression analysis for periods three and four.

Two Periods

3. Click on the "Three Periods" button to clear and set up regression analysis for period four.

Three Periods

4. The "Troubled Firm Demo" button returns the demo numbers to view a completed posting operation of a business that is in trouble and headed toward bankruptcy.

Troubled Firm

5. The "Prosperous Firm Demo" button returns the demo numbers to view a completed posting operation of a business that is in excellent condition.

Prosperous Firm

6. This button tells the system that your business is *publicly held*. This is used in determining your appropriate *Z-Score*.

Publicly Held

7. This button tells the system that your business is *privately held*. This is used in determining your appropriate *Z-Score*.

Privately Held

8. This button tells the system that your business is **non-manufacturing**. This is used in determining your appropriate **Z-Score**.

Non-Manufacturing

9. Click on a business category that best defines your firm's type:

1) Manufacturing,   **Manufacturer**

2) Service,   **Service**

3) Retail,   **Retailer**

4) Wholesale,   **Wholesaler**

5) Job Shop.   **Job Shop**

With the Master Data Entry worksheet still in view, scroll down placing the summary charts at the top of the Excel window.

This figure shows additional data entry cells and information generated by the Master Data Entry worksheet. Callouts explain additional features.

| | | Year |
| | | 2001 |

<table>
<tr><td colspan="2">Summary Charts:
These charts are instantly updated as data is entered in each column.</td></tr>
</table>

Summary Charts:
These charts are instantly updated as data is entered in each column.

Legend:
This is the legend for the summary charts showing the 8 data sources.

Summary Charts

Cost of Sales   □ Gross Profit   □ Fixed Expenses   ■ Other Expenses

Business Category:
This displays the business type selected by the appropriate button.

Business Category: Manufacturer	
Z-Score - Stock is Publicly Held	2.40
Breakeven Dollars	$636,455

Z-Score and Break-Even:
These numbers are displayed at the top of this sheet for quick viewing as the data is entered.

Break-Even Charts:
These charts are instantly updated as data is entered in each column.

Breakeven Charts

Column Headings:
Depending upon your choice these headings can Month, Quarter, or Year.

Chart of Accounts:
Depending upon your choice as to business type, these descriptions change to conform to the choice.

	Year
Cost of Sales	2001
Gross Sales	$2,010,000
Discounts/Allowances	($50,000)
Net Sales	$1,960,000
Direct Material Cost	$320,000
Direct Labor Cost	$300,000
Other Direct Costs	$125,000
Total Cost of Sales	$745,000

Let us review additional items on the worksheet.

1. Summary Charts:

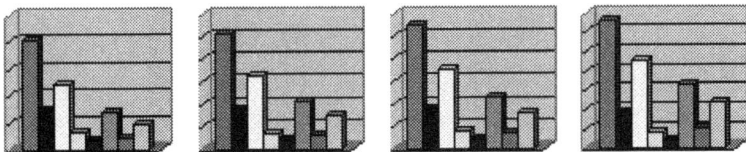

These charts are instantly updated as data is entered in each column.

2. Legend:

⊠ Sales Revenue	■ Cost of Sales	☐ Gross Profit	⊠ Fixed Expenses	■ Other Expenses	⊠ Income Before Tax	⊠ Income Taxes	⊠ Net Income (Loss)

This is the legend for the summary charts showing the 8 data sources.

3. Business Category:

> ### Business Category: Manufacturer

This displays the business type selected by the appropriate button.

4. Z-Score and Break-Even:

> ### Z-Score - Stock is Publicly Held
>
> ### Breakeven Dollars

These numbers are displayed at the top of this sheet for quick viewing as the data is entered.

These two concepts will be discussed later in the book.

5. Break-Even Charts:

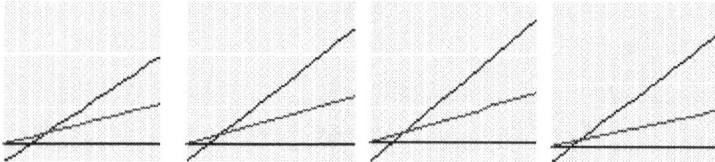

These charts are instantly updated as data is entered in each column.

6. Column Headings:

Year 2001	Year 2002	Year 2003	Year 2004

Depending upon your choice these headings can Month, Quarter, or Year.

7. Chart of Accounts Descriptions under "Sales & Cost of Sales" heading:

Sales & Cost of Sales
> Gross Sales
> Discounts/Allowances
> Net Sales
> Direct Material Cost
> Direct Labor Cost
> Other Direct Costs
> Total Cost of Sales

> **Gross Profit**

Depending upon your button choice as to business type, these descriptions change to conform to your choice.

Scrolling back to the top of the worksheet you will see a block of cells starting with **"Enter Your Firm's Name"** for additional information data entry.

Step 2		
Sheet Heading Information: The information entered in these cells appears as headings on all analysis worksheets.		
Special Entries: Self-explanatory, these items are important to sheet calcualtions.		

Enter Your Name	Bobby Jones	
Enter Your Business Name	The XYZ Company	
Address	6200 XYZ Drive	
City, State/Provice, Postal Code	ABC, Wyoming 00000-0000	
Phone Number	Phone: (000) 000-0000	
Fax Number	FAX: (000) 000-0000	
E-mail	E-mail: someone@xyz.com	
The Date on Each Report Page	June 22, 2005	
Enter Current Number of Employees		37
Enter Current Weekly Payroll		$6,732
Enter Current Average Weekly Sales		$65,384
"C" Corporation (Y/N)		Y
If "Y" enter tax percentage		30%
Enter Years or Quarters (Y or Q)		Y
If Years enter "Start Year" of Financials		2001

General instructions

The line items in this data entry block will appear on all of the analysis worksheets and include. They are in Bold Blue indicating information you need to enter manually:

1. Enter Your Name

This will appear in the heading of each analysis worksheet.

2. Enter Your Business Name:

This and the address, phone, FAX, and E-mail appear in the heading of each analysis worksheet.

3. Address:

Enter Business Address Information, Phone, FAX, and E-mail.

Example: 6200 XYZ Drive

4. Enter City, State/Province, And Postal Code:

Example: ABC, Wyoming 00000-0000

5. Enter Phone Number:

Example: Phone: (000) 000-0000

6. Enter Fax Phone Number:

Example: FAX: (000) 000-0000

7. Enter E-mail Address:

Example: someone@xyz.com

8. The Date on Each Report Page

Initially set to your clock's current date, enter the date you wish to appear on each linked analysis report sheet in this format 10/12/2005.

9. Enter Current Number of Employees

This is used to compute under or over-staffed conditions on the Payroll Analysis worksheet.

10. Enter Current Weekly Payroll

This includes Executive Payroll. This is used to compute Payroll Analysis.

11. Enter Current Average Weekly Sales

This is used to compute Payroll Analysis and other computations.

12. "C" Corporation (Y/N)

Be sure that 'Y' is entered if the company is a C-corporation. Otherwise, enter 'N' for an S-corporation, a sole proprietorship, or a partnership. Taxes will only be computed if you indicate that the company is a C-corporation.

13. If you entered "C" then enter the tax percentage

Enter the corporate tax rate for the year of projection. If you have chosen "N" no taxes will be calculated.

14. Enter Years or Quarters or Months (Y or Q or M)

Enter whether you want to post Annual, Quarterly, or Monthly financials with Y or Q or M.

15. Enter Start Year

If you entered a "Y" then enter "Start Year" of Financials, This is the earliest year that you want to start posting financial information.

The "What-if Master Data Entry" worksheet

With *Manager.xls* still open, go to the next worksheet entitled *What-if Master Data Entry*.

This figure shows the What-if Master Data Entry worksheet. It takes the data you entered in the Master Data Entry worksheet and you manipulate it for investigation and forecasting.

This worksheet is a powerful tool. You can experiment with increases and decreases to line items to improve the profit and B/E picture.

This is a mirror image of the Master Data Entry worksheet and linked so that the figures can be manipulated. The spinners are set at 100% to equal the entries on the Master Data Entry worksheet sheet.

By using the spinners, you can increase or decrease all cells to determine <u>what if</u> a change here or there will improve the bottom-line.

You can increase and decrease line items by increments of 1% and instantly see the changes to Profit and Break-even.

This feature was developed to demonstrate the impact of cumulative expense reductions on net income combined with only marginal increases in revenue.

Be sure to save often so as not to lose multiple spinner values.

All changes you make in this worksheet will be reflected in 30 linked worksheets including:

- What-if Master Data Entry
- What-if BE Adjusted
- What-if Breakdown of Costs
- What-if Breakeven 4 Periods
- What-if Breakeven Analysis
- What-if Breakeven Analysis (2)
- What-if Breakeven Analysis (3)
- What-if Breakeven Analysis (4)
- What-if Comp. Balance Sheet
- What-if Comp. Income Statement
- What-if Cover Sheet
- What-if Executive Summary
- What-if Expanded Ratios
- What-if Financial Summary
- What-if Forecast Analysis

- What-if H-Factor
- What-if Logit Analysis
- What-if Proforma Balance
- What-if Proforma Income
- What-if Projected Cash Flow
- What-if Sales vs. Expense
- What-if Springate
- What-if Stock Valuation
- What-if Z-Score (1) Chart
- What-if Z-Score (2) Chart
- What-if Z-Score (3) Chart
- What-if Z-Score Analysis (1)
- What-if Z-Score Analysis (2)
- What-if Z-Score Analysis (3)
- What-if Z-Score Explained

Spinners Reset Buttons:

1. You may reset the spinner values to 100% at any time with the reset buttons located in the upper left hand corner of both the Income Statement and Balance Sheet.

2. You may reset the Income or Balance Sheet cells separately or the entire worksheet with the buttons.

Toggling between the report sheets will give you a visible display of the changes.

Business Type Configurations

Returning to the Master Data Entry worksheet, we will configure the worksheets to the 5 business types.

With *Manager.xls* still open, go back to the Master Data Entry worksheet and click on the **Manufacturer** button. Several changes occur on multiple worksheets to conform to a manufacturer.

The Small Business Manufacturer

Manufacturer

Click on the **Manufacturer** button.

This figure shows the Comparative Income Statement that has been automatically configured as a manufacturer. This is accomplished by clicking the Manufacturer button on the Master Data Entry worksheet.

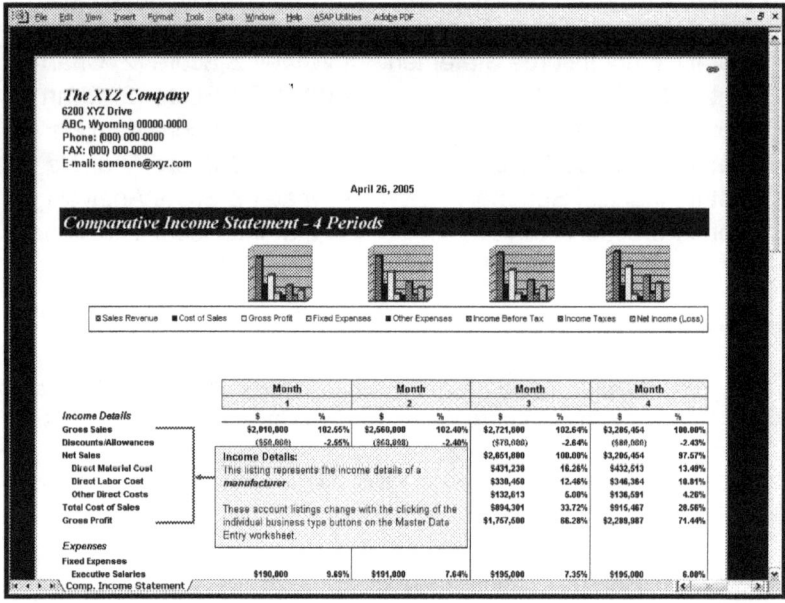

A manufacturer makes a profit by increasing sales and using cost controls in the realm of labor, materials, direct costs, and other manufacturing expenses.

The Small Business Service Firm

> **Service**

Click on the **Service** button.

This figure shows the Comparative Income Statement that has been automatically configured as a service business. This is accomplished by clicking the Service button on the Master Data Entry worksheet.

A service business makes a profit by increasing sales and using cost controls in general and administrative expenses.

The Small Business Retail Firm

Retailer

Click on the **Retailer** button.

This figure shows the Comparative Income Statement that has been automatically configured as a retail business. This is accomplished by clicking the Retail button on the Master Data Entry worksheet.

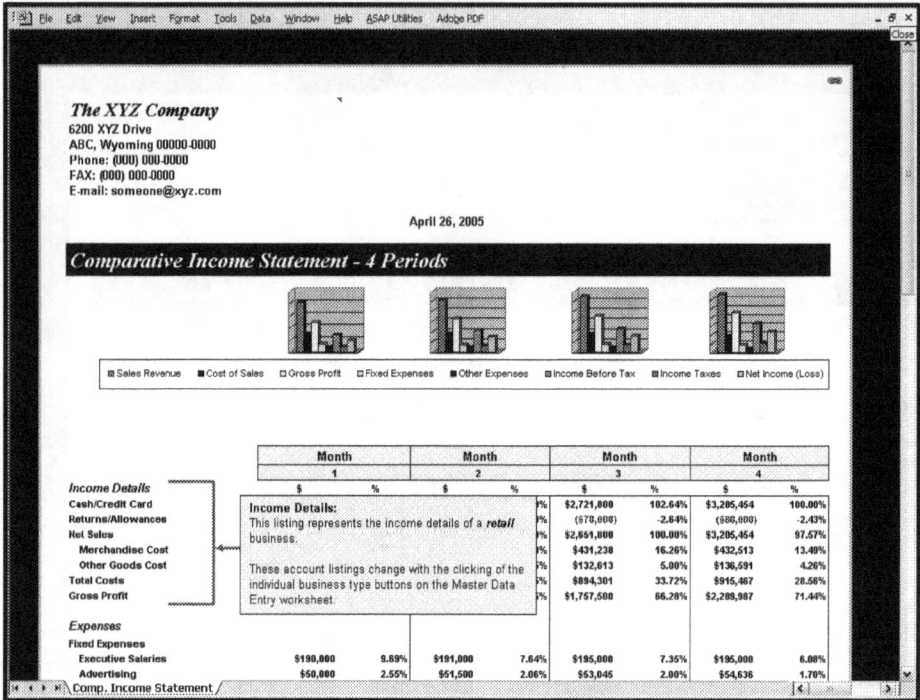

A retail business makes a profit by increasing sales and using controls in cost of goods and operating expenses.

The Small Business Wholesale Firm

Wholesaler

Click on the **Wholesaler** button.

This figure shows the Comparative Income Statement that has been automatically configured as a wholesale business. This is accomplished by clicking the Wholesale button on the Master Data Entry worksheet.

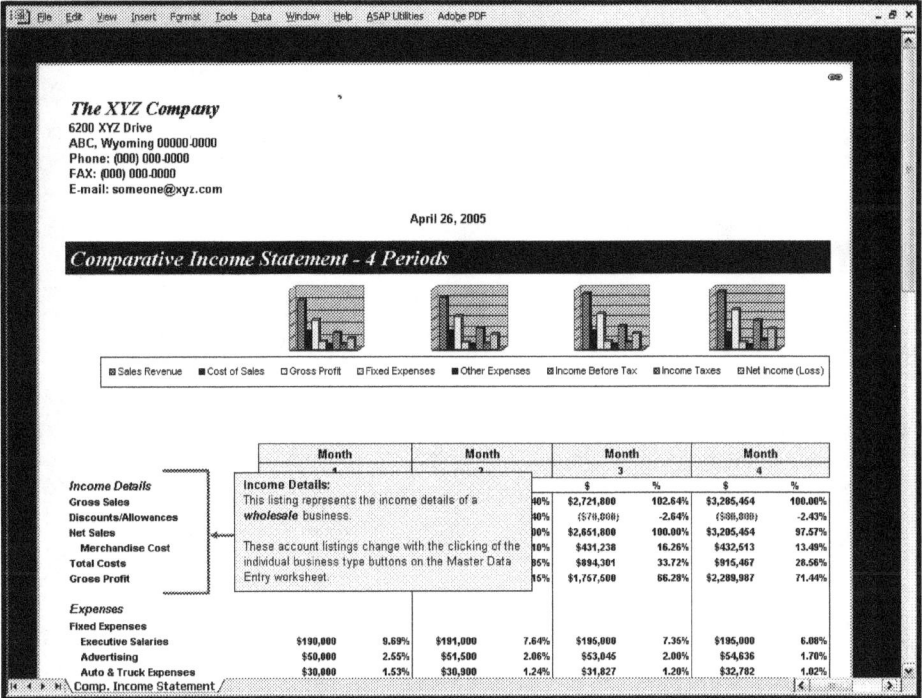

A wholesale business makes a profit by increasing sales and using controls in cost of goods and operating expenses.

The Small Business Job Shop

Job Shop

Click on the **Job Shop** button.

This figure shows the Comparative Income Statement that has been automatically configured as a job shop business. This is accomplished by clicking the Job Shop button on the Master Data Entry worksheet.

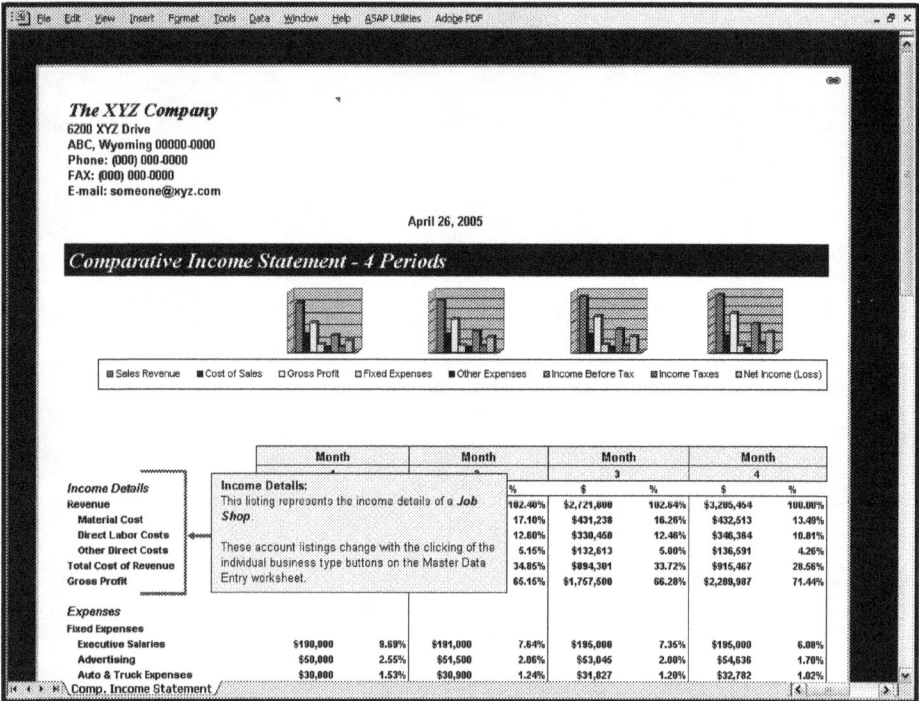

A job shop business makes a profit by increasing sales and using controls in cost of goods and operating expenses.

Financial Snapshot

This worksheet is a quick look at the financial health of the firm.

There are key ratios here that are driven from the "Master Data Entry" worksheet. The only item that is not linked is the Investment made to start and sustained the firm.

By habit, loan institutions look for one key ratio, the "Current Ratio". Unfortunately, this ratio will vary above and below the magic 2.0 depending on the industry.

The net profit ratios/percentages are also very important indicators (Upper Left Hand Corner).

In reality all of the numbers on this sheet are important and should be in sound health.

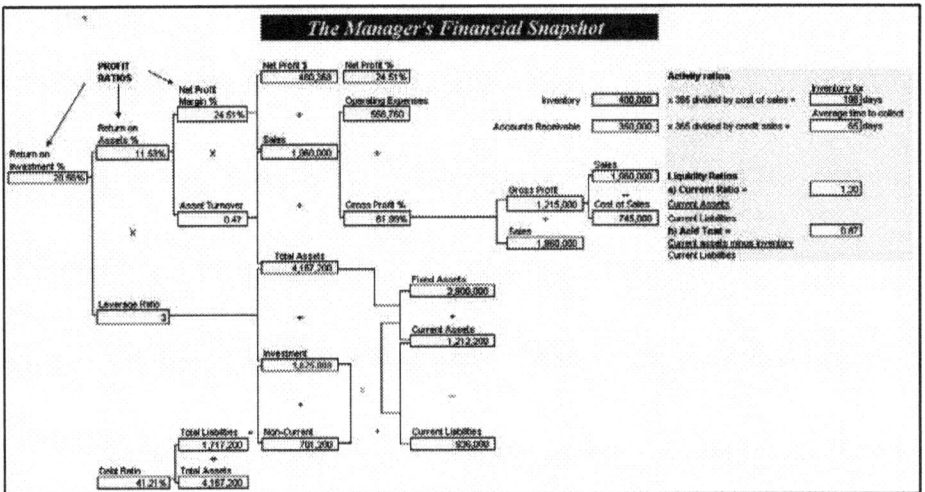

The Manager's Financial Snapshot

What-if Financial Snapshot

This worksheet is driven by the What-if Master Data Entry worksheet and is identical in layout to the Financial Snapshot sheet.

This sheet gives you an opportunity to see "What if this happens . . . ?" scenarios and how they will impact on your business.

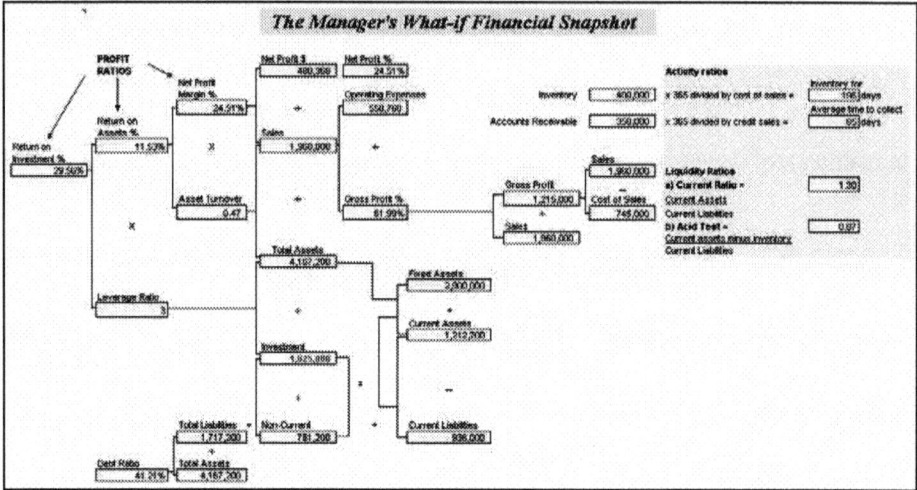

The Manager's What-if Financial Snapshot

Basic Financial Records

We now turn to the three basic financial records

1. Comparative Income Statement

2. Comparative Balance Sheet

3. Cash Flow – Current and Projected

The Income Statement

The income statement (or profit and loss statement or P&L) compares expenses against revenue to show your firm's net profit or loss. The annual P&L statement reports the profits for a fiscal calendar year.

Net profit or loss is the total revenue that flows into the business from sales of goods and services less total expenses.

The Manager has two income statements:

1. Comparative Income Statement

2. What-if Comparative Income Statement

With *Manager.xls* still open, go to the *Comp. Income Statement* worksheet.

---

1. Comparative Income Statement

This figure shows the Comparative Income Statement.

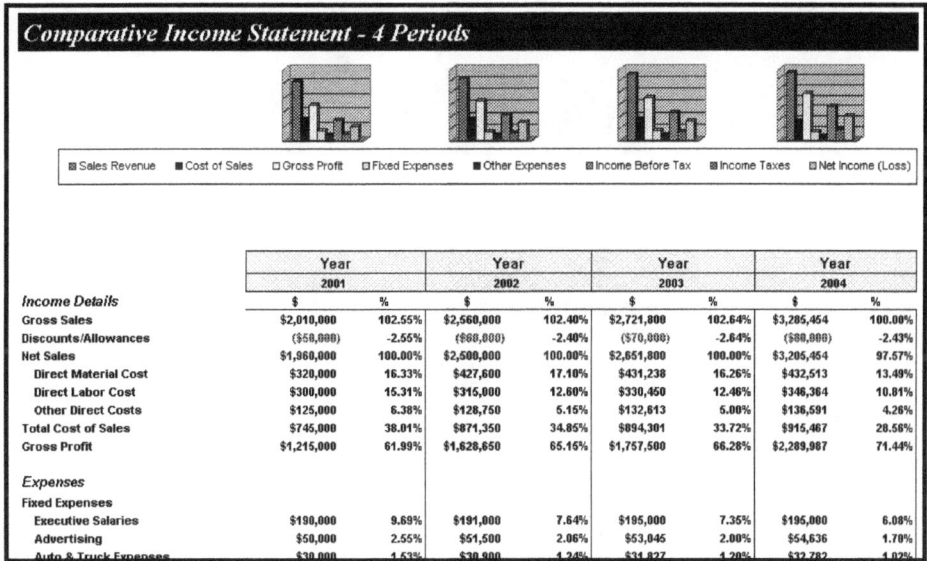

Income Details	Year 2001 $	%	Year 2002 $	%	Year 2003 $	%	Year 2004 $	%
Gross Sales	$2,010,000	102.55%	$2,560,000	102.40%	$2,721,800	102.64%	$3,285,454	100.00%
Discounts/Allowances	($50,000)	-2.55%	($60,000)	-2.40%	($70,000)	-2.64%	($80,000)	-2.43%
Net Sales	$1,960,000	100.00%	$2,500,000	100.00%	$2,651,800	100.00%	$3,205,454	97.57%
Direct Material Cost	$320,000	16.33%	$427,600	17.10%	$431,238	16.26%	$432,513	13.49%
Direct Labor Cost	$300,000	15.31%	$315,000	12.60%	$330,450	12.46%	$346,364	10.81%
Other Direct Costs	$125,000	6.38%	$128,750	5.15%	$132,613	5.00%	$136,591	4.26%
Total Cost of Sales	$745,000	38.01%	$871,350	34.85%	$894,301	33.72%	$915,467	28.56%
Gross Profit	$1,215,000	61.99%	$1,628,650	65.15%	$1,757,500	66.28%	$2,289,987	71.44%
Expenses								
Fixed Expenses								
Executive Salaries	$190,000	9.69%	$191,000	7.64%	$195,000	7.35%	$195,000	6.08%
Advertising	$50,000	2.55%	$51,500	2.06%	$53,045	2.00%	$54,636	1.70%
Auto & Truck Expenses	$30,000	1.53%	$30,900	1.24%	$31,827	1.20%	$32,782	1.02%

This worksheet compares 4 periods performance in both dollars and percentage. It is the results of your entries on the Master Data Entry worksheet.

Now, click on the *What-if Comp. Income Statement* tab to reveal the worksheet.

2. What-if Comparative Income Statement

This figure shows the What-if Comparative Income Statement.

What-if Comparative Income Statement - 4 Periods

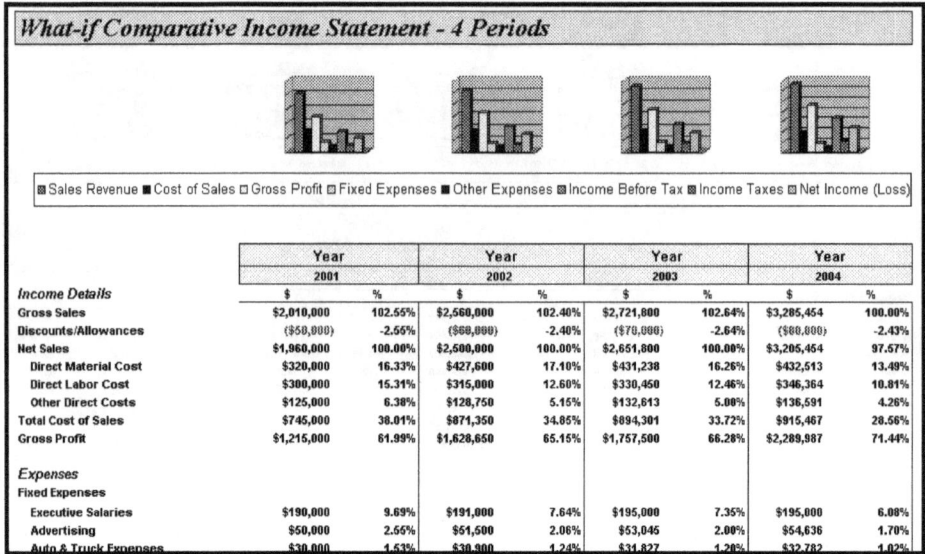

⊠ Sales Revenue ■ Cost of Sales ▢ Gross Profit ▢ Fixed Expenses ■ Other Expenses ⊠ Income Before Tax ⊠ Income Taxes ▢ Net Income (Loss)

	Year 2001		Year 2002		Year 2003		Year 2004	
Income Details	$	%	$	%	$	%	$	%
Gross Sales	$2,010,000	102.55%	$2,560,000	102.40%	$2,721,800	102.64%	$3,285,454	100.00%
Discounts/Allowances	($50,000)	-2.55%	($60,000)	-2.40%	($70,000)	-2.64%	($80,000)	-2.43%
Net Sales	$1,960,000	100.00%	$2,500,000	100.00%	$2,651,800	100.00%	$3,205,454	97.57%
Direct Material Cost	$320,000	16.33%	$427,600	17.10%	$431,238	16.26%	$432,513	13.49%
Direct Labor Cost	$300,000	15.31%	$315,000	12.60%	$330,450	12.46%	$346,364	10.81%
Other Direct Costs	$125,000	6.38%	$128,750	5.15%	$132,613	5.00%	$136,591	4.26%
Total Cost of Sales	$745,000	38.01%	$871,350	34.85%	$894,301	33.72%	$915,467	28.56%
Gross Profit	$1,215,000	61.99%	$1,628,650	65.15%	$1,757,500	66.28%	$2,289,987	71.44%
Expenses								
Fixed Expenses								
Executive Salaries	$190,000	9.69%	$191,000	7.64%	$195,000	7.35%	$195,000	6.08%
Advertising	$50,000	2.55%	$51,500	2.06%	$53,045	2.00%	$54,636	1.70%
Auto & Truck Expenses	$30,000	1.53%	$30,900	1.24%	$31,827	1.20%	$32,782	1.02%

This worksheet compares 4 periods performance in both dollars and percentage. It is the results of your what-if manipulations on the What-if Master Data Entry worksheet.

These two sheets allow you the ability to print two separate Comparable Income Statements:

> 1. The *actual* and

> 2. The *what-if* to demonstrate data manipulation for investigation and forecasting for improving the bottom-line.

The Balance Sheet

The balance sheet provides you with an estimate of your firm's worth on a given date. The balance sheet is built on the fundamental accounting equation:

Assets = Liabilities + Owner's Equity

Any increase or decrease on one side of the equation must be offset by an equal increase or decrease on the other side; therefore, the name *balance sheet*.

Assets are the total value of everything the business owns. Current assets consist of cash and items to be converted into cash. Intangible assets include items that, although valuable, do not have tangible value, such as goodwill, copyrights, and patents.

Liabilities are the creditors' claims against the firm's assets. Current liabilities are those debts that must be paid within one year.

Owner's equity is the value of your investment in the business.

The Manager has two balance sheets:

      1. Comparative Balance Sheet

      2. What-if Comparative Balance Sheet

Go to the ***Comp. Balance Sheet*** worksheet.

1. Comparative Balance Sheet

This figure shows the Comparative Balance Sheet.

Comparative Balance Sheet - 4 Periods

Legend: ■ Total Current Assets □ Total Fixed Assets □ Total Assets ■ Total Current Liabilities ▨ Total Liabilities ▨ Total Owners' Equity ▨ Total Liabilities and Equity

	Year 2001 $	Year 2001 %	Year 2002 $	Year 2002 %	Year 2003 $	Year 2003 %	Year 2004 $	Year 2004 %
ASSETS								
Current Assets								
Cash and cash equivalents	$451,000	10.82%	$464,530	11.35%	$478,466	8.75%	$492,820	7.98%
Accounts receivable	$350,000	8.40%	$460,500	11.25%	$871,315	15.94%	$1,382,464	22.40%
Notes receivable	$1,200	0.03%	$3,200	0.08%	$3,000	0.05%	$3,400	0.06%
Inventory	$400,000	9.60%	$612,000	14.95%	$824,360	15.08%	$937,091	15.18%
Other current assets	$10,000	0.24%	$10,300	0.25%	$10,609	0.19%	$10,927	0.18%
Total Current Assets	$1,212,200	29.09%	$1,550,530	37.87%	$2,187,750	40.01%	$2,826,692	45.80%
Fixed Assets								
Land	$1,000,000	24.00%	$1,030,000	25.16%	$1,106,090	20.23%	$1,109,273	17.97%
Buildings	$1,500,000	36.00%	$1,045,000	25.52%	$1,591,350	29.10%	$1,739,091	28.18%
Equipment	$800,000	19.20%	$824,000	20.13%	$948,720	17.35%	$874,182	14.16%
Subtotal	$3,300,000	79.19%	$2,899,000	70.81%	$3,646,160	66.68%	$3,722,545	60.31%
Less-accumulated depreciation	$400,000	9.60%	$412,000	10.06%	$424,360	7.76%	$437,091	7.08%
Total Fixed Assets	$2,900,000	69.59%	$2,487,000	60.74%	$3,221,800	58.92%	$3,285,464	53.23%
Intangible Assets								
Cost	$50,000	1.20%	$51,500	1.26%	$53,045	0.97%	$54,636	0.89%

This worksheet compares 4 periods performance in both dollars and percentage. It is the results of your entries on the Master Data Entry worksheet.

Go to the **What-if Comp. Balance Sheet** worksheet.

2. What-if Comparative Balance Sheet

This figure shows the What-if Comparative Balance Sheet.

What-if Comparative Balance Sheet - 4 Periods

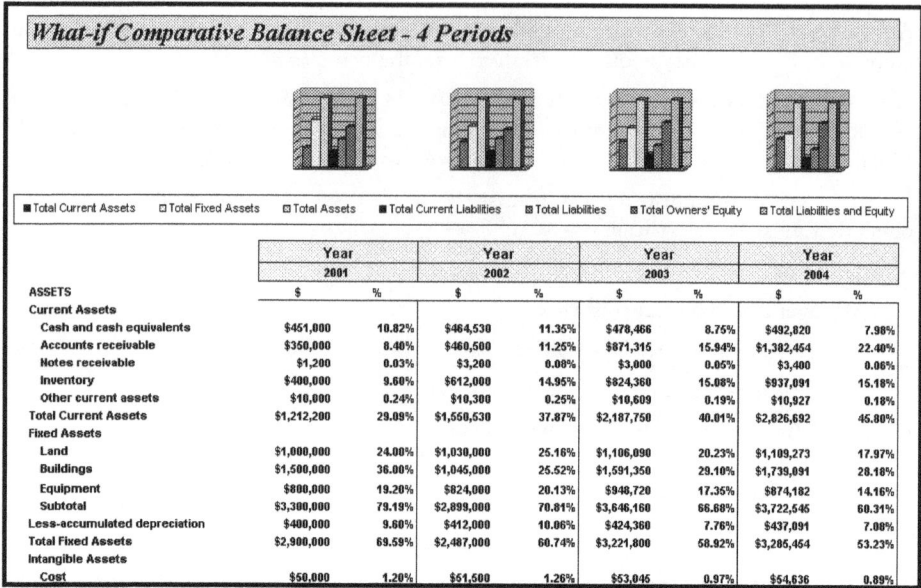

■ Total Current Assets ☐ Total Fixed Assets ☐ Total Assets ■ Total Current Liabilities ☒ Total Liabilities ☒ Total Owners' Equity ☐ Total Liabilities and Equity

	Year 2001		Year 2002		Year 2003		Year 2004	
	$	%	$	%	$	%	$	%
ASSETS								
Current Assets								
Cash and cash equivalents	$451,000	10.82%	$464,530	11.35%	$478,466	8.75%	$492,820	7.98%
Accounts receivable	$350,000	8.40%	$460,500	11.25%	$871,315	15.94%	$1,382,454	22.40%
Notes receivable	$1,200	0.03%	$3,200	0.08%	$3,000	0.05%	$3,400	0.06%
Inventory	$400,000	9.60%	$612,000	14.95%	$824,360	15.08%	$937,091	15.18%
Other current assets	$10,000	0.24%	$10,300	0.25%	$10,609	0.19%	$10,927	0.18%
Total Current Assets	$1,212,200	29.09%	$1,550,530	37.87%	$2,187,750	40.01%	$2,826,692	45.80%
Fixed Assets								
Land	$1,000,000	24.00%	$1,030,000	25.16%	$1,106,090	20.23%	$1,109,273	17.97%
Buildings	$1,500,000	36.00%	$1,045,000	25.52%	$1,591,350	29.10%	$1,739,091	28.18%
Equipment	$800,000	19.20%	$824,000	20.13%	$948,720	17.35%	$874,182	14.16%
Subtotal	$3,300,000	79.19%	$2,899,000	70.81%	$3,646,160	66.68%	$3,722,545	60.31%
Less-accumulated depreciation	$400,000	9.60%	$412,000	10.06%	$424,360	7.76%	$437,091	7.08%
Total Fixed Assets	$2,900,000	69.59%	$2,487,000	60.74%	$3,221,800	58.92%	$3,285,454	53.23%
Intangible Assets								
Cost	$50,000	1.20%	$51,500	1.26%	$53,045	0.97%	$54,636	0.89%

This worksheet compares 4 periods performance in both dollars and percentage. It is the results of your what-if manipulations on the What-if Master Data Entry worksheet.

This allows you the ability to print two separate Comparable Balance Sheets:

> 1. The **actual** and

> 2. The **what-if** to demonstrate data manipulation for investigation and forecasting for improving the bottom-line.

Cash Flow – Current and Projected

The Manager has two cash flow sheets:

> 1. Current and Projected Cash Flow Statement
> 2. What-if Current and Projected Cash Flow

For one final time, we return to our old friend **Manager.xls**.

Please view **Projected Cash Flow** and **What-if Projected Cash Flow** worksheets.

These two worksheets introduce you to **regression analysis**.

The concept of regression might sound strange because the term is normally associated with movement backward, whereas in the world of statistics, regression is often used to predict the future. Simply put, regression is a statistical technique that finds a mathematical expression that best describes a set of data.

Often businesses try to predict the future using sales and percent-of-sales projections based on history. A simple percent-of-sales technique identifies assets and liabilities that vary along with sales, determines the proportion of each, and assigns them percentages. Although using percent-of-sales forecasting is often sufficient for slow or steady short-term growth, the technique loses accuracy as growth accelerates.

Regression analysis uses more sophisticated equations to analyze larger sets of data and translates them into coordinates on a line or curve. In the not-so-distant past, regression analysis was not widely used because of the large volume of calculations involved. Since spreadsheet applications began offering built-in regression functions, the use of regression analysis has become more widespread.

As mentioned earlier, the second worksheet in *Manager.xls* is the What-if Master Data Entry worksheet that takes the data you entered in the Master Data Entry worksheet and manipulates it for investigation and forecasting.

The spinners are set at 100% to equal the entries on the Master Data Entry worksheet sheet. As you increase or decrease the spinners the ratio worksheets will respond instantly giving the ability to compare changes to what-if improvement goals for the *What-if Projected Cash Flow* worksheet.

1. Current and Projected Cash Flow Statement

This figure shows the Current and Projected Cash Flow Statement.

CURRENT & PROJECTED CASH FLOW STATEMENT

	Year 2001	Year 2002	Year 2003	Year 2004	Year 2005	Year 2006	Year 2007	Year 2008
Cash from operations								
Net earnings (loss)	$480,368	$753,034	$799,039	$1,162,043	$1,321,378	$1,530,481	$1,739,584	$1,948,687
Add-depreciation and amortization	$33,750	$34,763	$35,805	$36,880	$37,907	$38,950	$39,994	$41,037
Net cash from operations	$514,118	$787,797	$834,845	$1,198,922	$1,359,286	$1,569,432	$1,779,578	$1,989,724
Cash provided (used) by operating activities								
Accounts Receivable	$350,000	$460,500	$871,315	$1,382,454	$1,643,112	$1,993,930	$2,344,748	$2,695,565
Inventory	$400,000	$612,000	$824,360	$937,091	$1,149,271	$1,331,634	$1,513,997	$1,696,361
Other current assets	$10,000	$10,300	$10,609	$10,927	$11,232	$11,541	$11,850	$12,159
Other non-current assets	$25,000	$25,750	$26,523	$27,319	$28,079	$28,952	$29,625	$30,398
Accounts payable	$600,000	$618,000	$636,540	$640,563	$658,833	$672,856	$686,879	$700,902
Current portion of long-term debt	$100,000	$103,000	$106,090	$109,273	$112,318	$115,409	$118,499	$121,590
Income taxes	$30,000	$30,900	$31,827	$32,782	$33,695	$34,623	$35,550	$36,477
Accrued expenses	$90,000	$92,700	$95,481	$98,345	$101,086	$103,868	$106,649	$109,431
Other current liabilities	$16,000	$16,480	$16,974	$17,484	$17,971	$18,465	$18,960	$19,454
Distributions to shareholders	$0	$0	$0	$0	$0	$0	$0	$0
Net cash used by operations	$1,621,000	$1,969,630	$2,619,719	$3,256,237	$3,755,597	$4,311,177	$4,866,757	$5,422,337
Investment transactions Increases (decreases)								
Land	$0	$0	$0	$0	$0	$0	$0	$0
Buildings and improvements	$0	$0	$0	$0	$0	$0	$0	$0
Equipment	$0	$0	$0	$0	$0	$0	$0	$0
Intangible assets	$0	$0	$0	$0	$0	$0	$0	$0
Net cash from investments	$0	$0	$0	$0	$0	$0	$0	$0
Financing transactions								

This worksheet compares 8 periods performance in dollars. It is the results of your entries on the Master Data Entry worksheet and using current 4 years data it predicts with regression analysis the trends out an additional 4 years.

2. What-if Current and Projected Cash Flow

This figure shows the What-if Current and Projected Cash Flow Statement.

WHAT-IF CURRENT & PROJECTED CASH FLOW STATEMENT

	Year 2001	Year 2002	Year 2003	Year 2004	Year 2005	Year 2006	Year 2007	Year 2008
Cash from operations								
Net earnings (loss)	$480,368	$753,034	$799,039	$1,162,043	$1,321,378	$1,530,481	$1,739,584	$1,948,687
Add-depreciation and amortization	$33,750	$34,763	$35,805	$36,880	$37,907	$38,950	$39,994	$41,037
Net cash from operations	$514,118	$787,797	$834,845	$1,198,922	$1,359,286	$1,569,432	$1,779,578	$1,989,724
Cash provided (used) by operating activities								
Accounts Receivable	$350,000	$460,500	$871,315	$1,382,454	$1,643,112	$1,993,930	$2,344,748	$2,695,565
Inventory	$400,000	$612,000	$824,360	$937,091	$1,149,271	$1,331,634	$1,513,997	$1,696,361
Other current assets	$10,000	$10,300	$10,609	$10,927	$11,232	$11,541	$11,850	$12,159
Other non-current assets	$25,000	$25,750	$26,523	$27,318	$28,079	$28,852	$29,625	$30,398
Accounts payable	$600,000	$618,000	$636,540	$640,563	$658,833	$672,856	$686,879	$700,902
Current portion of long-term debt	$100,000	$103,000	$106,090	$109,273	$112,318	$115,409	$118,499	$121,590
Income taxes	$30,000	$30,900	$31,827	$32,782	$33,695	$34,623	$35,550	$36,477
Accrued expenses	$90,000	$92,700	$95,481	$98,345	$101,086	$103,868	$106,649	$109,431
Other current liabilities	$16,000	$16,480	$16,974	$17,484	$17,971	$18,465	$18,960	$19,454
Distributions to shareholders	$0	$0	$0	$0	$0	$0	$0	$0
Net cash used by operations	$1,621,000	$1,969,630	$2,619,719	$3,256,237	$3,755,597	$4,311,177	$4,866,757	$5,422,337
Investment transactions Increases (decreases)								
Land	$0	$0	$0	$0	$0	$0	$0	$0
Buildings and improvements	$0	$0	$0	$0	$0	$0	$0	$0
Equipment	$0	$0	$0	$0	$0	$0	$0	$0
Intangible assets	$0	$0	$0	$0	$0	$0	$0	$0
Net cash from investments	$0	$0	$0	$0	$0	$0	$0	$0
Financing transactions								

This worksheet compares 8 periods performance in dollars. It is the results of your manipulation of the spinners on the What-if Master Data Entry worksheet and using current 4 years data it predicts with regression analysis the trends out an additional 4 years.

Summary

The Manager has all of the ingredients for a business self-analysis that allows trial and error capabilities unlike any tool currently available to the small business owner. Its power will not become apparent until you have entered your own financial numbers.

The Executive Summary

Key to successfully operating a business is having the right information to make your decisions. This concept may appear elementary, but it can be one of the greatest strategic and operational obstacles your company faces. As any person who reads or analyzes financial statements knows, there are more financial indicators available than are needed. The trick is to choose the indicators that have the greatest relevance to your financial goals.

Management accounting as a profession concerns itself with the internal operations and drivers of business performance. One of its primary tools is an Executive Summary. This spreadsheet explores the relationships among key variables. It shows you how to use the Manager to identify which actions you can modify to meet your goals.

The Executive Summary of your business yields an overall picture of its financial health. The primary objective is to zero in on all of the positive and negative areas that are affecting your bottom line.

This worksheet can be used in conjunction with the Executive Summary created for your business plan in Chapter 9.

Go to the ***Manager's Index*** worksheet and click on the ***Executive Summary*** hyperlink.

This figure illustrates an example of The Executive Summary worksheet taken from the Manager.

The Executive Summary

For
The XYZ Company
June 30, 2005

The Executive Summary of your business yields an overall picture of its financial health. We have extracted, compiled, and entered into our analysis system all of the vital information that pertains to this specific business and yielded this summary. The primary objective is to zero in on all of the areas that might be detracting from the bottom line.

Knowledge is power, and knowledge of your company's value is the ultimate power tool. Item 9 is the summary results of your ***Market Value Analysis***. The Market Value Analysis uses the 6 standard methods endorsed by The American Society of Appraisers.

Category	Your Current Year 2001	Your Forecasted Year 2005	Comments
1. Net Revenue	$1,960,000	$3,641,354	The trend in this category is positive.
2. Cost of Revenue	$745,000	$990,118	The trend in this category is positive.
3. Gross Profit	$1,215,000	$2,561,236	The trend in this category is positive.
4. Total Operating Expenses	$558,760	$717,248	The trend in this category is positive.
5. Operating Profit	$656,240	$1,843,988	The trend in this category is positive.
6. Return on Ownership	$670,368	$1,518,878	The trend in this category is positive.
7. Current Ratio	1.30	3.20	The trend in this category is positive.
8. Z-Score - Publicly Held	2.40	3.03	The trend in this category is positive.

Business Valuation Summary

	Base Price	Base Price + Intangible Assets	Target Price
9. Average Valuation	$5,263,548	$5,395,548	$5,425,328
Median Valuation	$5,323,107	$5,455,107	

Overall Rating: You meet or exceed all industry standards.

The Financial Summary Analysis

The Financial Summary Analysis worksheet is a similar tool to an Executive Summary indicating key financial trends for your business. It is the summary of figures entered on the Master Data worksheet and then sent on an analysis trip throughout the Manager, and sent back to this one worksheet.

A key feature is the "Trend Assessment" column. Each line item is analyzed across the actual 4 periods and 4 forecasted periods and yields a simple "Upward" or "Downward" assessment. Upward indicators are good so long as they are in synchronization with other variables. There are good downward trends, for example, a downward trend in date of break-even is good.

Go to the *Manager's Index* worksheet and click on the *Financial Summary* hyperlink.

This figure illustrates The Financial Summary Analysis worksheet in the Manager.

Financial Summary Analysis

*EBIT is Earnings Before Interest and Taxes
**Ownership is the Total Reward for being the owner=Owner Salary + Bonus + Net Income + Other

	Year 2001	Year 2002	Year 2003	Year 2004	Year 2005	Year 2006	Year 2007	Year 2008	Trend ASSESSMENT
Income Statement					Forecast				
Net Sales	$1,960,000	$2,500,000	$2,651,800	$3,205,454	$3,641,354	$4,040,170	$4,438,986	$4,837,803	Upward
Cost of Goods Sold	$745,000	$871,350	$894,301	$915,467	$990,118	$1,043,553	$1,096,988	$1,150,423	Upward
Gross Profit (Margin)	$1,215,000	$1,628,650	$1,757,500	$2,289,987	$2,651,236	$2,996,617	$3,341,998	$3,687,379	Upward
G&A	$178,767	$197,222	$209,659	$221,095	$236,540	$250,482	$264,424	$278,366	Upward
Total Operating Expenses	$558,760	$583,787	$647,842	$672,707	$717,248	$757,838	$798,428	$839,018	Upward
EBIT*	$686,240	$1,075,763	$1,141,485	$1,660,061	$1,887,683	$2,186,402	$2,485,120	$2,783,839	Upward
Net Income After	$480,368	$753,034	$799,039	$1,162,043	$1,321,378	$1,530,481	$1,739,584	$1,948,687	Upward
Ownership**	$670,368	$944,034	$994,039	$1,357,043	$1,518,878	$1,729,881	$1,940,884	$2,151,887	Upward
Balance Sheet					Forecast				
Current Assets	$1,212,200	$1,550,530	$2,187,750	$2,826,692	$3,314,467	$3,862,537	$4,410,607	$4,958,676	Upward
Inventory	$400,000	$612,000	$824,360	$937,091	$1,149,271	$1,331,634	$1,513,997	$1,696,361	Upward
Other Assets	$10,000	$10,300	$10,609	$10,927	$11,232	$11,541	$11,850	$12,159	Upward
Total Assets	$4,167,200	$4,094,180	$5,467,899	$6,172,246	$6,822,596	$7,561,481	$8,300,367	$9,039,253	Upward
Current Liabilities	$936,000	$964,080	$993,002	$1,007,719	$1,036,220	$1,060,628	$1,085,037	$1,109,445	Upward
Non-current Liabilities	$781,200	$809,600	$836,592	$864,999	$892,695	$920,534	$948,373	$976,212	Upward
Total Liabilities	$1,717,200	$1,773,680	$1,829,594	$1,872,718	$1,928,916	$1,981,162	$2,033,409	$2,085,656	Upward
Equity	$2,450,000	$2,320,500	$3,638,305	$4,299,528	$4,893,680	$5,580,319	$6,266,958	$6,953,597	Upward
Cash Flow					Forecast				
Net Cash Flow	$1,175,318	$873,797	$1,489,319	$1,879,487	$2,036,487	$2,309,290	$2,562,093	$2,854,896	Upward
Breakeven					Forecast				
Break-Even	$636,455	$593,738	$668,999	$618,603	$634,875	$637,046	$839,217	$641,387	Upward
B/E %	32.47%	23.75%	25.23%	19.30%	15.68%	11.87%	8.07%	4.26%	Downward
DAY OF B/E	119	87	92	70	57	43	29	16	Downward
DATE OF B/E	Apr 27	Mar 26	Apr 01	Mar 10	Feb 26	Feb 12	Jan 29	Jan 15	Downward
Key Ratios					Forecast				
Current Ratio	1.30	1.61	2.20	2.81	3.20	3.64	4.06	4.47	Upward
Quick Ratio	0.87	0.97	1.37	1.88	2.09	2.39	2.67	2.94	Upward
Debt Ratio	0.41	0.43	0.33	0.30	0.28	0.26	0.24	0.23	Downward
Asset Turnover	0.47	0.61	0.48	0.52	0.53	0.53	0.53	0.54	Upward
Net Income/Sales	0.25	0.30	0.30	0.36	0.36	0.38	0.39	0.40	Upward
Debt/Equity	0.70	0.76	0.50	0.44	0.39	0.36	0.32	0.30	Downward
Return on Assets	0.15	0.24	0.18	0.23	0.23	0.24	0.24	0.25	Upward
Working Capital	$276,200	$586,450	$1,194,748	$1,818,973	$2,278,247	$2,801,909	$3,325,570	$3,849,232	Upward
Sales/Working Capital	7.10	4.26	2.22	1.76	1.60	1.44	1.33	1.26	Downward
Market Value					Forecast				
Book Market Value	$2,450,000	$2,320,500	$3,638,305	$4,299,528	$4,893,680	$5,580,319	$6,266,957	$6,953,596	Upward
Plus Ownership**	$3,120,368	$3,264,534	$4,632,344	$5,656,570	$6,412,558	$7,310,200	$8,207,842	$9,105,483	Upward
Altman Z-Score Analysis					Forecast				
Publicly Held Firm	2.40	2.94	3.04	3.51	3.83	4.17	4.52	4.86	Upward
Privately Held Firm	1.35	1.88	1.62	1.88	2.01	2.14	2.27	2.41	Upward
Non-Manufacturing	4.09	5.26	5.89	7.02	7.92	8.86	9.81	10.75	Upward

The Forecast Analysis - 12 Fiscal Periods

The Forecast Analysis- 12 Fiscal Periods worksheet can not be overemphasized in importance. Based on 4 periods of actual data, it forecasts the condition of your business out to 12 financial periods.

Combined with the other analysis sheets, it tells a loan officer, venture capitalist, Small Business Administration, etc. the success trend of your business.

Its single greatest attribute is magnifying the future trend of a business. Small variances become much larger and apparent in the 12th regression.

Go to the **Manager's Index** worksheet and click on the **Forecast Analysis** hyperlink.

This figure illustrates The Forecast Analysis worksheet in the Manager. Shown portions of the income and balance sheet statements.

Forecast Analysis- 12 Fiscal Periods

Income Statement
Manufacturer

	Year 2001	Year 2002	Year 2003	Year 2004	Year 2005	Year 2006	Year 2007	Year 2008	Year 2009	Year 2010	Year 2011	Year 2012
Gross Sales	$2,010,000	$2,560,000	$2,721,800	$3,285,454	$3,641,354	$4,040,170	$4,438,986	$4,837,803	$5,236,619	$5,635,436	$6,034,251	$6,433,067
Discounts/Allowances	($50,000)	($60,000)	($70,000)	($80,000)	($90,000)	($100,000)	($110,000)	($120,000)	($130,000)	($140,000)	($150,000)	($160,000)
Net Sales	$1,960,000	$2,500,000	$2,651,800	$3,205,454	$3,551,354	$3,940,170	$4,328,986	$4,717,803	$5,106,619	$5,495,436	$5,884,251	$6,273,067
Direct Material Cost	$320,000	$427,600	$431,236	$432,513	$488,132	$522,250	$556,367	$590,485	$624,603	$658,721	$692,838	$726,956
Direct Labor Cost	$300,000	$375,000	$330,450	$346,364	$361,599	$377,043	$392,497	$407,951	$423,405	$438,859	$454,313	$469,767
Other Direct Costs	$125,000	$128,750	$132,613	$136,591	$140,397	$144,261	$148,124	$151,988	$155,851	$159,715	$163,578	$167,442
Total Cost of Sales	$745,000	$871,350	$894,301	$915,467	$990,118	$1,043,553	$1,096,988	$1,150,423	$1,203,859	$1,257,294	$1,310,729	$1,364,164
Gross Profit	**$1,215,000**	**$1,628,650**	**$1,757,500**	**$2,289,987**	**$2,561,236**	**$2,896,617**	**$3,231,998**	**$3,567,379**	**$3,902,760**	**$4,238,141**	**$4,573,522**	**$4,908,903**

Expenses

	2001	2002	2003	2004	2005	2006	2007	2008	2009	2010	2011	2012
Fixed Expenses												
Executive Salaries	$190,000	$191,000	$195,000	$195,000	$197,500	$199,400	$201,300	$203,200	$205,100	$207,000	$208,900	$210,800
Advertising	$50,000	$51,500	$53,045	$54,636	$56,159	$57,704	$59,250	$60,795	$62,340	$63,886	$65,431	$66,977
Auto & Truck Expenses	$30,000	$30,900	$31,827	$32,782	$33,695	$34,623	$35,550	$36,477	$37,404	$38,332	$39,259	$40,186
Depreciation	$5,000	$5,150	$45,305	$50,464	$70,616	$88,270	$105,925	$123,580	$141,234	$158,889	$176,543	$194,198
Employee Benefits	$3,000	$3,090	$3,183	$3,278	$3,370	$3,462	$3,555	$3,648	$3,740	$3,833	$3,926	$4,019
Home Office Business Expenses	$1,000	$1,030	$1,061	$1,093	$1,123	$1,154	$1,185	$1,216	$1,247	$1,278	$1,309	$1,340
Insurance	$3,306	$3,754	$4,010	$3,994	$4,046	$4,098	$4,150	$4,202	$4,254	$4,306	$4,358	$4,410
Bank Charges	$2,133	$2,197	$2,263	$2,331	$2,396	$2,462	$2,528	$2,594	$2,659	$2,725	$2,791	$2,857
Legal & Professional Services	$1,000	$1,330	$1,670	$2,020	$2,355	$2,695	$3,035	$3,375	$3,715	$4,055	$4,395	$4,735
Meals & Entertainment	$4,000	$4,120	$4,244	$4,371	$4,493	$4,616	$4,740	$4,864	$4,987	$5,111	$5,235	$5,358
Office Expense	$6,000	$6,180	$6,365	$6,556	$6,729	$6,925	$7,110	$7,295	$7,481	$7,666	$7,852	$8,037
Retirement Plans	$1,000	$1,030	$1,061	$1,093	$1,123	$1,154	$1,185	$1,216	$1,247	$1,278	$1,309	$1,340
Rent - Equipment	$3,000	$3,090	$3,183	$3,278	$3,370	$3,462	$3,555	$3,648	$3,740	$3,833	$3,926	$4,019
Rent - Office & Business Property	$8,750	$9,110	$9,544	$9,929	$10,326	$10,723	$11,120	$11,517	$11,914	$12,311	$12,708	$13,105
Repairs	$1,000	$1,030	$1,061	$1,093	$1,123	$1,154	$1,185	$1,216	$1,247	$1,278	$1,309	$1,340
Supplies	$1,000	$1,030	$1,061	$1,093	$1,123	$1,154	$1,185	$1,216	$1,247	$1,278	$1,309	$1,340
Taxes - Business & Payroll	$1,000	$1,030	$1,061	$1,093	$1,123	$1,154	$1,185	$1,216	$1,247	$1,278	$1,309	$1,340
Travel	$8,230	$8,120	$6,010	$5,900	$5,790	$5,680	$5,570	$5,460	$5,350	$5,240	$5,130	$5,020
Utilities	$11,974	$12,374	$14,186	$16,974	$18,080	$19,761	$21,442	$23,124	$24,805	$26,486	$28,167	$29,848
Other Expenses	$0	$0	$0	$0	$0	$0	$0	$0	$0	$0	$0	$0
Total Fixed Expenses	$329,983	$335,065	$385,138	$396,977	$424,549	$443,651	$474,754	$499,958	$524,958	$550,081	$575,183	$600,286

Balance Sheet
ASSETS

	Year 2001	Year 2002	Year 2003	Year 2004	Year 2005	Year 2006	Year 2007	Year 2008	Year 2009	Year 2010	Year 2011	Year 2012
Current Assets												
Cash and cash equivalents	$451,000	$464,530	$478,466	$492,820	$506,953	$520,492	$534,432	$548,371	$562,311	$576,251	$590,190	$604,130
Accounts receivable	$250,000	$460,500	$871,315	$1,382,454	$1,643,112	$1,893,930	$2,244,746	$2,695,565	$3,046,383	$3,397,201	$3,749,019	$4,099,837
Notes receivable	$1,200	$3,200	$3,300	$3,400	$4,300	$4,940	$5,580	$6,220	$6,860	$7,500	$9,140	$8,780
Inventory	$400,000	$812,000	$924,360	$937,091	$1,149,271	$1,391,634	$1,593,997	$1,696,361	$1,878,724	$2,061,087	$2,243,450	$2,425,813
Other current assets	$10,000	$10,300	$10,609	$10,927	$11,232	$11,541	$11,850	$12,159	$12,468	$12,777	$13,086	$13,395
Total Current Assets	$1,212,200	$1,550,530	$2,197,750	$2,826,692	$3,314,467	$3,862,537	$4,410,607	$4,958,676	$5,506,746	$6,054,816	$6,602,886	$7,150,955

	2001	2002	2003	2004	2005	2006	2007	2008	2009	2010	2011	2012
Fixed Assets												
Land	$1,000,000	$1,030,000	$1,106,090	$1,109,273	$1,162,319	$1,202,709	$1,243,099	$1,283,490	$1,323,881	$1,364,272	$1,404,663	$1,445,053
Buildings	$1,500,000	$1,045,000	$1,591,350	$1,739,391	$1,784,766	$1,911,128	$2,037,490	$2,163,852	$2,290,214	$2,416,576	$2,542,938	$2,668,301
Equipment	$800,000	$824,000	$948,720	$874,182	$948,542	$983,268	$1,017,995	$1,052,721	$1,087,448	$1,122,174	$1,156,900	$1,191,627
Subtotal	$3,300,000	$2,899,000	$3,646,160	$3,722,845	$3,895,625	$4,097,104	$4,296,584	$4,500,063	$4,701,543	$4,903,022	$5,104,501	$5,305,981
Less-accumulated depreciation	$400,000	$412,000	$424,360	$437,091	$449,271	$461,634	$473,997	$486,361	$498,724	$511,087	$523,450	$535,813
Total Fixed Assets	$2,900,000	$2,487,000	$3,221,900	$3,285,454	$3,446,354	$3,635,470	$3,824,586	$4,013,703	$4,202,819	$4,391,935	$4,581,051	$4,770,167

	2001	2002	2003	2004	2005	2006	2007	2008	2009	2010	2011	2012
Intangible Assets												
Cost	$50,000	$51,500	$53,045	$54,636	$56,159	$57,704	$59,250	$60,795	$62,340	$63,886	$65,431	$66,977
Less-accumulated amortization	$20,000	$20,600	$21,218	$21,855	$22,464	$23,082	$23,700	$24,318	$24,936	$25,554	$25,173	$26,791
Total Intangible Assets	$30,000	$30,900	$31,827	$32,782	$33,695	$34,623	$35,550	$36,477	$37,404	$38,332	$39,259	$40,186

	2001	2002	2003	2004	2005	2006	2007	2008	2009	2010	2011	2012
Other assets	$25,000	$25,750	$26,523	$27,318	$28,078	$28,852	$29,625	$30,398	$31,170	$31,943	$32,716	$33,488
Total Assets	$4,167,200	$4,094,180	$5,467,999	$6,172,246	$6,822,596	$7,561,481	$8,300,367	$9,039,253	$9,778,138	$10,517,024	$11,255,910	$11,994,795

The Market Value Analysis

There is no single best method for determining a business's worth since each business sale is unique. The wisest approach is to compute a company's value using several techniques and then choose the one that makes the most sense.

There are three techniques and several variations for determining the value of a business:

Go to the **Manager's Index** worksheet and click on the **Market Value Analysis** hyperlink.

The Balance Sheet Technique.

Balance Sheet Technique. The balance sheet technique is one of the most commonly used methods of evaluating a business, although it is not highly recommended because it oversimplifies the valuation process. This method computes the company's net worth or owner's equity (net worth = assets - liabilities) and uses this figure as the value.

The problem with this technique is that it fails to recognize reality: Most small

Balance Sheet Technique			
Book Value of Net Worth	=	Assets minus Liabilities	
	=	$4,167,200	$1,717,200
	=	$2,450,000	

businesses have market values that exceed their reported book values.

The first step is to determine which assets are included in the sale. In most cases, the owner has some personal assets he does not want to sell. Remember that net worth on a financial statement will likely differ significantly from actual net worth in the market.

Adjusted Balance Sheet Technique			
Adjusted Net Worth	=	Adjusted Assets minus Liabilities	
	=	$3,601,700	$1,717,200
	=	$1,884,500	

The Adjusted Balance Sheet Technique.

Adjusted Balance Sheet Technique. A more realistic method for determining a company's value is to adjust the book value of net worth to reflect actual market value. The values reported on a company's books may overstate or understate the true value of assets and liabilities. Typical assets in a business sale include notes and accounts receivable, inventories, supplies, and fixtures. If a buyer purchases notes and accounts receivable, he should estimate the likelihood of their collection and adjust their value accordingly.

The Earnings Approach.

The Earnings Approach. The buyer of an existing business is essentially purchasing its future income. The earnings approach is more refined because it considers the future income potential of the business.

Three Variations of the earnings method:

1. Excess Earnings Method.

This method combines both the value of the firm's existing assets (over its liabilities) and an estimate of its future earnings potential to determine a business's selling price.

The excess earnings method provides a more consistent and realistic approach for determining the value of goodwill. It measures goodwill by the amount of profit the business earns above the average firm in the same industry. It also assumes that the owner is entitled to a reasonable return on the firm's adjusted tangible net worth.

Earnings Approach					
	Variation 1 - Excess Earnings Method				
	Step 1	Adjusted tangible net worth equals		$3,601,700	minus	$1,717,200
		equals		$1,884,500		
	Step 2	Opportunity Costs	equals	$596,125	
	Step 3	Estimated net earnings	equals	$1,325,783	
	Step 4	Extra earning power=estimated net earnings-opportunity cost =			
		equals		$729,658	
	Step 5	Value of intangibles=extra earning power X years of profit figure =			
		equals		$3,648,290	
	Step 6	Value of business tangible net worth + value of intangibles =			
		equals		$5,532,790	

2. Capitalized Earnings Approach.

Another earnings approach capitalizes expected net profits to determine the value of a business. The buyer should prepare his own pro forma income statement and should ask the seller to prepare one also. Use a five year weighted average of past sales (with the greatest weights assigned to the most recent years) to estimate sales for the upcoming year

Once again, the buyer must evaluate the risk involved in purchasing the business to determine the appropriate rate of return on the investment. The greater the risk involved, the higher the return the buyer requires. Risk determination is always somewhat subjective, but it is necessary for proper evaluation.

The capitalized earnings approach divides estimated net earnings (after subtracting the owner's reasonable salary) by the rate of return that reflects the risk level.

Clearly, firms with lower risk factors are more valuable. Most normal risk businesses use a rate of return factor ranging from 25 percent to 33 percent. The lowest risk factor most buyers would accept for any business ranges from 15 to 20 percent.

Variation 2 - Capitalized Earnings Approach	
Value =	net earnings
	---
	rate of return
Value =	$1,325,783

	0.25
Value =	$5,303,132

3. Discounted Future Earnings Approach.

This variation of the earnings approach assumes that a dollar earned in the future is worth less than that same dollar today. Therefore, using this approach, the buyer estimates the company's net income for several years into the future and then discounts these future earnings back to their present value. The resulting present value is an estimate of the company's worth. The reduced value of future dollars has nothing to do with inflation.

Instead, present value represents the cost of the buyer giving up the opportunity to earn a reasonable rate of return by receiving income in the future instead of today.

The primary advantage of this technique is that it values a business solely on the basis of its future earning potential, but its reliability depends on making forecasts of future earnings and on choosing a realistic present value rate.

The discounted cash flow technique is especially well suited for valuing service businesses (whose asset bases are often small) and for companies experiencing high growth rates.

Variation 3 - Discounted Future Earnings Approach

Step 1 Projected future earnings approach

Year	Pessimistic	Most Likely	Optimistic	Weighted Average
2005	$1,281,737	$1,321,378	$1,387,447	$1,325,783
2006	$1,484,567	$1,530,481	$1,607,005	$1,535,583
2007	$1,587,397	$1,739,584	$1,826,563	$1,745,383
2008	$1,890,226	$1,948,687	$2,046,121	$1,955,183
2009	$2,093,056	$2,157,790	$2,265,879	$2,164,983
			Total	$8,726,914

Step 2 Discount future earnings at the appropriate present value factor

Year	Forecasted Earnings	X	Present Value Factor	= Net Present Value
2005	$1,325,783	X	0.8000	$1,060,626
2006	$1,535,583	X	0.6400	$982,773
2007	$1,745,383	X	0.5120	$893,636
2008	$1,955,183	X	0.4096	$800,843
2009	$2,164,983	X	0.3277	$709,465
			Total	$3,737,878

Step 3 Estimate income stream beyond 4 years

$$\text{Income Stream} = \text{Fourth year income} \times \frac{1}{\text{Rate of Return}}$$

= $2,164,983 X 4.00
= $8,659,931

Step 4 Discount income stream beyond four years (using fifth year present value factor)

Present value of income stream =	$8,659,931	X	0.1854
equals	$1,605,205		

Step 5 Compute the Total Value

Total Value =	Step 2 + Step 4		
Total Value =	$3,737,878	+	$1,605,205
Total Value =	$5,343,083		

The Market (or price/earnings) Approach.

The market (or price/earnings) approach uses the price/earnings ratios of similar businesses to establish the value of a company. The buyer must use businesses whose stocks are publicly traded to get a meaningful comparison. A company's price/earnings ratio (or P/E ratio) is the price of one share of its common stock in the market divided by its earnings per share (after deducting preferred stock dividends). To get a representative P/E ratio, the buyer should average the P/Es of as many similar businesses as possible. To compute the company's value, the buyer multiplies the average price/earnings ratio by the private company's estimated earnings.

The biggest advantage of the market approach is its simplicity. However, this method suffers from several disadvantages, including the following:

Market Approach

Value =	estimated earnings x Representative price-earnings ratio		
Value =	$1,325,783	Times	8.3
Value =	$11,067,784		

1) **Necessary comparisons between publicly traded and privately owned companies**. The stock of privately owned companies is illiquid, and, therefore, the PIE ratio used is often subjective and lower than that of publicly held companies.

2) **Unrepresentative earnings estimates**. The private company's net earnings may not realistically reflect its true earning potential. To minimize taxes, owners usually attempt to keep profits low and rely on fringe benefits to make up the difference.

3) **Finding similar companies for comparison**. Often, it is extremely difficult for a buyer to find comparable publicly held companies when estimating the appropriate P/E ratio.

4) **Applying the after-tax earnings of a private company to determine its value**. If a prospective buyer is using an after-tax P/E ratio from public companies, he also must use after-tax earnings from the private company

Despite its drawbacks, the market approach is useful as a general guideline to establishing a company's value.

The Summary of Approaches.

Summary of Approaches			Base Price	Base Price + Intangibles
Balance Sheet Technique			$2,450,000	$2,582,000
Adjusted Balance Sheet Technique			$1,864,500	$2,016,500
Earnings Approach		Variation 1	$5,532,790	$5,664,790
		Variation 2	$5,303,132	$5,435,132
		Variation 3	$5,343,083	$5,475,083
Market Approach			$11,067,784	$11,199,784
		Average	$5,263,548	$5,395,548
		Median	$5,323,107	$5,455,107

Payroll Analysis.

Go to the *Manager's Index* worksheet and click on the *Payroll Analysis* hyperlink.

This comprehensive version analyzes whether your business is under or overstaffed. The key information for the sheet is linked from the Master Data Entry Worksheet.

This What-if section changes 4 variables by using the spinners. 100% in all 4 categories equals the numbers in the payroll analysis section.

Spinners Reset Button: You may reset the spinner values to 100% at any time with the Reset button in the upper right hand corner.

Comparative Payroll Analysis

Reset Spinners   Calculator

Payroll Analysis		What-if Payroll Analysis	
This analysis uses simple direct proportions. Refer to it as a payroll performance snapshot in positive & negative situations.		What-if Analysis Use the spinners to experiment with the payroll demand.	

CURRENT NUMBER OF EMPLOYEES	37	CURRENT NUMBER OF EMPLOYEES	37
CURRENT SALES ANNUALIZED (Weekly X 52 Weeks)	$3,399,968	CURRENT SALES ANNUALIZED (Weekly X 52 Weeks)	$3,399,968 100%
CURRENT COMPLETED YEAR SALES	$3,285,464	CURRENT COMPLETED YEAR SALES	$3,285,464 100%
CURRENT PAYROLL ANNUALIZED (Weekly X 52 Weeks)	$350,064	CURRENT PAYROLL ANNUALIZED (Weekly X 52 Weeks)	$350,064 100%
PRIOR YEAR PAYROLL	$313,647	PRIOR YEAR PAYROLL	$313,647 100%

SALES VOLUME REQUIRED, AT CURRENT PAYROLL LEVEL, TO PRODUCE PROFITS
EQUAL TO THE PREVIOUS YEAR PROFITS-------- $3,666,922

SALES DEFICIENCY = SALES REQUIRED MINUS CURRENT VOLUME
SALES DEFICIENCY IS---------------   ($266,954)

GROSS PAYROLL ALLOWABLE
UNDER PROJECTED CONDITIONS----- $324,579

GROSS PAYROLL BURDEN IS------   ($25,485)   OR   -8.1%

THE NUMBER OF EXCESS EMPLOYEES ON THE PAYROLL . . . .   -3.01

SALES VOLUME REQUIRED, AT CURRENT PAYROLL LEVEL, TO PRODUCE PROFITS
EQUAL TO THE PREVIOUS YEAR PROFITS-------- $3,666,922

SALES DEFICIENCY = SALES REQUIRED MINUS CURRENT VOLUME
SALES DEFICIENCY IS---------------   ($266,954)

GROSS PAYROLL ALLOWABLE
UNDER PROJECTED CONDITIONS----- $324,579

GROSS PAYROLL BURDEN IS------   ($25,485)   OR   -8.1%

THE NUMBER OF EXCESS EMPLOYEES ON THE PAYROLL . . . .   -3.01

Expense Analysis.

Go to the *Manager's Index* worksheet and click on the *Expense Analysis* hyperlink.

This worksheet allows you to work on one financial period at a time.

Select one of four periods by clicking the respective button. The expense data will be transferred from the Master Data Entry worksheet.

Use the spinners to experiment with raising and lowering individual expenses by line item.

The results are displayed on the spinner operated zone and under the What-if, Actual, Change boxes.

You can clear and start a new session by clicking on the Spinner Reset Button.

Expense Analysis

Choose a Financial Period and Click The Respective Button

2001	Click Here
2002	Click Here
2003	Click Here
2004	Click Here

Reset Spinners   Calculator

	What-if	Actual	Change
Net Sales	$1,960,000	$1,960,000	$0
Total Expenses	$1,303,760	$1,303,760	$0
Operating Income	$656,240	$656,240	$0

Type of Expense	Actual Expense Value	To a Value of:	Change Expense By Difference:		By Percentage	Percentage Of Actual Expenses
Net Sales	$1,960,000	$1,960,000	$0		0.00%	60.05%
Direct Material Cost	$320,000	$320,000	$0		0.00%	9.80%
Direct Labor Cost	$300,000	$300,000	$0		0.00%	9.19%
Other Direct Costs	$125,000	$125,000	$0		0.00%	3.83%
Executive Salaries	$190,000	$190,000	$0		0.00%	5.82%
Advertising	$50,000	$50,000	$0		0.00%	1.53%
Auto & Truck Expenses	$30,000	$30,000	$0		0.00%	0.92%
Depreciation	$5,000	$5,000	$0		0.00%	0.15%
Employee Benefits	$3,000	$3,000	$0		0.00%	0.09%
Home Office Business Expenses	$1,000	$1,000	$0		0.00%	0.03%
Insurance	$3,906	$3,906	$0		0.00%	0.12%
Bank Charges	$2,133	$2,133	$0		0.00%	0.07%
Legal & Professional Services	$1,000	$1,000	$0		0.00%	0.03%
Meals & Entertainment	$4,000	$4,000	$0		0.00%	0.12%

Pro Forma Balance Sheet.

Go to the *Manager's Index* worksheet and click on the *Proforma Balance* hyperlink.

This is a financial planning tool for businesses. It is especially useful for estimating long-term financial leverage and is widely used in Business Plans.

Years 1 through 3 are linked to the Master Data Entry worksheet. Year 4 is a regression analysis based on the preceding 3 years.

Pro Forma Balance Sheet

ASSETS Current Assets	Year 2001	Year 2002	Year 2003	Year 2004
Cash and cash equivalents	$451,000	$464,530	$478,466	$492,131
Accounts receivable	$350,000	$460,500	$871,315	$1,081,920
Notes receivable	$1,200	$3,200	$3,000	$4,267
Inventory	$400,000	$612,000	$824,360	$1,036,480
Other current assets	$10,000	$10,300	$10,609	$10,912
Total Current Assets	$1,212,200	$1,550,530	$2,187,750	$2,625,710

Fixed Assets	2001	2002	2003	2004
Land	$1,000,000	$1,030,000	$1,106,090	$1,151,453
Buildings	$1,500,000	$1,045,000	$1,591,350	$1,470,133
Equipment	$800,000	$824,000	$948,720	$1,006,293
Subtotal	$3,300,000	$2,899,000	$3,646,160	$3,627,880
Less-accumulated depreciation	$400,000	$412,000	$424,360	$436,480
Total Fixed Assets	$2,900,000	$2,487,000	$3,221,800	$3,191,400

Intangible Assets	2001	2002	2003	2004
Cost	$50,000	$51,500	$53,045	$54,560
Less-accumulated amortization	$20,000	$20,600	$21,218	$21,824
Total Intangible Assets	$30,000	$30,900	$31,827	$32,736

Other assets	$25,000	$25,750	$26,523	$27,280
Total Assets	$4,167,200	$4,094,180	$5,467,899	$5,877,125

Feel free to write over any formula to generate your own Pro Forma presentation.

What-if Pro Forma Balance Sheet.

Go to the *Manager's Index* worksheet and click on the *What-if Proforma Balance* hyperlink.

This is a financial planning tool for businesses. It is especially useful for estimating long-term financial leverage and is widely used in Business Plans.

Years 1 through 3 are linked to the *What-if* Master Data Entry worksheet. Year 4 is a regression analysis based on the preceding 3 years.

What-if Pro Forma Balance Sheet

				Forecasted
ASSETS	Year	Year	Year	Year
Current Assets	2001	2002	2003	2004
Cash and cash equivalents	$451,000	$464,530	$478,466	$492,131
Accounts receivable	$350,000	$460,500	$871,315	$1,081,920
Notes receivable	$1,200	$3,200	$3,000	$4,267
Inventory	$400,000	$612,000	$824,360	$1,036,480
Other current assets	$10,000	$10,300	$10,609	$10,912
Total Current Assets	$1,212,200	$1,550,530	$2,187,750	$2,625,710
Fixed Assets	2001	2002	2003	2004
Land	$1,000,000	$1,030,000	$1,106,090	$1,151,453
Buildings	$1,500,000	$1,045,000	$1,591,350	$1,470,133
Equipment	$800,000	$824,000	$948,720	$1,006,293
Subtotal	$3,300,000	$2,899,000	$3,646,160	$3,627,880
Less-accumulated depreciation	$400,000	$412,000	$424,360	$436,480
Total Fixed Assets	$2,900,000	$2,487,000	$3,221,800	$3,191,400
Intangible Assets	2001	2002	2003	2004
Cost	$50,000	$51,500	$53,045	$54,560
Less-accumulated amortization	$20,000	$20,600	$21,218	$21,824
Total Intangible Assets	$30,000	$30,900	$31,827	$32,736
Other assets	$25,000	$25,750	$26,523	$27,280
Total Assets	$4,167,200	$4,094,180	$5,467,899	$5,877,125

Feel free to write over formulas to generate your own Pro Forma presentation.

Pro Forma Income Statement.

At the *Manager's Index* worksheet, click on the *Proforma Income* hyperlink.

This is a financial planning tool for businesses. It is especially useful for estimating long-term financing needs and is widely used in Business Plans.

Years 1 through 3 are linked to the Master Data Entry worksheet. Year 4 is a regression analysis based on the preceding 3 years.

Feel free to write over formulae to generate your own Pro Forma presentation.

Pro Forma Income Statement

	Year 2001	Year 2002	Year 2003	Forecasted Year 2004
REVENUE				
Gross Sales	$2,010,000	$2,560,000	$2,721,800	$3,142,400
Discounts/Allowances	($50,000)	($60,000)	($70,000)	($80,000)
Net Sales	$1,960,000	$2,500,000	$2,651,800	$3,062,400
COST OF SALES	**2001**	**2002**	**2003**	**2004**
Direct Material Cost	$320,000	$427,600	$431,238	$504,184
Direct Labor Cost	$300,000	$315,000	$330,450	$345,600
Other Direct Costs	$125,000	$128,750	$132,613	$136,400
Total Cost of Sales	$745,000	$871,350	$894,301	$986,184
Gross Profit (Loss)	$1,215,000	$1,628,650	$1,757,500	$2,076,216
OPERATING EXPENSES	**2001**	**2002**	**2003**	**2004**
Executive Salaries	$190,000	$191,000	$195,000	$197,000
Advertising	$50,000	$51,500	$53,045	$54,560
Auto & Truck Expenses	$30,000	$30,900	$31,827	$32,736
Depreciation	$5,000	$5,150	$45,305	$58,789
Employee Benefits	$3,000	$3,090	$3,183	$3,274
Home Office Business Expenses	$1,000	$1,030	$1,061	$1,091
Insurance	$3,906	$3,754	$4,010	$3,994
Bank Charges	$2,133	$2,197	$2,263	$2,328
Legal & Professional Services	$1,000	$1,330	$1,670	$2,003
Meals & Entertainment	$4,000	$4,120	$4,244	$4,365
Office Expense	$6,000	$6,180	$6,365	$6,547
Retirement Plans	$1,000	$1,030	$1,061	$1,091
Rent - Equipment	$3,000	$3,090	$3,183	$3,274
Rent - Office & Business Property	$8,750	$9,110	$9,544	$9,929
Repairs	$1,000	$1,030	$1,061	$1,091
Supplies	$1,000	$1,030	$1,061	$1,091
Taxes - Business & Payroll	$1,000	$1,030	$1,061	$1,091

What-if Pro Forma Income Statement.

From the *Manager's Index* worksheet, click on the *What-if Proforma Income* hyperlink.

This is a financial planning tool for businesses. It is especially useful for estimating long-term financing needs and is widely used in Business Plans.

Years 1 through 3 are linked to the What-if Master Data Entry worksheet. Year 4 is a regression analysis based on the preceding 3 years.

Feel free to write over formulae to generate your own Pro Forma presentation.

What-if Pro Forma Income Statement

	Year 2001	Year 2002	Year 2003	Forecasted Year 2004
REVENUE				
Gross Sales	$2,010,000	$2,560,000	$2,721,800	$3,142,400
Discounts/Allowances	($50,000)	($60,000)	($70,000)	($80,000)
Net Sales	$1,960,000	$2,500,000	$2,651,800	$3,062,400
COST OF SALES	**2001**	**2002**	**2003**	**2004**
Direct Material Cost	$320,000	$427,600	$431,238	$504,184
Direct Labor Cost	$300,000	$315,000	$330,450	$545,600
Other Direct Costs	$125,000	$128,750	$132,613	$136,400
Total Cost of Sales	$745,000	$871,350	$894,301	$986,184
Gross Profit (Loss)	$1,215,000	$1,628,650	$1,757,500	$2,076,216
OPERATING EXPENSES	**2001**	**2002**	**2003**	**2004**
Executive Salaries	$190,000	$191,000	$195,000	$197,000
Advertising	$50,000	$51,500	$53,045	$54,560
Auto & Truck Expenses	$30,000	$30,900	$31,827	$32,736
Depreciation	$5,000	$5,150	$45,305	$58,789
Employee Benefits	$3,000	$3,090	$3,183	$3,274
Home Office Business Expenses	$1,000	$1,030	$1,061	$1,091
Insurance	$3,906	$3,754	$4,010	$3,994
Bank Charges	$2,133	$2,197	$2,263	$2,328
Legal & Professional Services	$1,000	$1,330	$1,670	$2,003
Meals & Entertainment	$4,000	$4,120	$4,244	$4,365
Office Expense	$6,000	$6,180	$6,365	$6,547
Retirement Plans	$1,000	$1,030	$1,061	$1,091
Rent - Equipment	$3,000	$3,090	$3,183	$3,274
Rent - Office & Business Property	$8,750	$9,110	$9,544	$9,929
Repairs	$1,000	$1,030	$1,061	$1,091
Supplies	$1,000	$1,030	$1,061	$1,091
Taxes - Business & Payroll	$1,000	$1,030	$1,061	$1,091

What-if Sales versus Expense Reduction.

Go to the *Manager's Index* worksheet and click on the *Sales vs. Expense* and *What-if Sales vs. Expense* hyperlinks.

A simple concept. Is it more efficient to cut expenses or build sales volume to accomplish increased profits? Use the spinner to experiment.

Increased Sales Versus Expense Reduction					
How Expenses Impact On Profits					
	Year 2001	Year 2002	Year 2003	Year 2004	Total Impact
A 2% reduction in expenses equals an additional profit of............	$29,593	$34,939	$37,055	$40,868	$142,455
OR					
at your present **net profit** of..................	$480,368	$753,034	$799,039	$1,162,043	$3,194,484
and your current net sales of..................	$1,960,000	$2,500,000	$2,651,800	$3,205,454	$10,317,254
your current total costs are.....................	$1,479,632	$1,746,966	$1,852,761	$2,043,411	$7,122,770
A cost reduction yields a new profit of......	$509,961	$787,974	$836,094	$1,202,911	$3,336,940
Therefore you would have to build an additional sales volume of..................... to equal the expense reduction.	$120,744	$115,995	$122,976	$112,734	$472,449

The Conclusion: A reduction in expenses is far more efficient than building additional sales volume.

Try another percentage........................ [2]

Driven from the What-if Master Data Entry, the same concept is applied.

What-if Increased Sales Versus Expense Reduction					
How Expenses Impact On Profits					
	Year 2001	Year 2002	Year 2003	Year 2004	Total Impact
A 2% reduction in expenses equals an additional profit of............	$29,593	$34,939	$37,055	$40,868	$142,455
OR					
at your present **net profit** of..................	$480,368	$753,034	$799,039	$1,162,043	$3,194,484
and your current net sales of..................	$1,960,000	$2,500,000	$2,651,800	$3,205,454	$10,317,254
your current total costs are.....................	$1,479,632	$1,746,966	$1,852,761	$2,043,411	$7,122,770
A cost reduction yields a new profit of......	$509,961	$787,974	$836,094	$1,202,911	$3,336,940
Therefore you would have to build an additional sales volume of..................... to equal the expense reduction.	$120,744	$115,995	$122,976	$112,734	$472,449

The Conclusion: A reduction in expenses is far more efficient than building additional sales volume.

Try another percentage........................ [2]

Breakdown of Operating Costs.

Go to the *Manager's Index* worksheet and click on the *Breakdown of Costs* hyperlink.

Control of costs is the key to increased profits. This worksheet reveals down to the minute the cost of running your business.

Breakdown of Operating Costs

TOTAL OPERATING COSTS

COMPARATIVE PERIODS	Year 2001	Year 2002	Year 2003	Year 2004	Trend 2005
Total For Period	$745,000	$871,350	$894,301	$915,467	$990,118
1 DAY	$2,041	$2,387	$2,450	$2,508	$2,713
1 HOUR	$85.05	$99.47	$102.09	$104.51	$113.03
1 MINUTE	$1.42	$1.66	$1.70	$1.74	$1.88

LABOR EXPENSE

COMPARATIVE PERIODS	Year 2001	Year 2002	Year 2003	Year 2004	Trend 2005
Total For Period	$300,000	$315,000	$330,450	$346,364	$361,589
1 DAY	$822	$863	$905	$949	$991
1 HOUR	$34.25	$35.96	$37.72	$39.54	$41.28
1 MINUTE	$0.57	$0.60	$0.63	$0.66	$0.69

MATERIAL EXPENSE

COMPARATIVE PERIODS	Year 2001	Year 2002	Year 2003	Year 2004	Trend 2005
Total For Period	$320,000	$427,600	$431,238	$432,513	$488,132
1 DAY	$877	$1,172	$1,181	$1,185	$1,337
1 HOUR	$36.53	$48.81	$49.23	$49.37	$55.72
1 MINUTE	$0.61	$0.81	$0.82	$0.82	$0.93

OTHER EXPENSES

COMPARATIVE PERIODS	Year 2001	Year 2002	Year 2003	Year 2004	Trend 2005
Total For Period	$125,000	$128,750	$132,613	$136,591	$140,397
1 DAY	$342	$353	$363	$374	$385
1 HOUR	$14.27	$14.70	$15.14	$15.59	$16.03
1 MINUTE	$0.24	$0.24	$0.25	$0.26	$0.27

Break-even Adjusted to Reduce Expenses on Sales.

Go to the *Manager's Index* worksheet and click on the *Breakdown of Costs* and *What-if Breakdown of Costs* hyperlinks.

This sheet demonstrates how with proper expense controls in place the business could improve. The emphasis here is Variable Expense reduction.

Since profit begins at Breakeven, the sooner you reach it, the higher the profits. **Expense Control is the key**.

B/E Adjusted By Reducing Expenses on Existing Sales Volume

Spin an Expense Reduction Here........................ | 0% | Reset | Calculator

Expense
Reduction of 0%

	Adjusted Expenses 2001	Current Year 2001	Total Impact of Reductions	
FOR THE PERIOD OF......				
BREAK-EVEN VOLUME (DOLLARS).....................	$636,455	$636,455	$0	
BREAK-EVEN POINT (PERCENT)........................	32.47%	32.47%	0.00%	
DATE OF BREAK-EVEN....................................	Apr 27	Apr 27	0 Days Less	
ON SALES VOLUME OF.................................	$1,960,000	$1,960,000	Profit Impact Over 1 Year	Profit Impact Over 4 Years
WITH VARIABLE COSTS OF............................	$943,767	$943,767		
AND FIXED EXPENSES OF..............................	$329,993	$329,993		
OPERATING PROFIT IS............................	$686,240	$686,240	$0	$0
OPERATING PROFIT (%) IS.............................	35.01%	35.01%		
			Impact Over 1 Year	Impact Over 4 Years
SALES VOLUME REQUIRED				
BEFORE PROFIT BEGINS.............................	$636,455 PER YEAR	$636,455 PER YEAR	$0	$0
	$53,038 PER MONTH	$53,038 PER MONTH	$0	$0
	$12,335 PER WEEK	$12,335 PER WEEK	$0	$0
	$2,467 PER DAY	$2,467 PER DAY	$0	$0
	$308 PER HOUR	$308 PER HOUR	$0	$0
	$5.14 PER MINUTE	$5.14 PER MINUTE	$0.00	$0.00

What-if B/E Further Adjusted By Reducing Expenses on Existing Sales Volume

Spin an Expense Reduction Here........................ | 0% | Reset | Calculator

Expense
Reduction of 0%

	Adjusted Expenses 2001	Current Year 2001	Total Impact of Reductions	
FOR THE PERIOD OF......				
BREAK-EVEN VOLUME (DOLLARS).....................	$636,455	$636,455	$0	
BREAK-EVEN POINT (PERCENT)........................	32.47%	32.47%	0.00%	
DATE OF BREAK-EVEN....................................	Apr 27	Apr 27	0 Days Less	
ON SALES VOLUME OF.................................	$1,960,000	$1,960,000	Profit Impact Over 1 Year	Profit Impact Over 4 Years
WITH VARIABLE COSTS OF............................	$943,767	$943,767		
AND FIXED EXPENSES OF..............................	$329,993	$329,993		
OPERATING PROFIT IS............................	$686,240	$686,240	$0	$0
OPERATING PROFIT (%) IS.............................	35.01%	35.01%		
			Impact Over 1 Year	Impact Over 4 Years
SALES VOLUME REQUIRED				
BEFORE PROFIT BEGINS.............................	$636,455 PER YEAR	$636,455 PER YEAR	$0	$0
	$53,038 PER MONTH	$53,038 PER MONTH	$0	$0
	$12,335 PER WEEK	$12,335 PER WEEK	$0	$0
	$2,467 PER DAY	$2,467 PER DAY	$0	$0
	$308 PER HOUR	$308 PER HOUR	$0	$0
	$5.14 PER MINUTE	$5.14 PER MINUTE	$0.00	$0.00

Chapter 5 – Financial Ratios! Are they important?

Financial ratios help you get a better handle on your operations, see when things are out of kilter, and set down milestones for the future. Financial ratios help you answer these questions: Do I have enough working capital? Will I be able to make payroll and the next flock of bills? Is my debt too high? Will I have any difficulty meeting long-term obligations? Am I using my assets wisely? Is my inventory too large, or does it take too long to turn over? How profitable is my business?

This chapter discusses 12 important financial ratios contained in the Manager and plus an expanded ratio worksheet. The 12 ratios discussed are usually thought of as belonging to four basic categories: *profitability*, *liquidity*, *activity*, and *leverage* ratios:

Category	*Ratio*
Profitability ratios	• Earnings Per Share
	• Gross Profit Margin
	• Net Profit Margin
	• Return on Assets
	• Return on Equity
Liquidity ratios	• Current Ratio
	• Quick Ratio
Activity ratios	• Average Collection Period
	• Inventory Turnover Ratio
Leverage ratios	• Debt Ratio
	• Equity Ratio
	• Times Interest Earned Ratio

This is by no means an exhaustive list of the ratios to help analyze your company's financial position and the way that it conducts business. It is, however, representative.

Before embarking upon the 12 ratios, please read these general explanations.

Analyzing Profitability Ratios

If you are considering buying a business, its profitability is a major concern. If the company intends to pay dividends to its stockholders, those dividends must come out of its profits. If the company hopes to increase its worth in the marketplace by enhancing or expanding its product line, then an important source of capital to make improvements is its profit margin. There are several different, but related, means of evaluating a company's profitability.

Analyzing Liquidity Ratios

The issue of liquidity, as you might expect, concerns creditors. Liquidity is a company's ability to meet its debts as they come due. A company may have considerable total assets, but if those assets are difficult to convert to cash it is possible that the company might be unable to pay its creditors in a timely fashion. Creditors want their loans to be paid in the medium of cash, not in a medium such as inventory or factory equipment.

Analyzing Activity Ratios

There are various ratios that can give you insight into how well a company manages its operating and sales activities. One primary goal-perhaps, the primary goal-of these activities is to produce income through effective use of its resources. Two ways to measure this effectiveness are the Average Collection Period and the Inventory Turnover rate.

Analyzing Leverage Ratios

The term "leverage" means the purchase of assets with borrowed money. Suppose that your company retails office supplies. When you receive an order for business cards, you pay one of your suppliers 50 percent of the revenue to print them for you. This is a variable cost: the more you sell, the greater your cost.

But if you purchase the necessary printing equipment, you could make the business cards yourself. So doing would turn a variable cost into a fixed cost: no matter how many cards you sell, the cost of printing them is fixed at however much you paid for the printing equipment. The more cards you sell, the greater your profit margin. This effect is termed operating leverage.

If you borrow money to acquire the printing equipment, you are using another type of leverage, termed financial leverage. The cost is still fixed at however much money you must pay, at regular intervals, to retire the loan. Again, the more cards you sell, the greater your profit margin. But if you do not sell enough cards to cover the loan payment, you could lose money. In that case, it might be difficult to find funds either to make the loan payments or to cover your other expenses. Your credit rating might fall, making it more costly for you to borrow other money.

Leverage is a financial tool that accelerates changes in income, both positive and negative. A company's creditors and investors are interested in how much leverage has been used to acquire assets. From the standpoint of creditors, a high degree of leverage represents risk because the company might not be able to repay a loan. From the investors' standpoint, if the return on assets is less than the cost of borrowing money to acquire assets, then the investment is unattractive. The investor could obtain a better return in different ways-one way would be to loan funds rather than to invest them in the company

The 12 Key Ratios

With *Manager.xls* still open, go the Master Index worksheet and click on Ratios Introduction. In addition to explanations, this worksheet is also a mini-index of the 12 key ratios. You may choose each ratio from the Master Index as well.

1. Current Ratio

The current ratio compares a company's current assets (those that can be converted to cash during the current accounting period) to its current liabilities (those liabilities coming due during the same period). The usual formula is:

Current Ratio = Current Assets / Current Liabilities

The current ratio measures the company's ability to repay the principal amounts of its liabilities.

The current ratio is closely related to the concept of working capital. Working capital is the difference between current assets and current liabilities.

Is a high current ratio good or bad? Certainly, from the creditor's standpoint, a high current ratio means that the company is well-placed to pay back its loans. Consider, though, the nature of the current assets: they consist mainly of cash and cash equivalents. Funds invested in these types of assets do not contribute strongly and actively to the creation of income. Therefore, from the standpoint of stockholders and management, a current ratio that is very high means that the company's assets are not being used to best advantage.

This figure is an example of the Current Ratio over 4 periods. The first set of numbers is from the Master Data Entry worksheet. The second set of numbers is the results of a what-if scenario performed on the What-if Master Data Entry worksheet.

Current ratio	Year 2001	Year 2002	Year 2003	Year 2004
Current assets	$1,212,200	$1,550,530	$2,187,750	$2,826,692
Current liabilities	$936,000	$964,080	$993,002	$1,007,719
Current ratio	1.30	1.61	2.20	2.81
What-if Current ratio	Year 2001	Year 2002	Year 2003	Year 2004
Current assets	$1,212,200	$1,550,530	$2,187,750	$2,826,692
Current liabilities	$936,000	$964,080	$993,002	$1,007,719
Current ratio	1.30	1.61	2.20	2.81

2. Quick Ratio

The quick ratio is a variant of the current ratio. It takes into account the fact that inventory, while it is a current asset, is not as liquid as cash or accounts receivable. Cash is completely liquid; accounts receivable can normally be converted to cash fairly quickly, by pressing for collection from the customer. But inventory cannot be converted to cash except by selling it. The quick ratio determines the relationship between quickly accessible current assets and current liabilities:

Quick Ratio = (Current Assets - Inventory) / Current Liabilities

The quick ratio shows whether a company can meet its liabilities from quickly accessible assets.

In practice, a quick ratio of 1.0 is normally considered adequate, with this caveat: the credit periods that the company offers its customers and those granted to the company by its creditor must be roughly equal. If revenues will stay in accounts receivable for as long as 90 days, but accounts payable are due within 30 days, a quick ratio of 1.0 will mean that accounts receivable cannot be converted to cash quickly enough to meet accounts payable.

It is possible for a company to manipulate the values of its current and quick ratios by taking certain actions toward the end of an accounting period such as a fiscal year. It might wait until the start of the next period to make purchases to its inventory, for example. Or, if its business is seasonal, it might choose a fiscal year that ends after its busy season, when inventories are usually low. As a potential creditor, you might want to examine the company's current and quick ratios on, for example, a quarterly basis.

Both a current and a quick ratio can also mislead you if the inventory figure does not represent the current replacement cost of the materials in inventory. There are various methods of valuing inventory. The LIFO method, in particular, can result in an inventory valuation that is much different from the inventory's current replacement value; this is because it assumes that the most recently acquired inventory is also the most recently sold.

If your actual costs to purchase materials are falling, for example, the LIFO method could result in an over-valuation of the existing inventory. This would tend to inflate the value of the current ratio, and to underestimate the value of the quick ratio if you calculate it by subtracting inventory from current assets, rather than summing cash and cash equivalents.

Table 6.2 is an example of the Quick Ratio over 4 periods. The first set of numbers is from the Master Data Entry worksheet. The second set of numbers is the results of a what-if scenario performed on the What-if Master Data Entry worksheet.

Quick ratio	Year 2001	Year 2002	Year 2003	Year 2004
Current Assets	$1,212,200	$1,550,530	$2,187,750	$2,826,692
Inventory	$400,000	$612,000	$824,360	$937,091
Current Assets Less Inventory	$812,200	$938,530	$1,363,390	$1,889,602
Current liabilities	$936,000	$964,080	$993,002	$1,007,719
Quick ratio	0.87	0.97	1.37	1.88
What-if Quick ratio	Year 2001	Year 2002	Year 2003	Year 2004
Current Assets	$1,212,200	$1,550,530	$2,187,750	$2,826,692
Inventory	$400,000	$612,000	$824,360	$937,091
Current Assets Less Inventory	$812,200	$938,530	$1,363,390	$1,889,602
Current liabilities	$936,000	$964,080	$993,002	$1,007,719
Quick ratio	0.87	0.97	1.37	1.88

3. Earnings per Share (EPS)

Depending on your financial objectives, you might consider investing in a company to obtain a steady return on your investment in the form of regular dividend payments, or to obtain a profit by owning the stock as the market value of its shares increases. These two objectives might both be met, but in practice they often are not. Companies frequently face a choice of distributing income in the form of dividends, or retaining that income to invest in research, new products, and expanded operations. The hope, of course, is that the retention of income to invest in the company will subsequently increase its income, thus making the company more profitable and increasing the market value of its stock.

In either case, Earnings Per Share (EPS) is an important measure of the company's income. Its basic formula is:

EPS = Income Available for Common Stock / Shares of Common Stock Outstanding

EPS is usually a poor candidate for vertical analysis, because different companies always have different numbers of shares of stock outstanding. It may be a good candidate for horizontal analysis, if you have access both to information about the company's income and shares outstanding. With both these items, you can control for major fluctuations over time in shares outstanding. This sort of control is important: it is not unusual for a company to purchase its own stock on the open market to reduce the number of outstanding shares. So doing increases the value of the EPS ratio, perhaps making the stock appear a more attractive investment.

Note that the EPS can decline steadily throughout the year. Because, the number of shares outstanding is constant throughout the year, the EPS changes are due solely to changes in net income.

Many companies issue at least two different kinds of stock: common and preferred. Preferred stock is issued under different conditions than common stock. Preferred stock is often callable at the company's discretion, it pays dividends at a different (usually, higher) rate per share, it might not carry voting privileges, and often has a higher priority than common stock as to the distribution of liquidated assets if the company goes out of business.

Calculating EPS for a company that has issued preferred stock introduces a slight complication. Because the company pays dividends on preferred stock before any distribution to shareholders of common stock, it is necessary to subtract these dividends from net income:

EPS (Net Income - Preferred Dividends) / Shares of Common Stock Outstanding

This figure is an example of the Earnings per Share over 4 periods. The first set of numbers is from the Master Data Entry worksheet. The second set of numbers is the results of a what-if scenario performed on the What-if Master Data Entry worksheet.

Earnings Per Share (EPS) Ratio	Year 2001	Year 2002	Year 2003	Year 2004
Net income	$480,368	$753,034	$799,039	$1,162,043
Shares of common stock outstanding	100,000	100,000	100,000	100,000
EPS	$4.80	$7.53	$7.99	$11.62
What-if Earnings Per Share (EPS) Ratio	**Year 2001**	**Year 2002**	**Year 2003**	**Year 2004**
Net income	$480,368	$753,034	$799,039	$1,162,043
Shares of common stock outstanding	$100,000	$100,000	$100,000	$100,000
EPS	$4.80	$7.53	$7.99	$11.62

4. Gross Profit Margin

The gross profit margin is a basic ratio that measures the added value that the market places on a company's non-manufacturing activities. Its formula is:

Gross profit margin = (Sales - Cost of Goods Sold) / Sales

The cost of goods sold is, clearly, an important component of the gross profit margin. It is usually calculated as the sum of the cost of materials the company purchases plus any labor involved in the manufacture of finished goods, plus associated overhead.

The gross profit margin depends heavily on the type of business in which a company is engaged. A service business, such as a financial services institution or a laundry, typically has little or no cost of goods sold. A manufacturing, wholesaling, or retailing company typically has a large cost of goods sold, with a gross profit margin that varies from 20 percent to 40 percent.

The gross profit margin measures the amount that customers are willing to pay for a company's product, over and above the company's cost for that product. As mentioned previously, the company adds this value to that of the products it obtains from its suppliers. This margin can depend on the attractiveness of additional services, such as warranties, that the company provides. The gross profit margin also depends heavily on the ability of the sales force to persuade its customers of the value added by the company.

This added value is, of course, created by other costs such as operating expenses. In turn, these costs must be met largely by the gross profit on sales. If customers do not place sufficient value on whatever the company adds to its products, there will not be enough gross profit to pay for the associated costs. Therefore, the calculation of the gross profit margin helps to highlight the effectiveness of the company's sales strategies and sales management.

This figure is an example of the Gross Profit Margin over 4 periods. The first set of numbers is from the Master Data Entry worksheet. The second set of numbers is the results of a what-if scenario performed on the What-if Master Data Entry worksheet.

Gross Profit Margin	Year 2001	Year 2002	Year 2003	Year 2004
Sales	$1,960,000	$2,500,000	$2,651,800	$3,205,454
Cost of sales	$745,000	$871,350	$894,301	$915,467
Gross profit margin	62.0%	65.1%	66.3%	71.4%
What-if Gross Profit Margin	Year 2001	Year 2002	Year 2003	Year 2004
Sales	$1,960,000	$2,500,000	$2,651,800	$3,205,454
Cost of sales	$745,000	$871,350	$894,301	$915,467
Gross profit margin	62.0%	65.1%	66.3%	71.4%

5. Net Profit Margin

The net profit margin narrows the focus on profitability, and highlights not just the company's sales efforts, but also its ability to keep operating costs down, relative to sales. The formula generally used to determine the net profit margin is:

Net Profit Margin = Earnings after Taxes / Sales

When net profit margin falls dramatically from the first to the fourth quarters, a principal culprit is cost of sales.

Another place to look when you see a discrepancy between gross profit margin and net profit margin is operating expenses. When the two margins covary closely, it suggests that management is doing a good job of reducing expenses when sales fall, and increasing expenses when necessary to support production and sales in better times.

This figure is an example of the Net Profit Margin over 4 periods. The first set of numbers is from the Master Data Entry worksheet. The second set of numbers is the results of a what-if scenario performed on the What-if Master Data Entry worksheet.

Net Profit Margin	Year 2001	Year 2002	Year 2003	Year 2004
Net Income	$480,368	$753,034	$799,039	$1,162,043
Sales	$1,960,000	$2,500,000	$2,651,800	$3,205,454
Net profit margin	24.51%	30.12%	30.13%	36.25%
What-if Net Profit Margin	Year 2001	Year 2002	Year 2003	Year 2004
Net Income	$480,368	$753,034	$799,039	$1,162,043
Sales	$1,960,000	$2,500,000	$2,651,800	$3,205,454
Net profit margin	24.5%	30.1%	30.1%	36.3%

6. Return on Assets

One of management's most important responsibilities is to bring about a profit by effective use of the resources it has at hand. One ratio that speaks to this question is return on assets. There are several ways to measure this return; one useful method is:

Return on Assets = Net Income/ Total Assets

This formula will return the percentage earnings for a company in terms of its total assets. The better the job that management does in managing its assets-the resources available to it-to bring about profits, the greater this percentage will be.

It's normal to calculate the return on total assets on an annual basis, rather than on a quarterly basis.

This figure is an example of the Return on Assets over 4 periods. The first set of numbers is from the Master Data Entry worksheet. The second set of numbers is the results of a what-if scenario performed on the What-if Master Data Entry worksheet.

Recession Proofing Your Business

Return on Assets	Year 2001	Year 2002	Year 2003	Year 2004
Net Income	$480,368	$753,034	$799,039	$1,162,043
Total assets	$4,167,200	$4,094,180	$5,467,899	$6,172,246
Return on assets	11.5%	18.4%	14.6%	18.8%
What-if Return on Assets	Year 2001	Year 2002	Year 2003	Year 2004
Net Income	$480,368	$753,034	$799,039	$1,162,043
Total assets	$4,167,200	$4,094,180	$5,467,899	$6,172,246
Return on assets	11.5%	18.4%	14.6%	18.8%

7. Return on Equity

Another related profitability measure to Return on Assets is the Return on Equity. Again, there are several ways to calculate this ratio; here, it is measured according to this formula:

Return on Equity = Net Income / Stockholder's Equity

You can compare return on equity with return on assets to infer how a company obtains the funds used to acquire assets.

The principal difference between the formula for return on assets and for return on equity is the use of equity rather than total assets in the denominator, and it is here that the technique of comparing ratios comes into play. By examining the difference between Return on Assets and Return on Equity, you can largely determine how the company is funding its operations.

Assets are acquired through two major sources: creditors (through borrowing) and stockholders (through retained earnings and capital contributions). Collectively, the retained earnings and capital contributions constitute the company's equity. When the value of the company's assets exceeds the value of its equity, you can expect that some form of financial leverage makes up the difference: i.e., debt financing.

Therefore, if the Return on Equity ratio is much larger than the Return on Assets ratio, you can infer that the company has funded some portion of its operations through borrowing.

This figure is an example of the Return on Equity over 4 periods. The first set of numbers is from the Master Data Entry worksheet. The second set of numbers is the results of a what-if scenario performed on the What-if Master Data Entry worksheet.

Return on Equity	Year 2001	Year 2002	Year 2003	Year 2004
Net Income	$480,368	$753,034	$799,039	$1,162,043
Stockholder's equity	$2,450,000	$2,320,500	$3,638,305	$4,299,528
Return on equity	19.6%	32.5%	22.0%	27.0%

What-if Return on Equity	Year 2001	Year 2002	Year 2003	Year 2004
Net Income	$480,368	$753,034	$799,039	$1,162,043
Total Stockholders' Equity	$2,450,000	$2,320,500	$3,638,305	$4,299,528
Return on equity	19.6%	32.5%	22.0%	27.0%

8. Average Collection Period

You can obtain a general estimate of the length of time it takes to receive payment for goods or services by calculating the Average Collection Period.

One formula for this ratio is:

Average Collection Period = Accounts Receivable / (Credit Sales / Days)

Where Days is the number of days in the period for which Accounts Receivable and Credit Sales accumulate.

You should interpret the average collection period in terms of the company's credit policies. If, for example, the company's policy as stated to its customers is that payment is to be received within two weeks, then an average collection period of 30 days indicates that collections are lagging. It may be that collection procedures need to be reviewed, or it is possible that one particularly large account is responsible for most of the collections in arrears. It is also possible that the qualifying procedures used by the sales force are not stringent enough.

The calculation of the Average Collection Period assumes that credit sales are distributed roughly evenly during any given period. To the degree that the credit sales cluster at the end of the period, the Average Collection Period will return an inflated figure. If you obtain a result that appears too long (or too short), be sure to check whether the sales dates occur evenly throughout the period in question.

Regardless of the cause, if the average collection period is over-long, it means that the company is losing profit. The company is not converting cash due from customers into new assets that can, in turn, be used to generate new income.

This figure is an example of the Average Collection Period over 4 periods. The first set of numbers is from the Master Data Entry worksheet. The second set of numbers is the results of a what-if scenario performed on the What-if Master Data Entry worksheet.

Average Collection Period	Year 2001	Year 2002	Year 2003	Year 2004
Accounts Receivable	$350,000	$460,500	$871,315	$1,382,454
Credit Sales	$2,010,000	$2,560,000	$2,721,800	$3,285,454
Days Per Year	365	365	365	365
Credit sales per day	$5,507	$7,014	$7,457	$9,001
Average Collection Period	63.56	65.66	116.85	153.58

What-if Average Collection Period	Year 2001	Year 2002	Year 2003	Year 2004
Accounts Receivable	$350,000	$460,500	$871,315	$1,382,454
Credit Sales	$2,010,000	$2,560,000	$2,721,800	$3,285,454
Days Per Year	365	365	365	365
Credit sales per day	$5,507	$7,014	$7,457	$9,001
Average Collection Period	63.56	65.66	116.85	153.58

9. Inventory Turnover Ratio

No company wants to have too large an inventory (the sales force excepted: salespeople prefer to be able to tell their customers that they can obtain their purchase this afternoon). Goods that remain in inventory too long tie up the company's assets in idle stock, often incur carrying charges for the storage of the goods, and can become obsolete while awaiting sale.

Just-in-Time inventory procedures attempt to ensure that the company obtains its inventory no sooner than absolutely required in order to support its sales efforts. That is, of course, an unrealistic ideal, but by calculating the inventory turnover rate you can estimate how well a company is approaching the ideal.

The formula for the Inventory Turnover Ratio is:

Inventory Turnover = Cost of Goods Sold / Average Inventory

where the Average Inventory figure refers to the value of the inventory on any given day during the period during which the Cost of Goods Sold is calculated. The higher an inventory turnover rate, the more closely a company conforms to just-in-time procedures.

The figures for cost of goods sold and average inventory are taken directly from the Income Statement's cost of sales and the Balance Sheet's inventory levels. In a situation where you know only the beginning and ending inventory-for example, at the beginning and the ending of a period-you would use the average of the two levels: hence the term "average inventory."

An acceptable inventory turnover rate can be determined only by knowledge of a company's business sector. If you are in the business of wholesaling fresh produce, for example, you would probably require an annual turnover rate in the 50s: a much lower rate would mean that you were losing too much inventory to spoilage. But if you sell computing equipment, you could probably afford an annual turnover rate of around 3 or 4, because hardware does not spoil, nor does it become technologically obsolete more frequently than every few months.

This figure is an example of the Inventory Turnover Ratio over 4 periods. The first set of numbers is from the Master Data Entry worksheet. The second set of numbers is the results of a what-if scenario performed on the What-if Master Data Entry worksheet.

Inventory Turnover Ratio	Year 2001	Year 2002	Year 2003	Year 2004
Cost of Goods Sold	$745,000	$871,350	$894,301	$915,467
Average Inventory	$400,000	$612,000	$824,360	$937,091
Inventory Turnover	1.86	1.42	1.08	0.98
What-if Inventory Turnover Ratio	Year 2001	Year 2002	Year 2003	Year 2004
Cost of Goods Sold	$745,000	$871,350	$894,301	$915,467
Average Inventory	$400,000	$612,000	$824,360	$937,091
Inventory Turnover	1.86	1.42	1.08	0.98

10. Debt Ratio

The debt ratio is defined by this formula:

Debt ratio = Total Liabilities / Total assets

It is a healthy sign when a company's debt ratio is falls, although both stockholders and potential creditors would prefer to see the rate of decline in the debt ratio more closely match the decline in return on assets. As the return on assets falls, the net income available to make payments on debt also falls. This company should probably take action to retire some of its short-term debt, and the current portion of its long-term debt, as soon as possible.

This figure is an example of the Debt Ratio over 4 periods. The first set of numbers is from the Master Data Entry worksheet. The second set of numbers is the results of a what-if scenario performed on the What-if Master Data Entry worksheet.

Debt ratio	Year 2001	Year 2002	Year 2003	Year 2004
Total Liabilities	$1,717,200	$1,773,680	$1,829,594	$1,872,718
Total Assets	$4,167,200	$4,094,180	$5,467,899	$6,172,246
Debt ratio	41.2%	43.3%	33.5%	30.3%
What-if Debt ratio	Year 2001	Year 2002	Year 2003	Year 2004
Total Liabilities	$1,717,200	$1,773,680	$1,829,594	$1,872,718
Total Assets	$4,167,200	$4,094,180	$5,467,899	$6,172,246
Debt ratio	41.2%	43.3%	33.5%	30.3%

11. Equity Ratio

The equity ratio is the opposite of the debt ratio. It is that portion of the company's assets financed by stockholders:

Equity Ratio = Total Equity / Total assets

It is usually easier to acquire assets through debt than to acquire them through equity. There are certain obvious considerations: for example, you might need to acquire investment capital from many investors; whereas you might be able to borrow the required funds from just one creditor. Less obvious is the issue of priority.

By law, if a firm ceases operations, its creditors have the first claim on its assets to help repay the borrowed funds. Therefore, an investor's risk is somewhat higher than that of a creditor, and the effect is that stockholders tend to demand a greater return on their investment than a creditor does on its loan. The stockholder's demand for a return can take the form of dividend requirements or return on assets, each of which tend to increase the market value of their stock.

But there is no "always" in financial planning. Because investors usually require a higher return on their investment than do creditors, it might seem that debt is the preferred method of raising funds to acquire assets. Potential creditors, though, look at ratios such as the return on assets and the debt ratio. A high debt ratio (or, conversely, a low equity ratio) means that existing creditors have supplied a large portion of the company's assets, and that there is relatively little stockholder's equity to help absorb the risk.

This figure is an example of the Equity Ratio over 4 periods. The first set of numbers is from the Master Data Entry worksheet. The second set of numbers is the results of a what-if scenario performed on the What-if Master Data Entry worksheet.

Equity ratio	Year 2001	Year 2002	Year 2003	Year 2004
Total Equity	$2,450,000	$2,320,500	$3,638,305	$4,299,528
Total Assets	$4,167,200	$4,094,180	$5,467,899	$6,172,246
Equity ratio	58.8%	56.7%	66.5%	69.7%
What-if Equity ratio	Year 2001	Year 2002	Year 2003	Year 2004
Total Equity	$2,450,000	$2,320,500	$3,638,305	$4,299,528
Total Assets	$4,167,200	$4,094,180	$5,467,899	$6,172,246
Equity ratio	58.8%	56.7%	66.5%	69.7%

12. Times interest Earned Ratio

One measure frequently used by creditors to evaluate the risk involved in loaning money to a firm is the Times Interest Earned ratio. This is the number of times in a given period that a company earns enough income to cover its interest payments. A ratio of 5, for example, would mean that the amount of interest payments is earned 5 times over during that period.

The usual formula is:

Times Interest Earned = *EBIT / Total Interest Payments

*EBIT stands for Earnings Before Interest and Taxes.

The Times Interest Earned ratio, in reality, seldom exceeds 10. A value of 44.1 is very high, although certainly not unheard of during a particularly good quarter. A value of 5.1 would usually be considered strong but within the normal range.

Notice that this is a measure of how deeply interest charges cut into a company's income. A ratio of 1, for example, would mean that the company earns enough income (after covering such costs as operating expenses and costs of sales) to cover only its interest charges. There would be no income remaining to pay income taxes (of course, in this case it's likely that there would be no income tax liability), to meet dividend requirements or to retain earnings for future investments.

This figure is an example of the Times Interest Earned Ratio over 4 periods. The first set of numbers is from the Master Data Entry worksheet. The second set of numbers is the results of a what-if scenario performed on the What-if Master Data Entry worksheet.

Times Interest Earned Ratio	Year 2001	Year 2002	Year 2003	Year 2004
EBIT	$686,240	$1,075,763	$1,141,485	$1,660,061
Interest charges	$16,250	$16,738	$17,240	$17,757
Times interest earned	42.2	64.3	66.2	93.5
What-if Times Interest Earned Ratio	**Year 2001**	**Year 2002**	**Year 2003**	**Year 2004**
EBIT	$686,240	$1,075,763	$1,141,485	$1,660,061
Interest charges	$16,250	$16,738	$17,240	$17,757
Times interest earned	42.23	64.27	66.21	93.49

Expanded Financial Ratios

Alphabetized by ratio description, this worksheet will help both you and any potential outside investor compare your business's performance.

The ratios can also be used as an aid in making future financial projections. For example, if you believe that it is prudent to hold the equivalent of a month's sales in inventory, once you have made the sales forecast for future years, the projections for inventory in the balance sheet follow logically.

Financial ratios help you get a better handle on your operations, see when things are out of kilter, and set down milestones for the future. Financial ratios help you answer these questions: Do I have enough working capital? Will I be able to make payroll and the next flock of bills? Is my debt too high? Will I have any difficulty meeting long-term obligations? Am I using my assets wisely? Is my inventory too large, or does it take too long to turn over? How profitable is my business?

This worksheet will also be helpful when you write your annual business plan and make strategies for the future, as well as being handy for setting monthly/annual goals.

This figure is an example of the Expanded Financial Ratios over 4 periods. This set of ratios is an addendum to those individually treated in the workbook. There is some repetition but this form can be used to an advantage in a business or strategic plan.

EXPANDED FINANCIAL RATIOS

Description	Year 2001	Year 2002	Year 2003	Year 2004
Amortization and Depreciation Expense to Net Sales	0.017	0.014	0.014	0.012
AP to Net Sales	0.31	0.25	0.24	0.20
Current Liabilities to Inventory	2.34	1.58	1.20	1.08
Current Liabilities to Net Worth	0.38	0.42	0.27	0.23
Current Ratio	1.30	1.61	2.20	2.81
Days Inventory	195.97	256.36	336.45	373.62
Days Purchases in AP	293.96	258.87	259.80	255.39
Days Sales in AR	65.18	67.23	119.93	157.42
Gross Profit Percentage	61.99%	65.15%	66.28%	71.44%
Income before tax to Net Worth	28.01%	46.36%	31.37%	38.61%
Income before tax to Total Assets	16.47%	26.28%	20.88%	26.90%
Interest Expense to Net Sales	0.01	0.01	0.01	0.01
Inventory Turnover	1.86	1.42	1.08	0.98
Net Sales to AR	65.18	67.23	119.93	157.42
Net Sales to Inventory	4.90	4.08	3.22	3.42
Net Sales to Net Fixed Assets	0.68	1.01	0.82	0.98
Net Sales to Net Worth	0.80	1.08	0.73	0.75
Net Sales to Total Assets	0.47	0.61	0.48	0.52
Net Sales to Working Capital	7.10	4.26	2.22	1.76
Net Worth to Total Liabilities	1.43	1.31	1.99	2.30
Operating Expenses as % of Net Sales	28.51%	23.35%	24.43%	20.99%
Quick Ratio	0.87	0.97	1.37	1.88
Retained Earning to Net Income	291%	205%	211%	149%
Return on Net Sales	24.51%	30.12%	30.13%	36.25%
Return on Net Worth	19.61%	32.45%	21.96%	27.03%
Return on Total Assets	11.53%	18.39%	14.61%	18.83%
Times Interest Earned	40.38	62.43	64.37	91.08
Total Assets to Net Sales	2.13	1.64	2.06	1.93
Total Liabilities to Net Worth	0.70	0.76	0.50	0.44
Working Capital	$276,200	$586,450	$1,194,748	$1,818,973

Summary

The Manager has some of the important financial ratios that are central to understanding how, and how well, a company conducts its business. There are variations on virtually every ratio discussed here, and there are ratios that were not covered at all, but their principal forms follow the formulas illustrated.

Only occasionally, can you calculate one of these indicators and gain immediate insight into a business operation. More frequently, it is necessary to know the sort of business that a company conducts, because the marketplace imposes different demands on different lines of business. Keep in mind that it's important to evaluate a financial ratio in terms of its trend over time, of a standard such as an industry average, and in light of other ratios that describe the company's operations and financial structure.

Chapter 6 - Cash Flow Management

Cash flow management is defined as the flow of cash into and out of a business over a period of time.

Cash is the word that defines the lifeblood of a small business. The lack of it has driven countless small companies into bankruptcy. Unfortunately, this could have been avoided if their owners had not neglected the principles of sound cash management.

It is vital to develop a cash flow forecast because some seasonal profit levels will not generate sufficient cash levels to keep a company afloat. The dynamic small business owner uses cash management techniques to foresee these problems and plan for them.

Go to the *Manager's Index* worksheet and click on the *Cash Flow Cycle* hyperlink. The Cash Flow Cycle worksheet allows you to manipulate two data entries that apply to your business.

This figure shows the cash flow cycle and it is defined as the time lag between paying suppliers for merchandise and receiving payment from customers-for a typical small business. The longer this cash flow cycle, the more likely the business owner is to encounter a cash crisis. Preparing a cash forecast that recognizes this cycle, however, will help avoid a crisis.

The central thought is to realize and see in a graph the lengthy process involved in

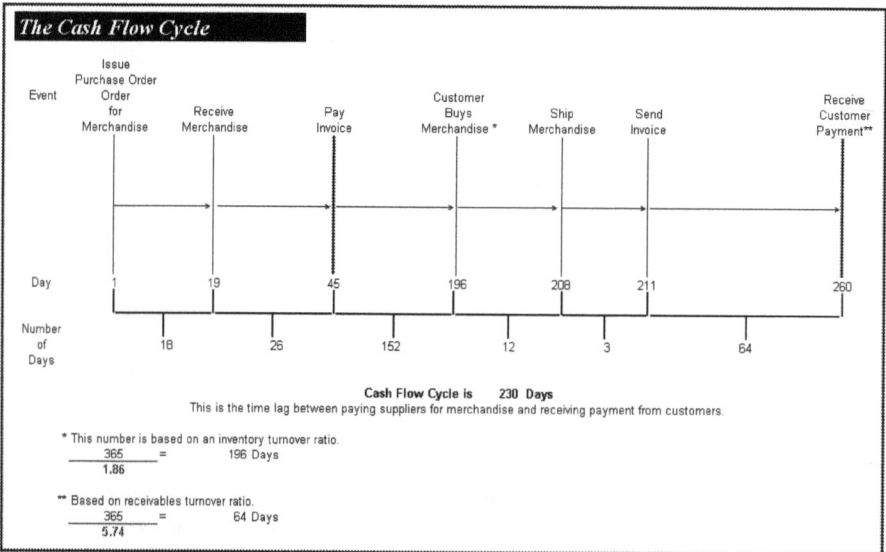

getting what belongs to you – cash!

In analyzing cash flow, the dynamic small business owner understands that cash and profits are not the same.

1. Profit is the difference between total revenue and total expenses, and can be tied up in many forms, such as inventory, computers, or machinery. Creditors, employees, and lenders cannot be paid in profits, but only in cash.

2. Cash is the money that flows through business in a continuous cycle without being tied up in any other asset.

You can have increasing profits but no cash. It is vital to look at the cash flow statement to measure how successful your business is operating. The income statement shows current profits and there may not be any cash. Why? You have look at where they went and there they are! In accounts receivable, assets, and inventory.

Next, go to the *Manager's Index* worksheet and click on the *Cash Flow Process* hyperlink..

This figure shows diagrammatically the flow of cash through a typical small business.

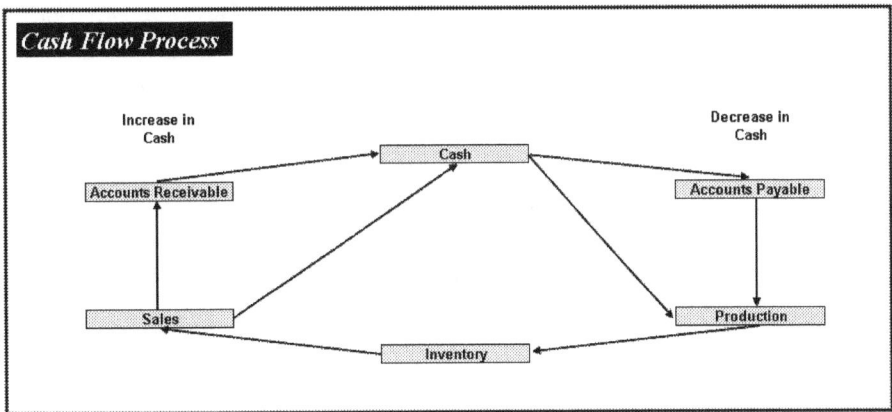

Cash Flow Process

What does this cash flow diagram indicate?

1. Cash flow is the volume of cash that comes into and goes out of the business during an accounting period.

2. Decreases in cash occur when the business purchases, on credit or for cash, goods for inventory or materials for use in production.

3. The resulting inventory from production is sold either for cash or on credit. When cash is taken in or when accounts receivable are collected, the firm's cash balance increases.

4. Notice that purchases for inventory and production lead sales; that is, these bills typically must be paid before sales are generated. Nevertheless, collection of accounts receivable lags behind sales; that is, customers who purchase goods on credit may not pay until next month.

The Cash Budget

The dynamic small business owner tracks, with eager curiosity, the flow of cash through their business so they can project the cash balance at specific intervals during the year.

Unfortunately, there are many owners who operate their businesses without knowing their cash flow pattern. Most feel that the task is too difficult and time consuming.

In fact, no small business owner can afford to neglect the practice of cash management. The owner must be sure that a sufficient, but not unwarranted, supply of cash is on hand to meet the need of their firm's operations.

The dynamic small business owner prepares a cash budget, which is a cash plan, showing the amount and timing of the cash receipts and the cash disbursements on a day-by-day, week-by-week, month-by-month, and quarterly/yearly.

1. Day-by-Day Cash Flow

Go to the *Manager's Index* worksheet and click on the *Cash Flow Forecast Daily* hyperlink.

This worksheet provides a cash flow tracking system on a *daily* basis. Enter your figures in the cells with Bold Blue numbers.

You can customize the form by changing the row labels or adding rows.

The shaded cells contain formulas to perform automatic calculations on your data. Do not enter data into these cells because doing so will erase the formulas in them.

This figure shows an expanded example and the Excel template file Daily Cash Flow.xls is provided for your actual use. This figure shows the flow of cash through a typical small business on a daily basis.

Daily Cash Flow Tracking

Day of Month:	Day 1	Day 2	Day 3	Day 4	Day 5	Day 6	Day 7	Week Totals	Day 8
Receipts									
Cash sales	20,875	42,585	64,295	88,280	109,990	132,383	154,775	613,183	177,168
Collections from credit sales	251	1,420	2,089	3,170	4,089	5,032	5,974	22,025	6,917
New equity inflow	0	0	0	0	0	0	0	0	0
Loans received	16,700	8,350	8,350	8,350	4,175	4,175	4,175	54,275	4,175
Other	0	0	0	0	0	0	0	0	0
Total Receipts	37,826	52,355	74,734	99,800	118,254	141,589	164,924	689,482	188,259
Payments									
Cash purchases	15,456	9,251	8,025	6,813	15,456	9,251	8,025	72,277	6,813
Payments to creditors	0	0	0	0	0	0	0	0	0
Salaries and wages	0	10,000	10,000	21,325	26,325	32,723	39,120	139,493	45,518
Employee benefits	893	534	464	393	893	534	464	4,175	393
Payroll taxes	7,022	4,203	3,646	3,095	7,022	4,203	3,646	32,837	3,095
Rent	2,276	1,362	1,183	1,002	2,276	1,362	1,183	10,644	1,002
Utilities	0	0	0	0	0	0	0	0	0
Repairs and maintenance	12,118	7,254	6,293	5,342	12,118	7,254	6,293	56,672	5,342
Insurance	0	0	0	0	0	0	0	0	0
Travel	2,113	1,265	1,098	932	2,113	1,265	1,098	9,884	932
Telephone	0	0	0	0	0	0	0	0	0
Postage	2,680	1,604	1,391	1,181	2,680	1,604	1,391	12,531	1,181
Office supplies	2,341	1,401	1,215	1,032	2,341	1,401	1,215	10,946	1,032
Advertising	978	584	506	431	978	584	506	4,567	431
Marketing/promotion	3,901	2,336	2,026	1,719	3,901	2,336	2,026	18,245	1,719
Professional fees	11,703	7,005	6,077	5,158	11,703	7,005	6,077	54,728	5,158
Training and development	1,301	779	675	574	1,301	779	675	6,084	574
Bank charges	14,044	8,406	7,292	6,191	14,044	8,406	7,292	65,675	6,191
Miscellaneous	29,225	0	0	0	0	0	0	29,225	0

2. Week-by-Week Cash Flow

Go to the *Manager's Index* worksheet and click on the *Cash Flow Forecast Weekly* hyperlink.

This worksheet provides a cash flow tracking system on a *weekly* basis. Enter your figures in the cells with Bold Blue numbers.

You can customize the form by changing the row labels or adding rows.

The shaded cells contain formulas to perform automatic calculations on your data. Do not enter data into these cells because doing so will erase the formulas in them.

This figure shows an 8-week example of the week-by-week cash flow tracking.

Weekly Cash Flow Tracking - One Year

Week:	Week 1	Week 2	Week 3	Week 4	Week 5	Week 6	Week 7	Week 8	Week 9
Receipts									
Cash sales	20,875	42,585	64,295	88,280	109,990	132,383	154,775	154,775	177,168
Collections from credit sales	251	1,420	2,089	3,170	4,089	5,032	5,974	5,974	6,917
New equity inflow	0	0	0	0	0	0	0	0	0
Loans received	16,700	8,350	8,350	8,350	4,175	4,175	4,175	4,175	4,175
Other	0	0	0	0	0	0	0	0	0
Total Receipts	37,826	52,355	74,734	99,800	118,254	141,589	164,924	164,924	188,259
Payments									
Cash purchases	15,456	9,251	8,025	6,813	15,456	9,251	8,025	8,025	6,813
Payments to creditors	0	0	0	0	0	0	0	0	0
Salaries and wages	0	10,000	10,000	21,325	26,325	32,723	39,120	39,120	45,518
Employee benefits	893	534	464	393	893	534	464	464	393
Payroll taxes	7,022	4,203	3,646	3,095	7,022	4,203	3,646	3,646	3,095
Rent	2,276	1,362	1,183	1,002	2,276	1,362	1,183	1,183	1,002
Utiltities	0	0	0	0	0	0	0	0	0
Repairs and maintenance	12,118	7,254	6,293	5,342	12,118	7,254	6,293	6,293	5,342
Insurance	0	0	0	0	0	0	0	0	0
Travel	2,113	1,265	1,098	932	2,113	1,265	1,098	1,098	932
Telephone	0	0	0	0	0	0	0	0	0
Postage	2,680	1,604	1,391	1,181	2,680	1,604	1,391	1,391	1,181
Office supplies	2,341	1,401	1,215	1,032	2,341	1,401	1,215	1,215	1,032
Advertising	978	584	506	431	978	584	506	506	431
Marketing/promotion	3,901	2,336	2,026	1,719	3,901	2,336	2,026	2,026	1,719
Professional fees	11,703	7,005	6,077	5,158	11,703	7,005	6,077	6,077	5,158
Training and development	1,301	779	675	574	1,301	779	675	675	574
Bank charges	14,044	8,406	7,292	6,191	14,044	8,406	7,292	7,292	6,191
Miscellaneous	29,225	0	0	0	0	0	0	0	0

3. Month-by-Month Cash Flow

Go to the *Manager's Index* worksheet and click on the *Cash Flow Forecast 12 Months* hyperlink.

This worksheet provides a cash flow tracking system on a *monthly* basis. Enter your figures in the cells with Bold Blue numbers.

You can customize the form by changing the row labels or adding rows.

The shaded cells contain formulas to perform automatic calculations on your data. Do not enter data into these cells because doing so will erase the formulas in them.

This figure shows is an 8-month example of the month-by-month cash flow tracking.

Monthly Cash Flow Tracking - One Year									
Month:	January	February	March	April	May	June	July	August	Septembe
Receipts									
Cash sales	20,875	42,585	64,295	88,280	109,990	132,383	154,775	154,775	177,16
Collections from credit sales	251	1,420	2,089	3,170	4,089	5,032	5,974	5,974	6,91
New equity inflow	0	0	0	0	0	0	0	0	
Loans received	16,700	8,350	8,350	8,350	4,175	4,175	4,175	4,175	4,17
Other	0	0	0	0	0	0	0	0	
Total Receipts	37,826	52,355	74,734	99,800	118,254	141,589	164,924	164,924	188,25
Payments									
Cash purchases	15,456	9,251	8,025	6,813	15,456	9,251	8,025	8,025	6,81
Payments to creditors	0	0	0	0	0	0	0	0	
Salaries and wages	0	10,000	10,000	21,325	26,325	32,723	39,120	39,120	45,51
Employee benefits	893	534	464	393	893	534	464	464	39
Payroll taxes	7,022	4,203	3,646	3,095	7,022	4,203	3,646	3,646	3,09
Rent	2,276	1,362	1,183	1,002	2,276	1,362	1,183	1,183	1,00
Utitities	0	0	0	0	0	0	0	0	
Repairs and maintenance	12,118	7,254	6,293	5,342	12,118	7,254	6,293	6,293	5,34
Insurance	0	0	0	0	0	0	0	0	
Travel	2,113	1,265	1,098	932	2,113	1,265	1,098	1,098	93
Telephone	0	0	0	0	0	0	0	0	
Postage	2,680	1,604	1,391	1,181	2,680	1,604	1,391	1,391	1,18
Office supplies	2,341	1,401	1,215	1,032	2,341	1,401	1,215	1,215	1,03
Advertising	978	584	506	431	978	584	506	506	43
Marketing/promotion	3,901	2,336	2,026	1,719	3,901	2,336	2,026	2,026	1,71
Professional fees	11,703	7,005	6,077	5,158	11,703	7,005	6,077	6,077	5,15
Training and development	1,301	779	675	574	1,301	779	675	675	57
Bank charges	14,044	8,406	7,292	6,191	14,044	8,406	7,292	7,292	6,19
Miscellaneous	20,225	0	0	0	0	0	0	0	

4. Quarterly/Yearly Cash Flow

Go to the *Manager's Index* worksheet and click on the *Cash Flow 4 Yrs Quarterly* hyperlink.

This worksheet provides a cash flow tracking system on a *quarterly* basis over 4 years. Enter your figures in the cells with Bold Blue numbers.

You can customize the form by changing the row labels or adding rows.

The shaded cells contain formulas to perform automatic calculations on your data. Do not enter data into these cells because doing so will erase the formulas in them.

This figure shows the flow of cash through a typical small business on a quarterly/yearly basis.

Preparing the Cash Budget

Quarterly Cash Flow - Four Years

	Year 1					Year 2			
	Qtr 1	Qtr 2	Qtr 3	Qtr 4	Totals	Qtr 1	Qtr 2	Qtr 3	Qtr 4
Receipts									
Cash sales	20,875	42,585	64,295	88,280	216,035	109,990	132,383	154,775	154,77
Collections from credit sales	251	1,420	2,089	3,170	6,930	4,089	5,032	5,974	5,97
New equity inflow	0	0	0	0	0	0	0	0	
Loans received	16,700	8,350	8,350	8,350	41,750	4,175	4,175	4,175	4,17
Other	0	0	0	0	0	0	0	0	
Total Receipts	37,826	52,355	74,734	99,800	264,715	118,254	141,589	164,924	164,92
Payments									
Advertising	15,456	9,251	8,025	6,813	39,545	15,456	9,251	8,025	8,02
Bank charges	0	0	0	0	0	0	0	0	
Capital purchases	0	10,000	10,000	21,325	41,325	26,325	32,723	39,120	39,12
Cash purchases	893	534	464	393	2,284	893	534	464	46
Employee benefits	7,022	4,203	3,646	3,095	17,966	7,022	4,203	3,646	3,64
Insurance	2,276	1,362	1,183	1,002	5,823	2,276	1,362	1,183	1,18
Loan repayments	0	0	0	0	0	0	0	0	
Marketing/promotion	12,118	7,254	6,293	5,342	31,007	12,118	7,254	6,293	6,29
Miscellaneous	0	0	0	0	0	0	0	0	
Office supplies	2,113	1,265	1,098	932	5,408	2,113	1,265	1,098	1,09
Owner's drawings	0	0	0	0	0	0	0	0	
Payments to creditors	2,680	1,604	1,391	1,181	6,856	2,680	1,604	1,391	1,39
Payroll taxes	2,341	1,401	1,215	1,032	5,989	2,341	1,401	1,215	1,21
Postage	978	584	506	431	2,499	978	584	506	50
Professional fees	3,901	2,336	2,026	1,719	9,982	3,901	2,336	2,026	2,02
Rent	11,703	7,005	6,077	5,158	29,943	11,703	7,005	6,077	6,07
Repairs and maintenance	1,301	779	675	574	3,329	1,301	779	675	67
Salaries and wages	14,044	8,406	7,292	6,191	35,933	14,044	8,406	7,292	7,29
Tax payments	29,225	0	0	0	29,225	0	0	0	

The dynamic small business owner prepares a projected monthly cash budget for at least one year into the future and a quarterly estimate several years in advance.

In one instance, we observed a business that had rapid seasonal fluctuations and required a weekly cash budget. The more variable the firm's sales pattern, the shorter its planning scope should be.

> Regardless of the period selected, the cash budget must be written down for the small business manager to visualize the firm's cash position.

There are 5 essentials in completing a cash budget.

1. Determine a sufficient minimum cash balance

2. Estimate future sales

3. Estimate future cash receipts

4. Estimate cash disbursements

5. Establish the end-of-month cash balance

1. Determine a sufficient minimum cash balance

The dynamic business owner does the due diligence in determining their cash on hand required for the end-of-the-month cash balance.

What is considered an unwarranted cash balance for one small business may be insufficient for another, even though the two firms are in the same trade and may even be in the same city.

There is a preponderance of rule-of-thumb clichés available for minimum cash balances. The one that seems the most common is the firm's cash balance should equal at least one fourth of its current debts. Yet, this may not work in all small businesses.

The most consistent method is based on analyzing past operating records. This should indicate the proper cash cushion needed to cover any unexpected expenses.

The startup business is at a disadvantage by having no financial history. In this instance there are many sources of advice with the primary source being your accountant. Secondary sources include your trade association, the Small Business Administration, Chamber of Commerce, and other local business owners.

2. Estimate future sales

The key to preparing the cash budget is producing a sales forecast. Since it is sales that are transformed into cash receipts and cash disbursements. The cash budget is only as accurate as the sales forecast from which it is derived.

In practical terms, the cash flow projections and the income statement projections are parallel tasks that are basically prepared from the same data.

The income statement shows the owner the income or loss based on the assumption that both sales income and the cost of making that sale are matched together in the same month.

The cash flow statement looks at the same transactions from the viewpoint that in reality the cost of the sale is incurred first (and paid for) and the income is received last, anywhere from one week to three months later.

Obviously, for a non-cash business the implications of this delay between making the sale and receiving the payment are crucial, especially in the first year of the business and when your business is growing quickly.

For the established business, the sales forecast can be based on past sales, but the owner must be careful not to be excessively optimistic in projecting sales. Many factors can come into play that can drastically alter sales patterns such as economic swings, increased competition, fluctuations in demand, and other factors

The job of forecasting sales for the new firm is more difficult, but not impossible. As mentioned earlier, there are many sources of advice with the primary source being your accountant. Secondary sources include your trade association, the Small Business Administration, Chamber of Commerce, and other local business owners. Additional sources may include census reports, newspapers, radio and television customer profiles, polls and surveys, and local government statistics.

It is important that you create three estimates-an optimistic, a pessimistic, and a most likely sales estimate-and then make a separate cash budget for each forecast. This dynamic forecast enables the owner to determine the range within which their sales will likely be as the year progresses.

To make this task easier for you, we have included several spreadsheet templates.

Go to the **Manager's Index** worksheet and click on the **Cash Flow Sensitivity Analysis** hyperlink.

This worksheet allows you to manipulate two data entries that apply to your business. This first template will help you in estimating an optimistic, a pessimistic, and a most likely sales and cash flow projection.

This figure shows the Basic Cash Flow Sensitivity worksheet for projecting cash flow scenarios with cash inflows and disbursements spanned over the 3 scenarios.

Cash Flow Sensitivity Analysis

% change in assumptions		5.0%		
		Most Likely	**Pessimistic**	**Optimistic**
Beginning Cash Balance		$12,000	$12,000	$12,000
Cash Inflows (Income):				
Accounts Receivable Collections		$264,600	251,370	277,830
Loan Proceeds		$0		
Cash Sales		$30,000	28,500	31,500
Total Cash Inflows		$294,600	$279,870	$309,330
Available Cash Balance		$306,600	$291,870	$321,330
Cash Outflows (Expenses):				
Subtotal		$64,322	$67,538	$61,106
Other Cash Out Flows:				
Subtotal		$6,000	$6,300	$5,700
Total Cash Outflows		$70,322	$73,838	$66,806
Ending Cash Balance		$236,278	$218,032	$254,524

This worksheet will automatically produce the 3 scenarios being controlled by the assumption percentage.

Enter a percentage to change the assumption. The template will automatically prepare a pessimistic and optimistic set of cash flow scenarios.

1. Under the pessimistic scenario, cash receipts will be lowered by the percentage and disbursements will be increased by the same percentage.

2. Under the optimistic scenario, receipts will be increased while disbursements will be decreased by the percentage assumption.

Enter your numbers in the cells where the figures are in Bold Blue. The shaded formula cells are protected from overwriting.

Unfortunately, there is another factor that has to be considered to make a proper forecast. It is called account receivables aging. This important variable is discussed in the next section.

3. Estimate future cash receipts

Go to the *Manager's Index* worksheet and click on the *Cash Flow Sensitivity AR* hyperlink.

There has to be accountability for goods or services sold and the actual cash is received. This called aging of accounts receivable.

This figure shows the Basic Cash Flow Sensitivity AR worksheet for projecting cash flow scenarios while taking into account the aging of sales sold on credit spanned over the 3 scenarios.

Cash Flow Sensitivity Analysis - Aged AR

100% Total Credit Sales	$270,000
60% 30 Days	$162,000
30% 60 Days	$81,000
5% 90 Days	$13,500
4% 120 Days	$10,800
1% Unrecoverable	($2,700)
Total Projected Collections	$264,600

% change in assumptions	5.0%

	Most Likely	Pessimistic	Optimistic
Beginning Cash Balance	$12,000	$12,000	$12,000
Cash Inflows (Income):			
Accounts Receivable Collections	$264,600	251,370	277,830
Loan Proceeds	$0		
Cash Sales	$30,000	28,500	31,500
Other:			
Enter description here	$0		
Enter description here	$0		
Enter description here	$0		
Total Cash Inflows	$294,600	$279,870	$309,330
Available Cash Balance	$306,600	$291,870	$321,330

Virtually identical to the Cash Flow Sensitivity Analysis worksheet, there is one important addition, the aging of credit sales block that yields its total into the calculation process.

Enter your credit sales total and then assign a percentage of possible recovery for each time period: 30, 60, 90, 120 days, or unrecoverable. The sheet will automatically produce the unrecoverable percentage dollars and calculate the appropriate scenarios.

4. Estimate cash disbursements

Go to the **Manager's Index** worksheet and click on the **Expense Budget** hyperlink.

Use this worksheet to plan the labor and operating expenses for your company or a department.

The purchase of inventory or raw materials; wages and salaries; rent, taxes, loans and interest; selling expenses; overhead expenses; and miscellaneous expenses are the typical disbursement categories.

They are recorded in the month that they will be paid, not when the purchase occurred.

"Management by cash crisis" can come about when an owner underestimates cash disbursements and forgets to cushion the appropriate outflow accounts.

This figure shows the Expense Budget worksheet. Properly and regularly used, you will be on top of your cash outflow and prevent a cash drought.

Expense Budget

Account	Budget	Actual	Difference ($)	Difference (%)
Labor				
Office	$25,000	$28,150	$3,150	12.6%
Store	$15,000	$16,260	$1,260	8.4%
Salespeople	$27,500	$23,220	($4,280)	-15.6%
Others	$12,000	$9,640	($2,360)	-19.7%
Operations				
Advertising	$48,000	$37,260	($10,740)	-22.4%
Bad Debts	$4,000	$6,130	$2,130	53.3%
Cash Discounts	$6,000	$9,260	$3,260	54.3%
Delivery Costs	$3,400	$5,150	$1,750	51.5%
Depreciation	$3,000	$2,570	($430)	-14.3%
Dues and Subscriptions	$500	$370	($130)	-26.0%
Employee Benefits	$14,000	$12,850	($1,150)	-8.2%
Insurance	$6,000	$4,520	($1,480)	-24.7%
Interest	$450	$440	($10)	-2.2%
Legal and Auditing	$1,000	$1,300	$300	30.0%
Maintenance and Repairs	$1,500	$1,420	($80)	-5.3%
Office Supplies	$300	$370	$70	23.3%
Postage	$125	$160	$35	28.0%
Rent or Mortgage	$2,500	$3,570	$1,070	42.8%
Sales Expenses	$1,200	$910	($290)	-24.2%
Shipping and Storage	$600	$890	$290	48.3%
Supplies	$250	$200	($50)	-20.0%
Taxes	$2,000	$1,320	($680)	-34.0%
Telephone	$250	$260	$10	4.0%
Utilities	$450	$450	$0	0.0%
Other	$2,000	$2,460	$460	23.0%
Total Expenses	$177,025	$169,130	($7,895)	-4.5%

Filled out in two steps, the worksheet compares estimated and actual expenses. Enter the company or department name then enter the remaining information into the cells provided with the numbers in Bold Blue.

The worksheet automatically calculates the dollar and percentage difference between estimated and actual figures.

You can customize the form by changing the row labels or adding rows.

Do not enter data into shaded cells because doing so will erase the formulas in them.

5. Establish the end-of-month cash balance

To estimate the firm's cash balance for each month, we refer back to two critically important worksheet tools.

> 1. Cash Flow Forecast Daily
>
> 2. Cash Flow Forecast 12 Months

Using these two worksheets will prevent almost all of your uncertainties regarding cash flow. The emphasis is on "using". The dynamic small business owner is eager to be exposed to new tools from everywhere and they use them until they select those that are best for them and their business.

Chapter 7 - Break-even Analysis

The dynamic business owner systematically runs break-even analyses to be sure that sales individual items or services are profitable. Let us explore this simple tool with a few explanations.

The break-even point is where your business neither earns a profit nor incurs a loss.

At this level of activity, sales revenue equals expenses-that is, the firm breaks even. By analyzing costs and expenses, the owner can calculate the minimum level of activity required to keep the firm in operation.

These techniques can then be refined to project the sales needed to generate the desired profit. Most potential lenders and investors will require the potential owner to prepare a break-even analysis to assist them in evaluating the earning potential of the new business.

And, in addition to its being a simple, useful screening device for financial institutions, break-even analysis can also serve as a planning device for the small business owner.

Key among its strengths is showing just how unprofitable a proposed business venture is likely to be.

The Manager has a large selection of Break-even tools. Choose one and use it constantly.

Breaking Even - Sales, Variable Costs, and Fixed Expenses

A formula for this calculation, which will save time for your own calculations, is as follows:

The break-even point is equal to the fixed costs divided by fixed costs + Profit (BE=Fixed/Fixed + Profit). The result is expressed as a percentage. Multiply the percentage times Sales to get the break-even point in dollars.

Go to the **Manager's Index** worksheet and click on the **Breakeven Analysis** hyperlink.

This figure illustrates an example used in the Manager for computing the Break-even point for one financial period.

Breakeven **Analysis - Period 1**

Revenues	Cost of Sales	Gross Profit	Fixed Exp.	Income Taxes	Net Income	Income Variance		
$1,960,000	$745,000	$1,215,000	$329,993	$205,872	$480,368	$0	Reset	Calculator

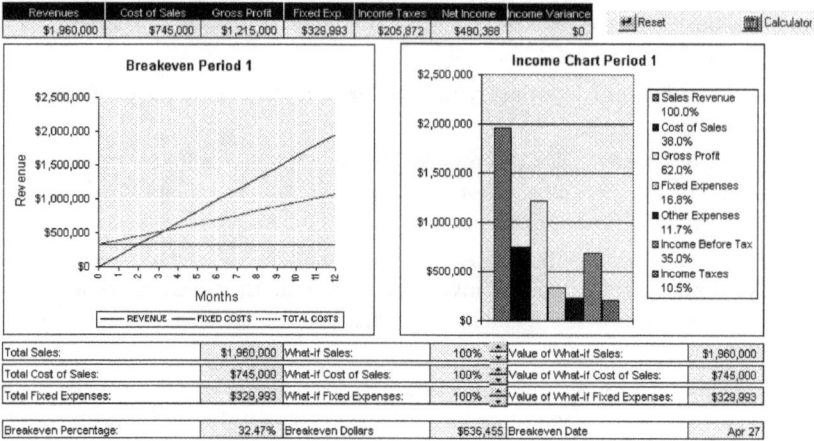

Breakeven Period 1 (chart: Revenue, Fixed Costs, Total Costs plotted against Months, $0 to $2,500,000)

Income Chart Period 1 (chart with legend:)
- Sales Revenue 100.0%
- Cost of Sales 38.0%
- Gross Profit 62.0%
- Fixed Expenses 16.8%
- Other Expenses 11.7%
- Income Before Tax 35.0%
- Income Taxes 10.5%

Total Sales:	$1,960,000	What-if Sales:	100%	Value of What-if Sales:	$1,960,000
Total Cost of Sales:	$745,000	What-if Cost of Sales:	100%	Value of What-if Cost of Sales:	$745,000
Total Fixed Expenses:	$329,993	What-if Fixed Expenses:	100%	Value of What-if Fixed Expenses:	$329,993

Breakeven Percentage:	32.47%	Breakeven Dollars	$636,455	Breakeven Date	Apr 27

Fixed costs and variable costs

A variable cost varies directly with the number of units produced. Each unit produced will incur a specific cost (materials required etc.), this cost to the company will increase in direct proportion to the number of units produced. That is, the more units that are produced, the greater the variable cost.

Typical variable costs are:

Materials, Commission/hourly wage, Variable utilities (machine power etc.)

A fixed cost remains constant for a particular range of activity. That is, regardless of the number of units produced within a range, the fixed costs will remain constant.

Typical fixed costs are:

Rent, mortgage, Equipment, Salary, Fixed utilities (factory lighting etc.)

Breaking Even - Using Units Calculations

Let us take an elementary example: A business plans to sell only one product and has only one fixed cost, which is the rent. In this example we plan to purchase goods at $3 per unit, which represents the variable cost, so every unit we sell adds that much to our fixed cost

Only one additional element is needed to calculate the break-even point: sales. We plan to sell at $5 per unit, so the sales are calculated by multiplying the number of units sold by the price per unit, or $5 in this case.

The break-even point is the stage when a business starts to make a profit. That is when the sales revenue begins to exceed both the fixed and variable costs.

A formula for this calculation, which will save time for your own calculations, is as follows: The break-even point is equal to the fixed costs divided by the difference between the unit selling price and the variable costs per unit.

So, in this case, the break-even point is $10,000 ÷ ($5 - $3), which equals 5000 units. Thus our example's break-even point is when 5000 units are sold.

From the templates folder, please open **Break-even Units.xls**.

This figure illustrates an example used for computing the Break-even point in units.

Break-even Units

Price Per Unit	$7.50			
Number of Units Sold	10000			
Total Sales	$75,000	100%		
Less: Variable Production Costs	$31,040	41%		
Less: Variable Selling Costs	$18,480	25%		
Total Variable Costs	$49,520	66%	$4.95 Per Unit	
Contribution Margin	$25,480	34%		
Less: Fixed Production Costs	$13,050	17%		
Less: Fixed Selling and Administrative Costs	$4,820	6%		
Total Fixed Costs	$17,870	24%	$1.79 Per Unit	
Income Before Taxes	$7,610	10%	$0.76 Per Unit	
Break-Even Point (units) =	7,013			
Break-Even Point ($'s) =	52,600			
Sales Price per Unit =	$7.50			

Break-Even Analysis Chart

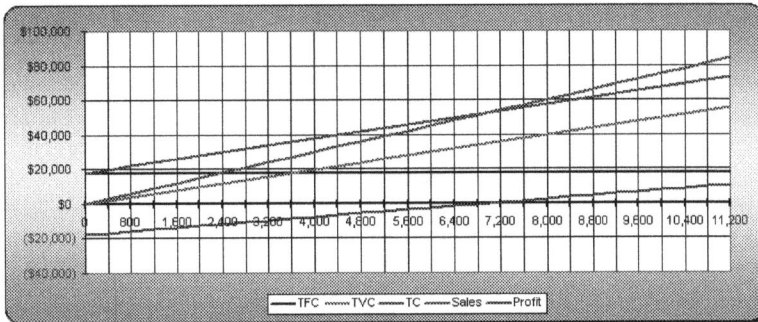

Breaking Even - Comprehensive Details

From the templates folder, please open *ManagerBreakeven.xls*.

Introduction

The key to successfully operating a business is having the right information to make your decisions. This concept may appear elementary, but it can be one of the greatest strategic and operational obstacles your company faces.

As any person who reads or analyzes financial statements knows, there are more financial indicators available than are needed. The trick is to choose the indicators that have the greatest relevance to your financial goals.

Management accounting as a profession concerns itself with the internal operations and drivers of business performance. One of its primary tools is contribution and break-even analysis, which uses financial indicators such as:

Contribution margin. This is usually defined as the sales revenue less the variable costs of production.

Unit contribution. This is the margin contributed by each unit sold.

Break-even point. This is the point in the sales process at which the revenues equal the costs of production.

These indicators enable you to make decisions about how you can:

- Increase product profitability
- Manage your product sales mix
- Optimize your resources to hold your costs down and raise your profits

These decisions often involve making assumptions about the profitability, resources, and product mix. You can test the assumptions by considering what effect they have on variables such as unit contribution.

For example, suppose that you manage a product whose contribution margin is $1 million per year. If your company is to meet its targeted profit for next year, you must assume that you can raise your product's contribution margin by 10 percent to $1.1 million. What options could you exercise that would cause your product to return an additional $100,000 profit?

To guide you in a search for your options, you could refer back to a contribution margin analysis and, perhaps, a unit contribution analysis. These analyses spell out the factors that tend to hold your revenues down and that keep your costs up. By examining these factors, you may be able to determine which costs, sales prices, and volume levels you can modify so as to achieve your assumed $1.1 million target.

This document in collaboration with the ***ManagerBreakeven.xls*** explores the relationships among these variables. It shows you how to use Excel to identify which inputs you can modify to meet your goals.

Calculating the Contribution Margin

All firms have costs that are directly associated with their products or services. One of the most powerful means of understanding and controlling those costs is contribution margin analysis. The contribution margin itself is calculated by subtracting the variable costs required to manufacture the product from the revenue achieved by selling that product.

Variable costs are those that change as production levels rise and fall: the cost of raw materials is a variable cost. Fixed costs are those that do not change along with differences in production levels: the cost of salaried workers is a fixed cost. (The next section discusses this distinction in more detail.)

In practice, the definition of the contribution margin is often expanded to "revenue minus directly traceable costs." This is because it can be extremely difficult to distinguish between some fixed and variable costs. But these directly traceable costs should include all those that are variable.

Case Study: Producing Compact Discs

MaxJax, Inc. produces CD-ROMs. To make the CDs, it costs MaxJax:

$5 per CD for the materials used in the CD itself

$1 per CD for the packaging materials (the jewel box, the paper insert, and the plastic wrapping)

$0.50 per CD for the factory employees

For a total production cost of $6.50 per CD. The contribution margin therefore would be calculated as shown in Figure 1.

Calculating The Contribution Margin - Figure 1

Sales (1000 CDs @ $10)	$10,000
Less: Costs associated with production:	
Employee costs (1000 CDs @ $0.50): $500	
Materials costs (1000 CDs @ $5): $5,000	
Packaging costs (1000 CDs @ $1): $1,000	
Total variable costs:	$6,500
Contribution margin:	$3,500

The $6.50 per unit in costs required to make each CD is called a variable cost. Remember that variable costs are the costs that vary with the level of production. When production goes down, variable costs decrease, and when production goes up, variable costs increase.

Besides variable costs, MaxJax also has fixed costs. Fixed costs do not vary with the level of production. For example, rent paid for a building, legal fees, and business insurance are usually the same regardless of how many CDs it makes. In contrast, when MaxJax makes more CDs, the total amount that it pays for materials such as blank CDs increases: it is a variable cost.

In practice, and even when you can separate variable from fixed costs, the distinction between them is not quite as crisp as this. Consider, for example, the $0.50 per CD that MaxJax pays its employees. There are several ways that MaxJax can incur that cost:

The employee is paid by the CD and (perhaps due to a negotiated contract) the payment cannot be changed. If that is the payment arrangement, the payment is a variable cost: the more CDs produced, the more the employee is paid.

The employee receives a fixed wage, regardless of the number of CDs produced, and the $0.50 per CD is just a long-term average. In this case, the employee represents a fixed cost. Unless you negotiate payment terms that are based directly on production, you should not include this cost in the contribution margin analysis.

The employee is paid by the CD, but the payment changes according to how many CDs are made. Up to 1,000 CDs made per day, you pay the employee $0.50 per CD, but you pay $0.60 per CD for anything over 1,000 CDs made. This is a semi-variable cost. A semi-variable cost changes with the number of units, but the change is not precisely proportional to the number of units.

Semi-variable costs are often step functions. A step function is one that changes suddenly when a variable reaches a certain threshold. In this example, when the production level reaches the threshold of 1,000 CDs, the employee cost jumps from $0.50 per unit to $0.60 per unit.

Up to 1,000 CDs, the ratio of total employee cost to units made is exactly $0.50. After 1,000 CDs, the ratio is exactly $0.60. But across the full range of production (say, from 0 to 10,000 CDs produced) the ratio is inexact: it depends on the number produced.

Figure 2 shows an example of how you might account for a semi-variable cost: in this case, an employee makes $0.50 for each CD sold up to and including 1,000 CDs per day, $0.60 per CD for 1,000 to 2,000, and so on.

Contribution Margin Analysis - Figure 2

		Employee cost calculation			Employee cost
CDs Sold:	4510	CDsMade		UnitCost	per quantity
Sales @ $10 per CD	$45,100.00		0	$0.50	$500.00
			1000	$0.60	$600.00
Less: Variable costs of production:			2000	$0.70	$700.00
			3000	$0.80	$800.00
Employee costs (semi-variable):	$3,059.00		4000	$0.90	$459.00
			5000	$1.00	$0.00
Materials costs (variable)	$22,550.00				
		MaterialsCost:		$5.00	
Packaging costs (variable)	$4,510.00				
		PackagingCost:		$1.00	
Total variable costs:	$30,119.00				
Contribution margin:	$14,981.00				

Click on cell P9. Notice the IF statements:

=IF(SalesLevel>CDsMade,MIN(1000,(SalesLevel-CdsMad))*UnitCost,0)

This formula uses three named ranges:

   1) SalesLevel

   2) CDsMade

   3) UnitCost

The MIN function appears in the formula because no more than 1,000 units should be counted for any level of CDsMade. In the Figure 2, SalesLevel is 4510. For the 4000

---

level of CDsMade, SalesLevel-CDsMade = 510, and this amount is multiplied by the corresponding UnitCost of $0.90 to return $51.00.

In contrast, at the 3000 level of CDsMade, SalesLevel-CDsMade = 1510. But this is too many units to count: 1000 is the maximum number of units to count for any given level. Therefore, the formula makes use of the MIN function to return the smaller of 1000, or the difference between SalesLevel and CDsMade.

The smaller of those two values (1000, or SalesLevel-CDsMade), is multiplied by the corresponding UnitCost to return the cost of the CDs made at that level of production.

Finally, SalesLevel can be less than any given level of CDsMade.In the figure, 4510 is less than 5000, so no units should be counted for that level. The IF function returns 0 in that case.

Using Unit Contribution

The analysis of contribution margin in the case study of CD production involved total variable costs and total revenues. You can also break the information down to a per unit and percent of sales basis. This gives you a different perspective on the relationship between your costs and revenues.

To continue the MaxJax example, consider the same information from a different perspective shown in *Figure* *3.*

Per Unit and Percent of Sales Contribution Analysis - Figure 3			
CDs Sold 4510			
	Total	Per Unit	% of Margin
Sales (CDs @ $10 each)	$45,100.00	$10.00	100.00%
Less:			
Labor (CDs at semi-variable per CD)	$3,059.00	$0.68	6.78%
Materials (CDs at $5 per CD)	$22,550.00	$5.00	50.00%
Packaging costs @ $1 per CD	$4,510.00	$1.00	10.00%
Contribution Margin	$14,981.00	$3.32	33.22%
CDs Sold 5510			
	Total	Per Unit	% of Margin
Sales (CDs @ $10 each)	$55,100.00	$10.00	100.00%
Less:			
Labor (CDs at semi-variable per CD)	$4,010.00	$0.73	7.28%
Materials (CDs at $5 per CD)	$27,550.00	$5.00	50.00%
Packaging costs @ $1 per CD	$5,510.00	$1.00	10.00%
Contribution Margin	$18,030.00	$3.27	32.72%

The detailed per unit and percent of margin information gives you a better idea of:

- The product's individual contribution to total revenue

- The source of the greatest percentage of variable costs

- The relationships among the magnitudes of the variable costs

The detail that you obtain from this type of analysis is valuable information because it gives you the tools you need to make decisions that maximize your profits. Figure 3, for example, makes it clear. Suppose that MaxJax wants to increase the contribution margin from 33.22% to 35%. By analyzing the information shown previously, MaxJax notices that if it can lower the cost of its materials from $5.00 per CD to $4.82 per CD, it can increase the contribution margin to 35%. One way of doing so might be by using a different supplier. Lowering the cost of materials will decrease the direct material cost to 48.2% of total costs. This enables MaxJax to achieve its desired margin of 35%.

In summary, a contribution margin analysis provides the following advantages when you must make operational decisions:

The analysis helps you decide what price to charge for your product. For example, if you want an additional $10 contribution margin on every unit you sell, you will have to either increase your price by $10 or reduce your unit variable costs by $10.

The analysis helps you control those costs that are directly related to manufacturing the product. For example, if you are currently using a vendor who charges $50 per each 10 units of materials, you may be able to find a vendor that charges $45, and yet obtain the same quality that your current vendor offers.

The analysis helps you understand the relationships among the volume of products produced and sold, their costs, and your profits. This is especially useful in the case of semi-variable costs, which are usually difficult to account for without doing the formal analysis.

Creating an Operating Income Statement

Once created, an Excel worksheet can make performing a contribution analysis very easy. The first thing you should do is create your Operating Income Statement on a worksheet. The worksheet contains your Sales, Variable Cost, and volume information on a total, per unit, and percent of margin basis. This portion of the worksheet contains the values that depend on unit pricing.

The formulas used to create the information in Figure 4 are shown in Figure 5.

	Total	Per unit	Percent of margin
Sales	$2,000	$20	100%
Less:			
Materials	$400	$4	20%
Labor	$900	$9	45%
Variable Overhead	$300	$3	15%
Contribution margin:	$400	$4	20%
Quantity Sold or Produced	100		

	Total	Per unit	Percent of margin
Sales	AN16*AO8	$20	100%
Less:			
Material	$AN$16*AO10	$4	AO10/$AO$8
Labor	$AN$16*AO11	$9	AO11/$AO$8
Variable Overhead	$AN$16*AO12	$3	AO12/$AO$8
Contribution margin:	AN8-SUM(AN10:AN12)	AO8-SUM(AO10:AO12)	AO13/$AO$8
Quantity Sold or Produced	100		

By separating your price, cost, and quantity information from your Operating Income Statement, you can easily make changes to selling prices, costs, and quantities. These changes will be reflected in the Operating Income Statement, and will therefore raise or lower your calculated contribution margin.

Finding the Break-even Point

One of the key benefits of the information acquired from management ac- counting is the ability to perform a cost/volume/profit analysis. Creating this analysis is nothing more than the manipulation of the information derived from your contribution analysis. In this way, you can determine the optimal production volume and sales price that will enable you to maximize your profits and minimize your costs.

One way to manipulate your contribution margin to perform a cost/volume/ profit analysis is to calculate the Break-Even point. This is the point where total revenues equal total expenses, both fixed and variable. Thus, the Break-Even point is the point at which total revenues equal total costs:

Total Revenues (Price * Quantity) = Total Costs

(Fixed Costs + (Variable Costs * Quantity)

Break-Even information allows you to plan for the level of sales that you need to cover your total costs. It also provides you with information on the level of sales that will be necessary to achieve your desired level of profitability.

There are several ways to calculate the Break-Even point. Each calculation method provides you with a different slant, and your choice should depend on your information requirements. The Break-Even calculations include Break-Even in units, Break-Even in dollars, and Break-Even with an expected level of profit.

Calculating Break-Even In Units

Break-Even in units is the number of units that must be sold at current price levels to cover fixed and variable costs. The Break-Even point measured in units is:

Break-Even point (units) = Total fixed costs/(Unit Sales Price -Unit Variable costs)

Calculating the Break-Even point in units is most useful when managers need to analyze current or projected volume levels. You might know, for example, that with your current sales force you can expect to sell 10 units per month. By calculating Break-Even in units, you can determine whether your company can be profitable at 10 units sold per month. If your company cannot be profitable at that level, you might decide that you need to add sales staff.

Suppose that total fixed costs are $50, unit sales price is $20 and unit variable costs are $15. You can calculate the Break-Even point in units by means of this formula:

Break-Even point (units) = $50/ ($20- $15)

The result is 10. Therefore, the company needs to sell 10 units during the period when the fixed costs are incurred to break even. With this information, you can manipulate the pricing and costs to calculate the number of units that need to be sold to break even.

Or, you might find it useful to turn this relationship around. Suppose that you know that your total fixed costs will increase by $10 per month, from $50 to $60. You do not want to change your unit sales price, and your unit variable costs will not change. How many units must you sell to break even?

Begin by rearranging the formula for Break-Even point in units, as follows:

Total Fixed Costs = Break-Even point (units) * (Sales Price -Unit Variable Costs)

You can use Excel's Goal Seek function to determine your new Break-Even point in units. See Figure 6 for a sample worksheet layout. Refer to the spreadsheet for procedures in using Goal Seek.

Fixed costs	Sales price	Variable cost	Break-Even units
50	20	15	10

Calculating Break-Even In Sales

Break-Even in Sales is the number of dollars of sales revenue that are needed to cover fixed and variable costs. There are several ways to calculate Break-Even in sales. Each provides the same result, but each method uses slightly different inputs. One method is:

Break-Even in Sales = (Break-Even Units * Unit Sales Price)

Suppose that the Break-Even units is 10 and the unit sales price is $20. These data result in Break-Even in sales dollars of $200:

$200 = (10 * $20)

Here, you already know how many units you need to sell so as to break even,

and you simply multiply that by the price of each unit.

Another formula that you can use if you haven't yet calculated Break-Even units is:

Break-Even in Sales = Total Fixed Costs / ((Unit Sales Price -Unit Variable Costs) / Unit Sales Price)

Here, the total fixed costs is $50, unit sales price is $20, and unit variable costs is $10. The data result in:

$200 = $501 (($20- $15)1 $20)

$200 = $501 ($51 $20)

$200 = $501 .25

In this case, you find your profit per unit ($20 - $15 = $5) and divide by the unit sales price: $5 / $20, or .25. This is the proportion of unit sales price that is profit over and above your variable costs. Dividing the additional costs that you need to cover, your total fixed costs, by that profit proportion results in the sales dollars needed to meet total costs.

A third approach is:

Break-Even in Sales = (Break-Even Units * Unit Variable Cost) + Total Fixed Costs

or, where Break-Even Units is 10, Unit Variable Cost is 15, and total Fixed Costs is $50:

$200 = (10 * $15) + $50

$200 = $150 + 50

This formula simply determines the Total Variable Cost for Break-Even units, and adds to that the Total Fixed Cost.

In each case, you find that you need $200 in sales to break even.

Break-Even as measured in sales dollars will provide you with valuable information regarding how much sales revenue is required to cover your operating costs. It can give you an understanding of how aggressively you must market your product to meet your operating costs. It also gives you some indication of how efficiently you are using your resources. For example, if your sales expectations are higher than the Break-Even point, and yet you are just meeting it, you may need to reevaluate how efficiently you are using the resources that are available to you.

> In practice, it is easiest to set up one formula that involves each component as a named cell reference. The formula might be:
>
> = Units * (Unit Price -Unit Cost) -Fixed Costs
>
> Then, you can use Goal Seek to set the value of the formula to zero (the Break-Even point) by varying anyone of the formula's precedent cells.

Calculating Break-Even in Sales Dollars with an Expected Level of Profit

Break-Even in sales dollars represents the sales revenue needed to cover fixed and variable costs, and still return a profit at the level that you require. Conceptually, this is similar to treating profit as a cost. You need to meet your fixed costs, and you need to meet your variable costs; you simply consider that profit is another cost category that you need to meet.

You can calculate Break-Even in sales dollars by using this formula:

Break-Even in Sales Dollars = Variable Costs + Fixed Costs + Expected Profit

Suppose that a company wants to make a $5 profit on every unit it sells. The Variable Cost is $15 per unit, 10 units are sold, the Fixed Costs total $50, and the expected profit is $5 per unit. Then, the formula that provides the Break- Even point in terms of sales dollars is:

Break-Even = (Unit Variable Cost * Units) + Fixed Costs + (Expected Profit * Units)

= ($15 * 10) + $50 + ($5 * 10)

= $250

and the company's Break-Even point, measured in sales dollars, is $250 for 10 units with a profit of $5 per unit.

Charting the Break-Even Point

Besides using equations to perform a Break-Even analysis, a graphic depiction of your Break-Even point is another valuable tool to analyze your cost/Volume/Profit relationship. Figures 7 through 9 display graphs that depict the elements of a Cost/Volume/Profit analysis.

Figure 7 shows a company's fixed costs by way of a straight line, at $50, regardless of sales volume.

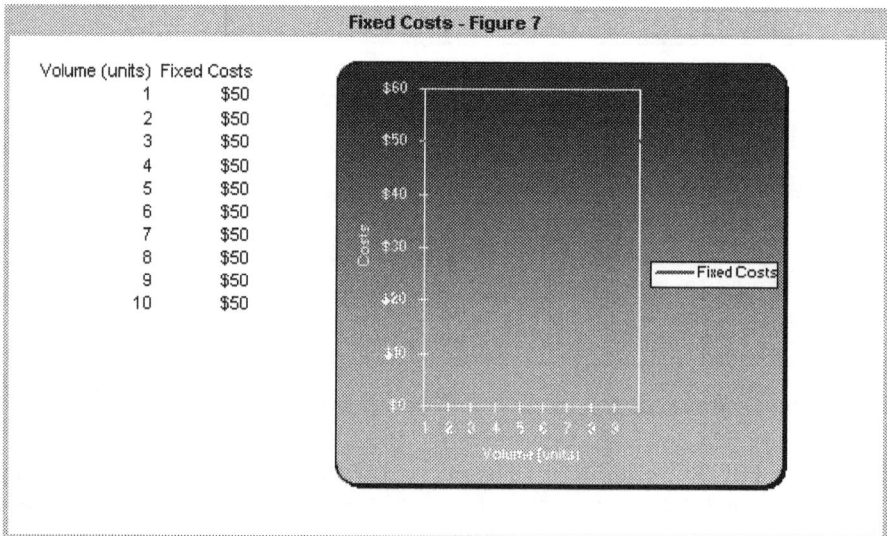

Fixed Costs - Figure 7

Volume (units)	Fixed Costs
1	$50
2	$50
3	$50
4	$50
5	$50
6	$50
7	$50
8	$50
9	$50
10	$50

To create this chart from the data shown by figure 7, follow these steps:

Select the range that contains the data.

Click the Chart Wizard button on the main toolbar. Or, choose Insert, Chart, and select On this sheet from the cascading menu.

The cursor will change to crosshairs with a depiction of a column chart below and right of the crosshairs. Place the crosshairs where you want the upper-left corner of your chart on the worksheet. Holding down the mouse button, drag right and down until you have outlined the location where you want your chart. Then, release the mouse button.

Step 1 of the Chart Wizard allows you to confirm or change the range address of the cells that you want to chart. Choose Next.

Step 2 of the Chart Wizard displays IS different chart types from which to choose. Click the Line chart type, and then choose Next.

Click format 2 in Step 3 of the Chart Wizard, and choose Next.

In Step 4 of the Chart Wizard, enter the number of columns to use for Category (X) Labels. Either click the spinner until the spin box contains 1, or type 1 directly in the Use First... Columns for Category (X) Labels box. Set Use First...Rows for Legend Text to 1.

In Step 5 of the Chart Wizard, type Volume (Units) in the Category (X) box. Type Costs in the Value (Y) box. Choose Finish.

After Excel has drawn the chart on your worksheet, double-click the chart. This opens the chart for editing.

Click on the (automatic) title at the top of the chart. Press the Delete key, or choose Clear from the Edit menu, and select All from the cascading menu.

Click inside the chart's plot area. Move your cursor to the handle at the center of the top border of the plot area. Your cursor changes to a double arrow. Hold down the mouse button, and drag the top border toward the top of the chart. Release the mouse button

Click the value axis. Choose Selected Axis...from the Format menu. If necessary , click the Scale tab at the top of the Format Axis dialog box. Type 140 in the Maximum edit box, and type 10 in the Major Unit edit box. Choose OK.

Click somewhere in the worksheet outside the embedded chart to deselect it.

You can create the charts shown in figures 8 and 9 by taking similar steps. Figure 8 illustrates how variable costs increase as production volume increases.

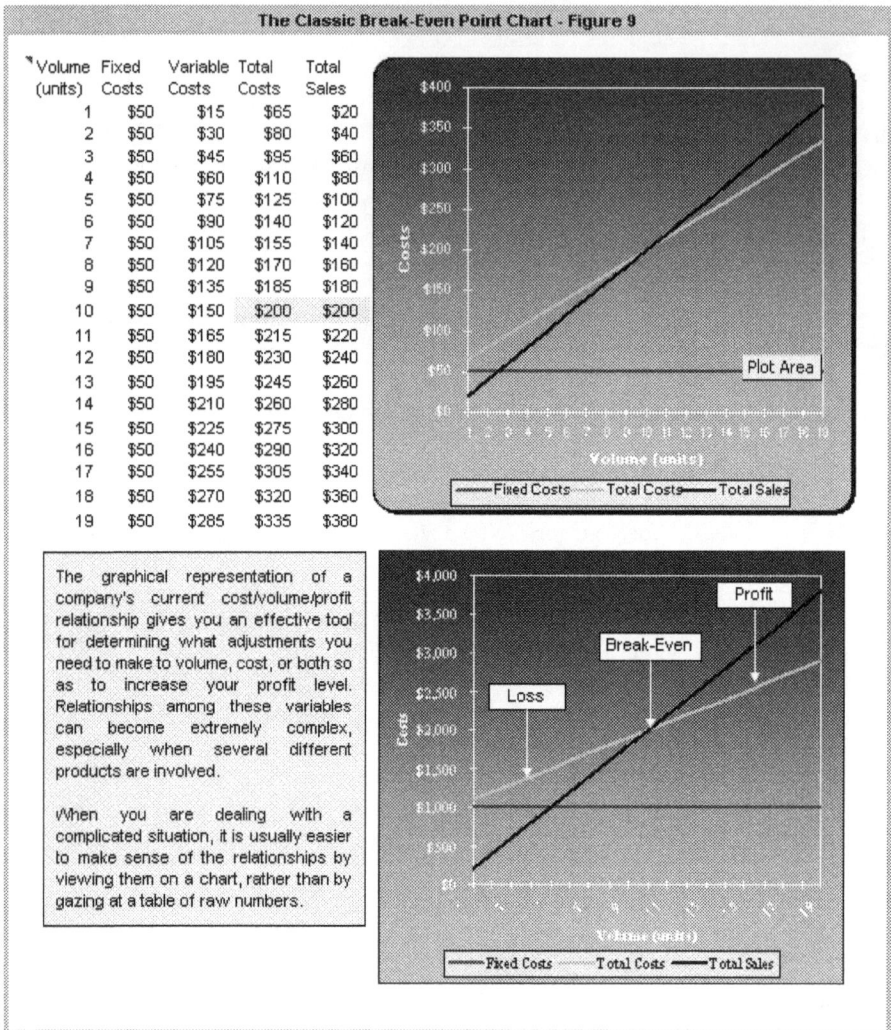

The Classic Break-Even Point Chart - Figure 9

Volume (units)	Fixed Costs	Variable Costs	Total Costs	Total Sales
1	$50	$15	$65	$20
2	$50	$30	$80	$40
3	$50	$45	$95	$60
4	$50	$60	$110	$80
5	$50	$75	$125	$100
6	$50	$90	$140	$120
7	$50	$105	$155	$140
8	$50	$120	$170	$160
9	$50	$135	$185	$180
10	$50	$150	$200	$200
11	$50	$165	$215	$220
12	$50	$180	$230	$240
13	$50	$195	$245	$260
14	$50	$210	$260	$280
15	$50	$225	$275	$300
16	$50	$240	$290	$320
17	$50	$255	$305	$340
18	$50	$270	$320	$360
19	$50	$285	$335	$380

The graphical representation of a company's current cost/volume/profit relationship gives you an effective tool for determining what adjustments you need to make to volume, cost, or both so as to increase your profit level. Relationships among these variables can become extremely complex, especially when several different products are involved.

When you are dealing with a complicated situation, it is usually easier to make sense of the relationships by viewing them on a chart, rather than by gazing at a table of raw numbers.

Figure 9 represents the relationship between Total Costs and Total Sales at different levels of production.

The figure illustrates the quantity at which Loss, Break-Even, and Profit are achieved. Below 10 units on the X-axis, the company loses money because the unit profit has yet to make up for the fixed costs. At 10 units, there is exactly enough unit profit to cover fixed costs, and the Total Sales equals Total Costs. Above 10 units, the company is making a profit at the rate of $5 per unit over 10.

The graphical representation of a company's current cost/volume/profit relationship gives you an effective tool for determining what adjustments you need to make to volume, cost, or both so as to increase your profit level. Relationships among these variables can become extremely complex, especially when several different products are involved. When you are dealing with a complicated situation, it is usually easier to make sense of the relationships by viewing them on a chart, rather than by gazing at a table of raw numbers.

Making Assumptions in Contribution Analysis

The analysis of contribution margin, Break-Even points, and the relationships among costs, volume, and profit makes some assumptions that must be met before you can fully trust the results of the analysis. The assumptions that follow are particularly important.

Linear Relationships

Contribution margin analysis assumes that revenues and expenses are linear across the relevant range of volume. Suppose that you offer volume discounts to your customers. In that case, when you sell more goods, each additional, incremental sale generates less revenue per unit than when you sell fewer units.

The revenue line would be similar to that in Figure 10. Notice that it is no longer straight (linear), but that it increases more slowly as volume in- creases (curvilinear).

Non-linear Revenue Growth From Giving Discounts - Figure 10

Sales Price per Unit = $20

Volume (units)	Discount	Revenue
5	0.0%	$100
10	2.5%	$195
15	5.0%	$285
20	7.5%	$370
25	10.0%	$450
30	12.5%	$525
35	15.0%	$595
40	17.5%	$660
45	20.0%	$720
50	22.5%	$775
55	25.0%	$825
60	27.5%	$870
65	30.0%	$910
70	32.5%	$945
75	35.0%	$975
80	37.5%	$1,000
85	40.0%	$1,020
90	42.5%	$1,035

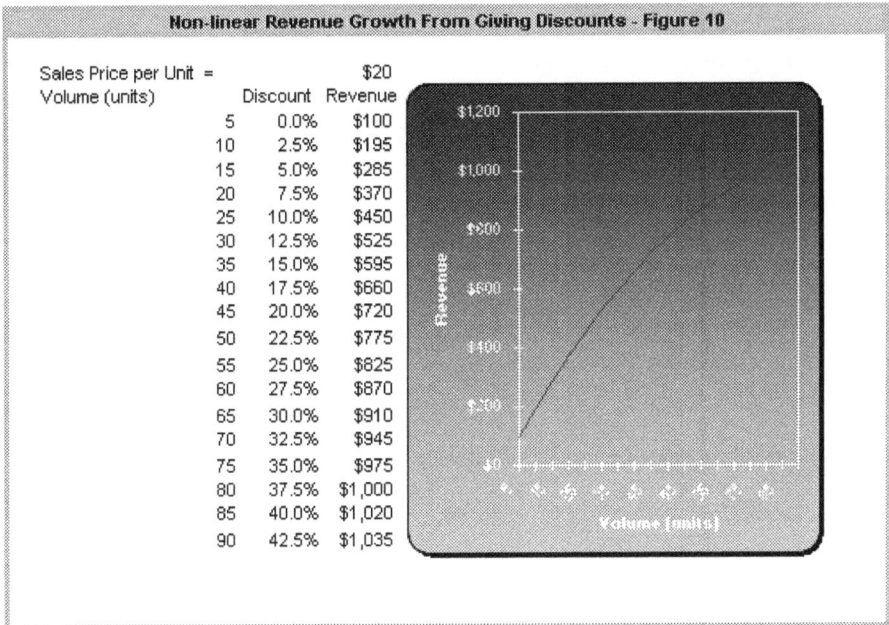

On the other hand, suppose that you take advantage of volume discounts from your suppliers-in that case, the more supplies you buy, the less you pay in unit costs.

The contribution margin line might be similar to that in Figure 11.

Sales Price per Unit = $20

Volume (units)	Supplier Discount	Variable Costs	Sales	Contribution margin
5	0.0%	$75	$100	$25
10	2.5%	$146	$200	$54
15	5.0%	$214	$300	$86
20	7.5%	$278	$400	$123
25	10.0%	$338	$500	$163
30	12.5%	$394	$600	$206
35	15.0%	$446	$700	$254
40	17.5%	$495	$800	$305
45	20.0%	$540	$900	$360
50	22.5%	$581	$1,000	$419
55	25.0%	$619	$1,100	$481
60	27.5%	$653	$1,200	$548
65	30.0%	$683	$1,300	$618
70	32.5%	$709	$1,400	$691
75	35.0%	$731	$1,500	$769
80	37.5%	$750	$1,600	$850
85	40.0%	$765	$1,700	$935
90	42.5%	$776	$1,800	$1,024

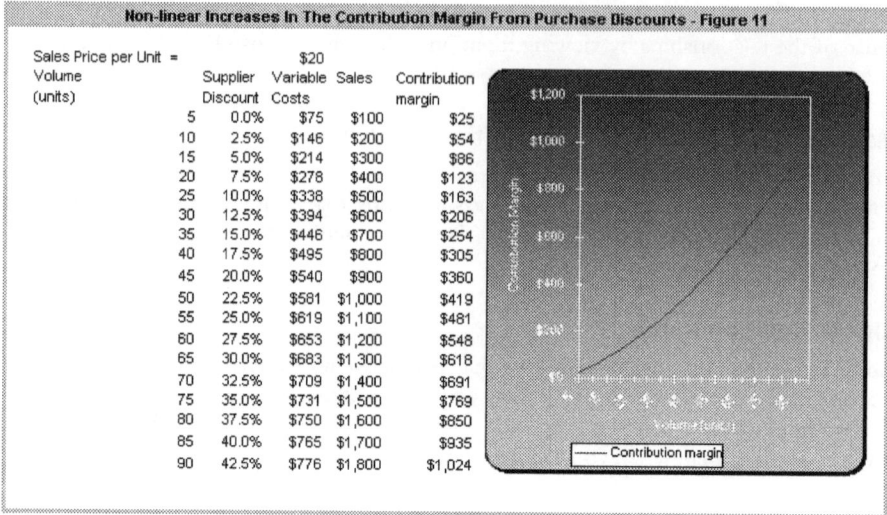

Assignment of Costs

Contribution margin analysis assumes that you can accurately divide expenses between fixed and variable costs. In most cases you will be able to assign an expense to one category or another. For example, up to the point that you need to acquire additional space, your monthly office lease is fixed regardless of how many units you sell. In some cases, however, it can be difficult to decide whether to treat a particular expense as fixed or variable. In particular, it can be difficult to assign an expense that bears a relationship to volume but not necessarily a direct, one-to-one relationship.

An example is your monthly long-distance phone bill. Unless your sales are restricted to your local phoning area, it is likely that the more you sell, the higher your bill will be. But some of those long-distance calls probably have nothing to do with incremental sales volume.

The accuracy of your analysis of contribution margin and Break-Even will depend on how accurately you can assign a portion of the long distance charges to fixed costs vs. variable costs.

Constant Sales Mix

The analysis assumes that the sales mix is constant: that, from one period to the next, your total sales are based on the same percent of each product line. Sales mix is discussed in greater detail in the section, "Determining Sales Mix," but here note that different products usually have different cost and profit structures. If the sales mix changes so that, overall, either costs or contribution margins also change, then the Break-Even points will vary.

Constant Inventory

The analysis assumes that inventories do not change in Break-Even computations. Inventory costs can change over time, or as your sales volume rises and falls, for a variety of reasons: the overall inventory level might rise due to slowing sales or fall with increasing sales, or the mix of inventory for different product lines might change (creating a change in the mix of both fixed and variable costs), or the carrying costs might change. Any of these can bring about a change in your Break-Even points.

Worker Productivity

The analysis assumes that worker productivity does not change. If, at a constant rate of pay, your workers begin to produce: more product per period of time, then the structure of your variable costs will change: the Break-Even points will drop, and the product's contribution margin will rise. Conversely, if your workers begin to produce less per period of time, due perhaps to ill- ness or procedural changes, variable costs will increase, as will your Break-Even points.

Determining Sales Mix

More often than not, a company manufactures, or offers for sale, more than one product line. In these cases, you should consider the sales and costs value of each of those product lines as you analyze the company's sales value as a whole.

For example, suppose that a company sells three product lines. besides the vases, the ceramics company also produces and sells figurines and frames. A side-by-side analysis of each of these products' price and cost information is a valuable way to analyze each product's impact on the bottom line.

Sales Mix Analysis - Figure 12

Fixed costs = $34,000

Package size	8-oz.	Per Unit	6-oz.	Per Unit	4-oz.	Per Unit	Total
Sales (units)	10,000		15,000		20,000		
Sales (dollars)	$74,000	$7.40	$94,050	$6.27	$102,600	$5.13	$270,650
Less variable costs	$37,500	$3.75	$50,850	$3.39	$60,600	$3.03	$148,950
(as % of Sales)	51%		54%		59%		55%
Contribution margin	$36,500	$3.65	$43,200	$2.88	$42,000	$2.10	$121,700
(as % of Sales)	49%		46%		41%		45%
Sales mix	27%		35%		38%		100%
Break-Even	$68,932		$74,021		$83,057		$75,613

For a sample analysis, see Figure 12.

A sales mix analysis helps you analyze the relative value of the products in your current sales mix. You can determine which of your products provides the greatest contribution to your company's total sales. Suppose that your company produces an over-the-counter medicine in three different package sizes: 8-ounce, 6-ounce, and 4-ounce.

Figure 12 shows that it costs twice as much to make figurines as it does to make vases ($30 per unit versus $15 per unit), and 1.25 times as much to make figurines as it does to make frames ($30 per unit versus $24 per unit).

However, the contribution margin from selling figurines is four times greater than from selling vases ($200 versus $50), and more than 3 times greater than from selling frames ($200 versus $60).

Figure 12 shows that the variable costs to make the 8-ounce package are 1.10 times greater than to make the 6-ounce package ($3.75 per unit versus $3.39 per unit)] and 1.24 times greater than the 4-ounce package ($3.75 per unit versus $3.03 per unit). However, the contribution margin from selling the 8-ounce package is 1.27 times greater than from selling the 6-ounce pack- age ($3.65 versus $2.88), and 1.74 times greater than from selling the 4-ounce package ($3.65 versus $2.10).

The difference in contribution margin is due to the fact that variable costs are only 51% of the selling price for the 8-ounce package, whereas they are 54% of the selling price for the 6-ounce package and 59% of the selling price for the 4-ounce package. So even though it costs more to make the larger pack- age, the sales price of the 8,.ounce package is high enough to recover more of its variable costs than does the sales price of the other sizes.

This type of analysis is valuable in helping you determine which products you want to market most actively, which products (if any) you should discontinue, and which products you wish to keep but at a reduced level of production.

For example, if you focused sales and production efforts on the larger sizes, and de-emphasized the 4-ounce size, your total profit might appear as in Figure 13.

Redistribution of Sales Mix To Increase Profits - Figure 13								
Fixed costs =	$34,000							
Package size	8-oz.	Per Unit	6-oz.	Per Unit	4-oz.	Per Unit	Total	
Sales (units)	15,000		20,000		5,000			
Sales (dollars)	$111,000	$7.40	$125,400	$6.27	$25,650	$5.13	$262,050	
Less variable costs	$56,250	$3.75	$67,800	$3.39	$15,150	$3.03	$139,200	
(as % of Sales)	51%		54%		59%		53%	
Contribution margin	$54,750	$3.65	$57,600	$2.88	$10,500	$2.10	$122,850	
(as % of Sales)	49%		46%		41%		47%	
Sales mix	42%		48%		10%		100%	
Break-Even	$68,932		$74,021		$83,057		$72,525	

In Figure 13, sales and production efforts have been shifted from the 4-ounce package to the 8- and 6-ounce packages. The effect has been to de- crease sales of the 4-ounce package by 15,000 units, and to increase sales of the 8-ounce package and 6-ounce package by 5,000 each. The total sales revenue has dropped by $8,600, but the total contribution margin has increased by $1,150.

This result, of course, is achieved by selling more of the higher-profit products and fewer of the lower-profit products. And while it is obvious that doing so will increase profit, it is useful to carry out this sort of analysis: both to quantify the potential results and to focus attention not just on the revenues but on the contribution margins as well.

The previous analysis is a very basic snapshot of the impacts that are associated with discontinuing a product line. In addition, you should also consider such issues as:

The incremental costs of discontinuing a product line-for example, the value of an existing contract to purchase the materials used.

The ease of shifting resources to a different product line-for example, can those employees who produce one product also produce another product with no additional training?

There can be a variety of reasons that you might want to change the sales mix. An obvious one is that discontinuing a low-margin product can create additional profit. Another is that discontinuing a product that is out of line with the company's long-range strategic goals might outweigh the associated incremental costs. In either case, the best decision is probably to change your sales mix to achieve your profit target and strategic goals.

Achieving the optimum sales mix is a more difficult task in reality than it is in a book. Nevertheless, it is wise to monitor your sales mix closely. The wrong mix can prevent your company from being profitable. Using the tools that have been presented in this chapter, and extending them to your actual line of business, will help you achieve the optimum sales mix for your company's expectations, both short- and long-term.

Analyzing Segment Margin

Suppose that a ceramics company has three divisions: household ceramics, ceramic tiles, and ceramic conductors. It may be that each division uses a different physical plant, employs different operating and sales staff, has a different overhead structure, and so on.

If so, the divisions' fixed costs are likely to differ. An analysis of segment margin-so called because each division is termed a segment-is primarily an extension of contribution margin analysis for products to segments.

You can determine the segment margin by deducting the direct fixed costs from the segment's contribution margin, as shown in Figure 14.

Analyzing Segment Margin - Figure 14			
	Household Ceramics	Ceramic Tiles	Ceramic Conductors
Sales	$1,100	$3,500	$5,000
Less variable costs	$690	$2,000	$3,750
Contribution margin	$410	$1,500	$1,250
Less direct fixed costs	$200	$1,000	$1,000
Segment margin	$210	$500	$250

Unlike a contribution margin analysis, which focuses on short-term impacts, the segment margin can help you understand a segment's long-term profitability. It gives you information on how much revenue is available after a segment has covered all its direct costs. The remaining revenue can be used to cover the common costs incurred by the total company, and any extra represents the segment's contribution to the company's total net income.

By deducting direct fixed costs from the segment's contribution margin, you have a better picture of each segment's contribution to the cost/volume/ profit relationship for the company as a whole.

Summary

This chapter has discussed several important tools that can help you under- stand how your company's profit picture is structured:

The Contribution Margin analysis gives you a snapshot of how a particular product is performing, in terms of both its variable costs (which increase with each additional unit produced) and its contribution margin (sales revenue less variable costs).

The Unit Contribution analysis puts you in a position to consider the profitability of a given product in greater detail.

The Break-Even point in sales tells you how much revenue you must generate to cover both your products' variable costs as well as your fixed costs. This may imply that you need to lower your costs, increase your sales price, or increase the number of units sold.

The Break-Even point in units tells you how many units you need to sell to cover your fixed and variable costs. You may find that you need to increase sales staff to reach the Break-Even point in units. This can be a complex decision when increasing staff leads to a concomitant increase in fixed costs.

The Sales Mix analysis helps you understand how your product lines combine to result in a profit or loss. It can help pinpoint which products are performing best, and where you may need to make adjustments to costs so as to lift the performance of a given product.

The Segment analysis gives you a broader perspective on a company with several divisions, each with its own set of products. You would typically use this sort of analysis to gain a longer-term understanding of the source of a company's profits.

Chapter 8 - Dynamic Strategic Planning.

Let's jump to a new dimension in thinking. Instead of the day-to-day operations let's think about your firm's future.

The recession savvy business owner has a vision for their firm's future. It is difficult translating a vision into a plan. This chapter provides you the "yellow brick road" to making your vision a reality. It is called **Dynamic Strategic Planning**. It is dynamic in that it is a living tool you continually update and share with your management and employees.

A special tool has been created for this chapter that enables you to learn by doing. You will be using the *DynamicStrategicPlanner.xls* workbook template. It is a straightforward, step-by-step workbook that allows you to plan for your firm's future.

Dynamic Strategic Planning is the process of defining what you or your organization would like to be, then devising a way to get there. The plan will vary for each business but the process is the same.

There are 10 steps to creating your Strategic Plan:

1. Develop a clear vision and translate it into a meaningful mission statement.

2. Define the Company's Driving Force and Identify Its Market Position.

3. Access your company's strengths and weaknesses.

4. Scan the environment for significant Opportunities and Threats facing your Business.

5. Identify the Key Factors for success in your business.

6. Analyze the Competition.

7. Create company goals and objectives.

8. Formulate Strategic Options and select the appropriate strategies.

9. Translate Strategic Plans into Action Plans.

10. Establish Accurate Controls.

Please go to the template folder and open

DynamicStrategicPlanner.xls workbook template.

> We suggest you keep this workbook open on your desktop. It contains all of the worksheets that are used as you read this chapter.

The workbook opens with the worksheet **Assessment** in view.

This figure shows the first worksheet of the Dynamic Strategic Planner workbook template. The Assessment worksheet guides you through the creative process.

Strategic Plan Assessment

Summary Sheet

Instructions:
1. Enter your business address in the cells with bold blue lettering.
2. Answer the 10 questions either Yes or No by clicking on the appropriate box.
   Click in Yes boxes as you complete the exercise worksheets.
   The No response will trigger a jump to the appropriate topic for reading and completion.

Business Name: Quadrant Surveying & Equipment Company
Address: 600 Madison Drive
City: Hamilton, New York 13346

Yes	No	Assessment Questions
☐	☐	1. Have you developed a clear sense of direction or mission statement?
☐	☐	2. Have you clearly defined your company's driving force and identified its market position?
☐	☐	3. Have you assessed your firm's strengths and weaknesses?
☐	☐	4. Have you scanned the environment for significant opportunities and threats facing your business?
☐	☐	5. Have you identified the key factors for success in your business?
☐	☐	6. Have you analyzed your competition?
☐	☐	7. Have you created company goals and objectives?
☐	☐	8. Have you formulated strategic options and selected the appropriate strategies?
☐	☐	9. Have you translated strategic plans into action plans?
☐	☐	10. Have you established accurate controls?

You will note the text in Bold Blue. Please select each and enter your business name and address. This information will appear as linked headings on all data entry worksheets and the Summary worksheet.

This Assessment worksheet starts the creative process. Answer with a checkmark for "Yes" or "No" for each of the assessment questions.

A "Yes" checkmark will generate an encouragement message and a "No" checkmark will automatically jump you to the appropriate worksheet for completion.

Each step has an explanation worksheet followed by a data entry worksheet.

All worksheets have transportation buttons for returning to the Assessment worksheet or you can use the tabs.

It is suggested that you start with the first question and work your way down the list since they sequentially build on each other.

All of the data entry worksheets are linked to the Summary worksheet. Each time you enter data in any step it will automatically appear on the Summary sheet at the appropriate location.

This workbook is always a "work in progress" project since it should be updated regularly.

When you have all of the "Yes" boxes checked you have your completed Dynamic Strategic Plan.

> Various versions of this workbook are in daily use in scores of small businesses throughout the world.
>
> Its purpose is to develop a discipline that becomes routine in making strategic management decisions.

Steps for creating a dynamic strategic plan

Step 1 – From clear vision to a meaningful mission statement

This step should locate the firm's present position in the marketplace as well as suggest its future direction. The mission statement's focus should be on creating a competitive advantage for the firm by identifying a new, better, or different way to satisfy customer needs.

This bottom-up approach for defining the scope of the business operation should include identifying segments of the market to target as customer bases as well as positioning the company (and its goods and services) to reach these market segments most effectively. In essence, the mission statement answers the question-What business am I in?

A sound mission statement need not be lengthy to be effective. It should, however, answer certain important questions:

1. What are the basic beliefs and values of the organization? What does your business stand for?

2. Who are the company's target customers, and what are they like?

3. What needs and wants do they satisfy when they buy from you?

4. How can you better satisfy these needs and wants?

5. What constitutes value to the customer? How can you offer your customers better value?

6. What are the firm's basic products and services?

7. In which markets (or market segments) do you compete?

8. What is your desired public image for your business?

By answering such basic questions, the company can focus on what it is and what it wants to be.

This fictitious land surveying firm defines its mission as:

"To meet the spectrum of surveying and engineering needs of private landowners, large tract owners, financial institutions, attorneys, realtors, and timber companies with high-quality service, rapid turnaround, and unparalleled professionalism, at a profit."

This figure shows the Mission Statement explanation worksheet.

Step 1 - Create a Mission Statement

This step should locate the firm's present position in the marketplace as well as suggest its future direction. The mission statement's focus should be on creating a competitive advantage for the firm by identifying a new, better, or different way to satisfy customer needs. This bottom-up approach for defining the scope of the business operation should include identifying segments of the market to target as customer bases as well as positioning the company (and its goods and services) to reach these market segments most effectively. *In essence, the mission statement answers the question-What business am I in?*

A sound mission statement need not be lengthy to be effective. It should, however, answer certain key questions:
1. What are the basic beliefs and values of the organization? What does your business stand for?
2. Who are the company's target customers, and what are they like?
3. What needs and wants do they satisfy when they buy from you?
4. How can you better satisfy these needs and wants?
5. What constitutes value to the customer? How can you offer your customers better value?
6. What are the firm's basic products and services?
7. In which markets (or market segments) do you compete?
8. What is your desired public image for your business?
By answering such basic questions, the company can focus on what it is and what it wants to be.

Sample mission statement of a small surveying company.
To meet the spectrum of surveying and engineering needs of private landowners, large tract owners, financial institutions, attorneys, realtors, and timber companies with high-quality service, rapid turnaround, and unparalleled professionalism, at a profit.

This worksheet reiterates the explanation in this chapter so that you will not have to refer back to this chapter when working on your mission statement.

This figure shows the Step 1 Worksheet. This worksheet has been preformatted for you to enter your mission statement.

Step 1 - Exercise Worksheet for Creating a Mission Statement

Quadrant Surveying & Equipment Company
600 Madison Drive
Hamilton, New York 13346

Mission Statement

This box is preformatted for easy entry.
1) To enter your text, double click inside the box and select this text with your mouse and start typing.
   Your text will automatically wrap at the end of the right margin inside the box.
2) To edit your text, double click inside the box.
3) To add a paragraph break, hold down the Alt key and tap the Enter key for each break. After entering your
   text, tap the Enter key to finish.
4) To remove the box border, click on the box once, select Format>Cells>Border Tab>None.

The mission statement should not be so lengthy as to overflow from the borders of this box. Remember that "Less is More".

Follow the directions in the data entry box or hover your mouse over the red comment triangle. Any data (text) entered will be reflected on the Summary worksheet.

This is a good time to mention that this workbook is an exercise of working on your business and not in your business. It is a healthy diversion from day-to-day stress that creates a road map for a successful business future.

Step 2 - What is your firm's driving force?

When choosing a driving force, you must consider several vital issues.

1. How many competitors do you have?

2. How broad is your customer base?

3. How vulnerable would your business be to sudden changes in economic, social, or political conditions?

4. To what extent does this focus build on skills that your firm already has?

5. How will this focus affect your financial structure?

Sample Driving Force statement of a small surveying company. Quadrant has been extremely successful in carving out a specialty niche for itself as well as in meeting the surveying needs of the general public. The company has earned a reputation as the expert in surveying and planning golf courses.

Quadrant has been extremely successful in carving out a specialty niche for itself as well as in meeting the surveying needs of the general public. The company has earned a reputation as the expert in surveying and planning golf courses. After completing work on two local courses, Quadrant obtained a contract on a large, "upscale" golf course 125 miles west of Hamilton. The work is progressing on schedule and will be finished on time and within budget.

Please click on the Driving Force tab.

This figure shows the Step 2 Driving Force worksheet. This worksheet explains how to mine the driving forces in your business.

Step 2 - Define Driving Force

Define the company's driving force and identify its market position. The driving force is what the company does best; it is the focal point of the strategy. This step must identify target market segments and outline how to positiorn the firm in those markets. The The dynamic business owner must identify some way to differentiate their business from competitors.

When choosing a driving force, several vital issues must be considered.
1. How many competitors do you have?
2. How broad is your customer base?
3. How vulnerable would your business be to sudden changes in economic, social, or political conditions?
4. To what extent does this focus build on skills that your firm already has?
5. How will this focus affect your financial structure?

Sample Driving Force statement of a small surveying company.

Quadrant has been extremely successful in carving out a specialty niche for itself as well as in meeting the surveying needs of the general public. The company has earned a reputation as the expert in surveying and planning golf courses.

Quadrant has been extremely successful in carving out a specialty niche for itself as well as in meeting the surveying needs of the general public. The company has earned a reputation as the expert in surveying and planning golf courses. After completing work on two local courses, Quadrant obtained a contract on a large, "upscale" golf course 125 miles west of Hamilton. The work is progressing on schedule and will be finished on time and within budget.

This worksheet reiterates the explanation in this chapter so that you will not have to refer back to this chapter when working on your driving force statement.

Figure 2.5 shows the Step 2 Worksheet. This worksheet has been preformatted for you to enter your Driving Force statement.

Quadrant Surveying & Equipment Company
600 Madison Drive
Hamilton, New York 13346

Driving Force

This box is preformatted for easy entry.
1) To enter your text, double click inside the box select all of this text with your mouse and start typing. Your text will automatically wrap at the end of the right margin inside the box.
2) To edit your text, double click inside the box.
3) To add a paragraph break hold down the Alt key and tap the Enter key for each break. After entering your text, tap the Enter key to finish.
4) To remove the box border, click on the box once, select Format>Cells>Border Tab>None

The Driving Force statement should not be so lengthy as to overflow from the borders of this box. Remember that "Less is More".

Follow the directions in the data entry box or hover your mouse over the red comment triangle. Any data (text) entered will be reflected on the Summary worksheet.

Step 3 - Your company's strengths and weaknesses.

Having identified the firm's driving force and desired position in the market, you can turn your attention to determining the company's strengths and weaknesses.

Building a successful competitive strategy demands that a business expand its strengths and compensate for its weaknesses.

1. Strengths are positive internal factors that contribute to the accomplishment of objectives;

2. Weaknesses are negative internal factors that inhibit the accomplishment of objectives.

Identifying strengths and weaknesses helps you understand your business as it exists. One very effective technique for taking this strategic inventory is to prepare a balance sheet of company strengths and weaknesses.

This figure shows an example of a balance sheet of company strengths and weaknesses.

Having identified the firm's driving force and desired position in the market, the business you can turn your attention to assessing company strengths and weaknesses. Building a successful competitive strategy demands that a business amplify its strengths and compensate for its weaknesses.

Strengths are positive internal factors that contribute to the accomplishment of objectives; weaknesses are negative internal factors that inhibit the accomplishment of objectives. Identifying strengths and weaknesses helps you understand their business as it exists.

One very effective technique for taking this strategic inventory is to prepare a balance sheet of company strengths and weaknesses. The positive side should reflect important skills, knowledge, or resources that contribute to the firm's success. The negative side should record honestly key limitations that detract from the company's ability to compete.

Balance Sheet - Internal strengths and weaknesses of my business

Strengths (+)	Weaknesses (-)
1. Specific skills of the firm	1. Lacking in skills
2. Unique knowledge	2. What do we know about our business or customers?
3. Special resources of the firm	3. Resources the firm is lacking--e.g. cash

The positive side should reflect important skills, knowledge or resources that contribute to the firm's success. The negative side should record honestly key limitations that detract from the company's ability to compete.

This exercise can help you move from your present position to future actions. Please click on the Step 3 Worksheet tab.

This worksheet has been preformatted for you to enter your strengths and weaknesses in a preformatted comparative balance sheet.

Step 3 - Exercise Worksheet for Strengths and Weaknesses

Quadrant Surveying & Equipment Company
600 Madison Drive
Hamilton, New York 13346

Strengths and Weaknesses Balance Sheet

Strengths (+)	Weaknesses (-)
1 Specific skills of the firm	1 Lacking in skills
2 Unique knowledge	2 What do we know about our business or customers?
3 Special resources of the firm	3 Resources the firm is lacking--e.g. cash

Follow the directions in the data entry box or hover your mouse over the red comment triangle. Any data (text) entered will be reflected on the Summary worksheet.

Step 4 - Determine your company's opportunities and threats.

Once you have taken an internal inventory of company strengths and weaknesses, you must turn to the external environment to identify any opportunities and threats that might have a significant impact on the business. Opportunities are positive external options the firm could employ to accomplish its objectives.

The number of potential opportunities is limitless, so managers must analyze only factors significant to the business (probably two or three at most). For example, the owner of a small auto lube business concluded that he faced two realistic opportunities: opening a second shop across town or buying a franchised outlet from a national company.

When identifying opportunities, the owner must pay close attention to new potential markets. Are competitors overlooking a niche in the market? Threats are negative external forces that inhibit the firm's ability to achieve its objectives. Threats to the business can take a variety of forms, such as new competitors entering the local market, a government mandate regulating a business activity, an economic recession, rising interest rates, and technological advances making a company's product obsolete. The owner must prepare a plan for shielding their business from such threats.

The positive side should reflect factors significant to the business, paying close attention to potential markets and important trends.

The negative side should reflect new competitors, government regulation, economic recession, interest rates, obsolescence, etc..

Please click on the Opportunities and Threats tab.

This figure shows the Step 4 Worksheet. This worksheet has been preformatted for you to enter your strengths and weaknesses in a preformatted comparative balance sheet.

Quadrant Surveying & Equipment Company
600 Madison Drive
Hamilton, New York 13346

Opportunities and Threats Balance Sheet

Opportunities (+)	Threats (-)
Consider 2 or 3 factors significant to the business, paying close attention to potential markets and important trends.	New competitors, government regulation, economic recession, interest rates, obsolescence, etc.

Follow the directions in the data entry box or hover your mouse over the red comment triangle. The data (text) entered will be reflected on the Summary worksheet.

Step 5 - Key factors for success of the company.

Every business is characterized by a set of controllable variables that determine the relative success of market participants.

Identifying these variables and manipulating them is how a small business gains a competitive advantage Such factors lead to what are often dramatic differences in performance levels within the same business.

Companies that understand these key success factors tend to be leaders of the pack, while those who fail to recognize them become also-rans.

For example this small surveying company lists these key success characteristics:

1. Providing services in a timely fashion.

2. Accuracy of work.

3. "Guaranteed satisfaction."

4. Professional image.

5. Capable work force.

Please click on the Key Factors tab.

This figure shows the Step 5 Key Factors worksheet. This worksheet explains how to extract controllable variables that determine the relative success of market participants.

Step 5 - Key factors for success of the company

Every business is characterized by a set of controllable variables that determine the relative success of market participants. Identifying these variables and manipulating them is how a small business gains a competitive advantage Such factors lead to what are often dramatic differences in performance levels within the same business. Companies that understand these key success factors tend to be leaders of the pack, while those who fail to recognize them become also rans.

Sample Key Factors statement of a small surveying company.
The owners see the following factors playing a critical role in the success of the company:
1. Providing services in a timely fashion.
2. Accuracy of work.
3. "Guaranteed satisfaction."
4. Professional image.
5. Capable work force.

This figure shows the Step 5 Worksheet. This worksheet has been preformatted for you to enter your key factors for success of your business.

Step 5 - Exercise Worksheet for Key Factors

Quadrant Surveying & Equipment Company
600 Madison Drive
Hamilton, New York 13346

Key Factors

This box is preformatted for easy entry.
1) To enter your text, double click inside the box select all of this text with your mouse and start typing Your text will automatically wrap at the end of the right margin inside the box.
2) To edit your text, double click inside the box.
3) To add a paragraph break hold down the Alt key and tap the Enter key for each break. After entering your text, tap the Enter key to finish.
4) To remove the box border, click on the box once, select Format>Cells>Border Tab>None.

The key factors list should not be so lengthy as to overflow from the borders of this box. Remember that "Less is More".

Follow the directions in the data entry box or hover your mouse over the red comment triangle. The data (text) entered will be reflected on the Summary worksheet.

Step 6 - Analyze Competition.

How can a small business owner gather competitive information?

1. Devote a specific time for managers to evaluate the competition. A monthly meeting designed to share information is ideal.

2. Create an intelligence file on key competitors. This helps keep the information organized in a useful manner.

3. Check industry and trade publications for information on competitors. Articles can be a tremendous source of valuable data.

4. Listen to customers and sales people. "Customers and salespeople are our best sources of information," says one successful small business owner "We listen to our customers and act on what we hear."

5. Attend industry trade shows, exhibits, and conferences. You can learn a great deal from competitors' booths at such shows.

6. Read the local papers where major competitors are located.

7. Study competitors' literature. Sales, product, and service brochures offer valuable information on rivals' strategies and how they position themselves in the market.

8. Buy competitors' products. Purchasing rivals' products and taking them apart-benchmarking-is a rich source of information.

9. Obtain credit reports on competitors.

10. Avoid ethical dilemmas. Unethical means of gathering information-bribery, payoffs, wiretaps may produce short-term benefits, but in the long term, these owners and their companies lose-often dramatically. One business owner who regularly monitors his competitors' actions says, "What we do here is not covert in nature; it's more a matter of keeping your ear to the ground."

Here is a sample competitive analysis of a small surveying company.

Quadrant Surveying & Engineering Company faces no direct competition in its hometown, Hamilton, New York, but there are three primary competitors conducting similar operations in towns within a fifty-mile diameter of Hamilton.

1. Geodetic Survey, Inc. A small corporation (three principals) whose primary focus is surveying large land tracts for timber companies. Serves 28% of local markets.

2. Photogrammetry Engineers, Ltd. A small partnership that performs all types of surveying jobs and specializes in surveying by aerial photography. Controls 22% of local market.

3. Land Surveyors, Inc. A relatively new, aggressive company that also performs all types of surveying jobs and specializes in surveying for local architectural firms, Controls 18% of the local market.

Please click on the Analyze Competition tab.

This figure shows the Step 6 Analyze Competition worksheet. This worksheet explains how to gather competitive information.

This figure shows the Step 6 Worksheet. This worksheet has been preformatted for you to enter your competitive information.

Step 6 - Analyze Competition

In a recent national survey, small business owners cited competition as the single biggest challenge facing their companies in the next decade. Another survey, from the Conference Board, found that 68 percent of the companies believed it was "very important" to monitor competitors' activities.

How can a small business owner gather competitive information?
1. Devote a specific time for managers to evaluate the competition. A monthly meeting designed to share information is ideal.
2. Create an intelligence file on key competitors. This helps keep the information organized in a useful manner.
3. Check industry and trade publications for information on competitors. Articles can be a tremendous source of valuable data.
4. Listen to customers and sales people. "Customers and salespeople are our best sources of information," says one successful small business owner "We listen to our customers and act on what we hear."
5. Attend industry trade shows, exhibits, and conferences. You can learn a great deal from competitors' booths at such shows.
6. Read the local papers where major competitors are located.
7. Study competitors' literature. Sales, product, and service brochures offer valuable information on rivals' strategies and how they position themselves in the market.
8. Buy competitors' products. Purchasing rivals' products and taking them apart-benchmarking-is a rich source of information.
9. Obtain credit reports on competitors.
10. Avoid ethical dilemmas. Unethical means of gathering information-bribery, payoffs, wiretaps may produce short-term benefits, but in the long term, these owners and their companies lose-often dramatically. One business owner who regularly monitors his competitors' actions says, "What we do here is not covert in nature; it's more a matter of keeping your ear to the ground."

Step 6 - Exercise Worksheet for Competition Analysis

Sample competitive analysis of a small surveying company.
Quadrant Surveying & Engineering Company faces no direct competition in its hometown, Hamilton, New York, but there are three primary competitors conducting similar operations in towns within a fifty-mile diameter of Hamilton.

Geodetic Survey, Inc. A small corporation (three principals) whose primary focus is surveying large land tracts for timber companies. Serves 28% of local markets.

Photogrammetry Engineers, Ltd. A small partnership that performs all types of surveying jobs and specializes in surveying by aerial photography. Controls 22% of local market.

Land Surveyors, Inc. A relatively new, aggressive company that also performs all types of surveying jobs and specializes in surveying for local architectural firms. Controls 18% of the local market.

Using the sample above and the explanation in step 6, create your own competitive analysis for your business. This page is setup to print on most ink jet printers.

Competitive Analysis
Quadrant Surveying & Equipment Company
600 Madison Drive
Hamilton, New York 13346

Opening statement
Opening statement

Competitor 1
Competitor 1 + supportive information

Competitor 2
Competitor 2 + supportive information

Competitor 3
Competitor 3 + supportive information

Follow the directions in the data entry box or hover your mouse over the red comment triangle. The data (text) entered will be reflected on the Summary worksheet.

Step 7 - Goals and Objectives.

Goals

Goals are the broad, long range attributes the business seeks to accomplish; they tend to be general and sometimes even abstract.

Goals are not intended to be specific enough for a manager to act on, but simply state the general level of accomplishment sought.

Addressing these broad issues will help you focus on the next phase, developing specific, realistic objectives.

Objectives

Objectives are more detailed, specific targets of performance. Common objectives concern profitability, markets, productivity, growth, efficiency, financial resources, physical facilities, organizational structure, employee welfare, and social responsibility.

Because some of these objectives might conflict with one another, the manager must establish priorities. Which objectives are most important? Which are least important? Arranging objectives in a hierarchy according to their priority can help the small business manager resolve conflicts when they arise.

Well written objectives have the following characteristics.

They are S M A R T

S-pecific,

M-easurable,

A-chievable,

R-ealistic, and

T-imely.

Sample Key Objectives statement of a small surveying company.

The overall mission of Quadrant is more clearly defined by dissecting it into the following objectives:

1. To boost annual sales to $480,000.

---

2. To increase market share from 31 percent to 36 percent of the local market.

3. To obtain a contract for another golf course.

4. To increase by 10% the number of engineering jobs performed for local towns and districts (e.g., water and sewage systems design).

5. To improve profit margin from 13 percent to 17 percent.

Please click on the Goals & Objectives tab.

This figure shows the Step 7 Goals and Objectives worksheet. This worksheet explains how to analyze and create your goals and objectives.

Step 7 - Goals and Objectives

Goals
Goals are the broad, long range attributes the business seeks to accomplish; they tend to be general and sometimes even abstract. Goals are not intended to be specific enough for a manager to act on, but simply state the general level of accomplishment sought. Addressing these broad issues will help you focus on the next phase, developing specific, realistic objectives.

Objectives
Objectives are more detailed, specific targets of performance. Common objectives concern profitability, markets, productivity, growth, efficiency, financial resources, physical facilities, organizational structure, employee welfare, and social responsibility. Because some of these objectives might conflict with one another, the manager must establish priorities. Which objectives are most important? Which are least important? Arranging objectives in a hierarchy according to their priority can help the small business manager resolve conflicts when they arise.

Well written objectives have the following characteristics.
They are S M A R T
S-pecific,
M-easurable,
A-chievable,
R-ealistic, and
T-imely.

This figure shows the Step 7 Worksheet. This worksheet has been preformatted for you to enter your goals and objectives information.

Step 7 - Exercise Worksheet for Goals And Objectives

Sample key goals statement of a small surveying company.
The overall mission of Quadrant is more clearly defined by dissecting it into the following goals:
1. To boost annual sales to $480,000.
2. To increase market share from 31 percent to 36 percent of the local market.
3. To obtain a contract for another golf course.
4. To increase by 10% the number of engineering jobs performed for local towns and districts (e.g., water and sewage systems design).
5. To improve profit margin from 13 percent to 17 percent.

Using the sample above and the explanation in step 7, create your own goals and objectives for your business. This page is setup to print on most ink jet printers.

Quadrant Surveying & Equipment Company
600 Madison Drive
Hamilton, New York 13346

Goals
Enter goals here.

Objectives
Enter objectives here

Follow the directions in the data entry box or hover your mouse over the red comment triangle. The data (text) entered will be reflected on the Summary worksheet.

Step 8 - Formulate Options and Strategies.

By now, you should have a clear picture of what your business does best and what are its competitive advantages.

Similarly, you should know your firm's weaknesses and limitations as well as those of its competitors. The next step is to evaluate strategic options and then prepare a game plan designed to accomplish the business's objectives.

A strategy is a road map of the actions you develop to achieve the firm's mission, goals, and objectives. In other words, the mission, goals, and objectives spell out the ends, and the strategy defines the means for reaching them. Strategy is the master plan that covers all of the major parts of the organization and ties them together into a unified whole.

Obviously, the number of strategies from which you can choose is infinite. When all the glitter is stripped away, however, three broad-based, generic strategies remain:

1. Cost leadership

There are many ways to build a low-cost strategy, but the most successful cost leaders know where they have cost advantages over their competitors, and they use these as the foundation for their strategies.

2. Differentiation

There are many ways to create a differentiation strategy, but the key concept is to be special at something that is important tothe customer If a small company can either improve the product's (or service's) performance, reduce the customer's cost and risk of purchasing it, or both, it has the potential to differentiate.

3. Focus

A focus strategy recognizes that not all markets are homogeneous. In fact, within any given market, there are many different customer segments, each having different needs, wants, and characteristics. The primary idea of this strategy, is to select one (or more) segment(s), identify, customers' special needs, wants, and interests, and approach them with a good or service designed excel in meeting these needs, wants, and interests. Focus strategies build on differences among market segments.

Sample key objectives statement of a small surveying company.

To obtain these objectives, Quadrant will employ a business strategy designed to exploit the four key factors for success in the surveying business-to maintain:

1. Prompt turnaround time on jobs;

2. Professional image with the clientele;

---

3. Continuous relationship with "return customers"; and

4. Healthy customer mix to ensure a steady flow of work.

The following key points illustrate this strategy:

1. To utilize equipment offering the latest technological advances.

2. To train employees in implementing advanced survey techniques into their work.

3. To provide the opportunity for clients to consult with project managers (or principals, if desired) on all projects.

4. To keep the customer informed of the job's progress on a timely basis.

5. To "crack the engineering market" by obtaining small jobs with cities, districts, and subdivisions.

6. To increase the number of government contracts bid on.

7. To acquire and to develop "regional accounts"-clients with large land holdings (e.g., large timber companies).

Please click on the Options & Strategies tab.

This figure shows the Step 8 Options and Strategies worksheet. This worksheet explains how to analyze and create your Options and Strategies.

Step 8 - Formulate Options and Strategies

By now, you should have a clear picture of what your business does best and what are its competitive advantages. Similarly, you should know your firm's weaknesses and limitations as well as those of its competitors. The next step is to evaluate strategic options and then prepare a game plan designed to accomplish the business's objectives.

A strategy is a road map of the actions you develop to achieve the firm's mission, goals, and objectives. In other words, the mission, goals, and objectives spell out the ends, and the strategy defines the means for reaching them. Strategy is the master plan that covers all of the major parts of the organization and ties them together into a unified whole.

Obviously, the number of strategies from which you can choose is infinite. When all the glitter is stripped away, however, three broad-based, generic strategies remain:

1. Cost leadership
There are many ways to build a low-cost strategy, but the most successful cost leaders know where they have cost advantages over their competitors. The next step is to use these as the foundation for their strategies.

2. Differentiation
There are many ways to create a differentiation strategy, but the key concept is to be special at something that is important to the customer If a small company can either improve the product's (or service's) performance, reduce the customer's cost and risk of purchasing it, or both, it has the potential to differentiate.

3. Focus
A focus strategy recognizes that not all markets are homogeneous. In fact, within any given market, there are many different customer segments, each having different needs, wants, and characteristics. The primary idea of this strategy, is to select one (or more) segment(s), identify, customers' special needs, wants, and interests, and approach them with a good or service designed excel in meeting these needs, wants, and interests. Focus strategies build on differences among market segments.

This worksheet reiterates the explanation in this chapter so that you will not have to refer back to this chapter when working on your Options & Strategies.

This figure shows the Step 8 Worksheet. This worksheet has been preformatted for you to enter your Options and Strategies information.

Step 8 - Exercise Worksheet for Options and Strategies

Sample key objectives statement of a small surveying company.

To obtain these objectives, Quadrant will employ a business strategy designed to exploit the four key factors for success in the surveying business-to maintain: (1) a prompt turnaround time on jobs; (2) a professional image with the clientele; (3) a continuous relationship with "return customers"; and (4) a healthy customer mix to ensure a steady flow of work.
The following key points illustrate this strategy:

1. To utilize equipment offering the latest technological advances.
2. To train employees in implementing advanced survey techniques into their work.
3. To provide the opportunity for clients to consult with project managers (or principals, if desired) on all projects.
4. To keep the customer informed of the job's progress on a timely basis.
5. To "crack the engineering market" by obtaining small jobs with cities, districts, and subdivisions.
6. To increase the number of government contracts bid on.
7. To acquire and to develop "regional accounts"-clients with large land holdings (e.g., large timber companies).

Using the sample above and the explanation in step 8, create your own options and strategies for your business. This page is setup to print on most ink jet printers.

Quadrant Surveying & Equipment Company
600 Madison Drive
Hamilton, New York 13346

Opening statement

List key strategies

Follow the directions in the data entry box or hover your mouse over the red comment triangle. The data (text) entered will be reflected on the Summary worksheet.

Step 9 - Translate Strategy Plans into Action Plans.

No strategic plan is complete until it is put into action. The small business manager must convert strategic plans into operating plans that guide the company on a daily basis and become a visible, active part of the business. The small business does not benefit from a strategic plan sitting on a shelf collecting dust.

Sample action plan by purchasing new equipment of a small surveying company.

1. Reduce the number of field personnel by one-third.

2. Reduce office personnel by the immediate transferring field data to the home office via telephone.

3. Minimize the number of return trips to the job site, a significant cost of doing business.

4. Improve productivity by performing more jobs in less time.

---

5. Improve the firm's professional image with its clientele by employing the latest, most advanced equipment.

6. Obtain golf course that requires a level accuracy attainable only with EDM devices.

Please click on the Plans into Actions tab.

This figure shows the Step 9 Plans into Actions worksheet. This worksheet explains how to translate strategy plans into action plans.

Step 9 - Translate Strategy Plans into Action Plans

No strategic plan is complete until it is put into action. The small business manager must convert strategic plans into operating plans that guide the company on a daily basis and become a visible, active part of the business. The small business does not benefit from a strategic plan sitting on a shelf collecting dust.

Sample action plan by purchasing new equipment of a small surveying company.
1. Reduce the number of field personnel by one-third.
2. Reduce office personnel by the immediate transferring field data to the home office via telephone.
3. Minimize the number of return trips to the job site, a significant cost of doing business.
4. Improve productivity by performing more jobs in less time.
5. Improve the firm's professional image with its clientele by employing the latest, most advanced equipment.
6. Obtain golf course that requires a level accuracy attainable only with EDM devices.

This figure shows the Step 9 Worksheet. This worksheet has been preformatted for you to enter your strategy plans into action plans information.

Step 9 - Exercise Worksheet for Moving Strategy Plans into Action Plans

Quadrant Surveying & Equipment Company
600 Madison Drive
Hamilton, New York 13346

Opening statement

List key action plans

Follow the directions in the data entry box or hover your mouse over the red comment triangle. The data (text) entered will be reflected on the Summary worksheet.

Step 10 - Establish Accurate Controls.

So far, the planning process has created company objectives and developed a strategy for reaching them. Rarely, if ever, will the company's actual performance match stated objectives. The manager quickly realizes the need to control actual results that deviate from plans.

Planning without control is of little operational value. A sound planning program requires a practical control process. The plans created in this process become the standards against which actual performance is measured. It is important for everyone in the organization to understand and to be involved in the planning- controlling process.

Controlling projects and keeping them on schedule means that the owner must identify and track key performance indicators.

The source of these indicators is the operating data from the company's normal business activity; they are the guideposts for detecting deviations from established standards.

Accounting, production, sales, inventory, and other operating records are primary sources of data the manager can use for controlling activities. For example, on a customer service project, performance indicators might include customer complaints, orders returned, on-time shipments, order accuracy, and others.

Please click on the Establish Accurate Controls tab.

This figure shows the Step 10 Establish Accurate Controls worksheet. This worksheet explains how to establish accurate controls in executing the strategic projects.

Step 10 - Establish Accurate Controls

Establishing Accurate Controls.

So far, the planning process has created company objectives and developed a strategy for reaching them. Rarely, if ever, will the company's actual performance match stated objectives. The manager quickly realizes the need to control actual results that deviate from plans.

Planning without control is of little operational value. A sound planning program requires a practical control process. The plans created in this process become the standards against which actual performance is measured. It is important for everyone in the organization to understand and to be involved in the planning- controlling process.

Controlling projects and keeping them on schedule means that the owner must identify and track key performance indicators. The source of these indicators is the operating data from the company's normal business activity; they are the guideposts for detecting deviations from established standards.

Accounting, production, sales, inventory, and other operating records are primary sources of data the manager can use for controlling activities. For example, on a customer service project, performance indicators might include customer complaints, orders returned, on-time shipments, order accuracy, and others.

This worksheet reiterates the explanation in this chapter so that you will not have to refer back to this chapter when working on establishing accurate controls in executing the strategic projects.

This figure shows the Step 10 Worksheet. This worksheet has been preformatted for you to enter your project controls information.

Step 10 - Exercise Worksheet for Establishing Accurate Controls

Quadrant Surveying & Equipment Company
600 Madison Drive
Hamilton, New York 13346

Opening statement

List key control measures

Follow the directions in the data entry box or hover your mouse over the red comment triangle. The data (text) entered will be reflected on the Summary worksheet.

Summary Analysis Worksheet

This figure shows the Summary Analysis worksheet. This worksheet is linked to all the data entry worksheets.

Strategic Plan Summary Analysis

Quadrant Surveying & Equipment Company
600 Madison Drive
Hamilton, New York 13346

Mission Statement

This box is preformatted for easy entry.
1) To enter your text, double click inside the box and select this text with your mouse and start typing.
   Your text will automatically wrap at the end of the right margin inside the box.
2) To edit your text, double click inside the box.
3) To add a paragraph break, hold down the Alt key and tap the Enter key for each break. After entering your
   text, tap the Enter key to finish.
4) To remove the box border, click on the box once, select Format>Cells>Border Tab>None.

The mission statement should not be so lengthy as to overflow from the borders of this box. Remember that "Less is More".

Driving Force

This box is preformatted for easy entry.
1) To enter your text, double click inside the box select all of this text with your mouse and start typing. Your text will
automatically wrap at the end of the right margin inside the box

Mentioned earlier, all of the data entry worksheets are linked to the Summary worksheet. Each time you enter data in any step it will automatically appear on the Summary sheet at the appropriate location.

This worksheet is preset for printing on most ink jet printers and prints 4 pages. When you have completed your strategic planning steps, print this worksheet for monitoring the progress of your project.

It is the ideal document for making or adding changes during the project period. Keep it nearby and read it often.

Chapter 9 - The Business Plan – "Recession Fighter"

You have successfully completed your **Dynamic Strategic Plan** and you have made a personal commitment to use it on a routine basis to improve your business operations.

Creating a strategic plan is a good first step in producing your business plan. The strategic planning process permitted you to dig deep into your firm's structure and reveal its true personality. It answered the questions of what is my business and where is it going?

Care has been taken in this chapter to "cut to the chase" in this potentially voluminous subject matter.

A recent Google search revealed over 132,000,000 documents found for the phrase "Business Plan". Another search using the phrase "Business Plan Software" returned 37,700,000 finds.

As you can see there is literally a glut of information and help for producing a business plan; however, its real advantage is seldom mentioned and that is **your business plan is a marketing tool**. It allows your business to make the most of the opportunities that arises in its life from start-up to maturity.

We have researched thousands of publications from the business, academic, financial, and public realms to give you examples of excellent business plan formats. Later in the chapter, we will discuss Excel worksheet templates for inclusion in the financial sections of your business plan.

There are three sections to this charter.

1. Section 1 is "Preparing Your Business Plan".

2. Section 2 is our example of an excellent business plan.

3. Section 3 is an example of a concise business plan.

Section 1 - Preparing Your Business Plan

To establish a solid financial base when starting a business, most entrepreneurs must look to lenders and investors for external funds. However, it is not always easy to convince people to invest their money in another's business. The entrepreneur first must convince potential lenders and investors that her business idea is promising, the market accessible, the firm's management capable, and the return on investment attractive. To accomplish these objectives, the entrepreneur should develop an attractive business plan. Often, the presence or absence of such a plan is the critical factor in a lender's or investor's decision to invest or not to invest in a small business.

In addition, a business plan is a valuable managerial tool, helping the entrepreneur focus on developing a course for the business in the future. In fact, the primary purpose of building a business plan is to improve managerial control over the company and to avoid the pitfalls commonly leading to business failure. Unfortunately, most small business owners never create business plans, and the result often is failure. According to one business consultant, "One of the reasons we feel business failure is as great as it is, is businesses are so concerned with meeting a payroll each week, they never take the time to make a business plan." This lack of planning starts a vicious cycle that is extremely difficult for owners to break: Failure to plan leads to business crises, which drive planning out of the owner's schedule, which leads to more crises, which I see a direct relationship between the absence of a business plan and the failure of a business," says one consultant.

Building a plan forces management to consider the long-term aspects of the company in a comprehensive fashion; using it to raise money is secondary. One business development consultant emphasizes, "When I speak of business plans, raising money is the last thing I talk about." When prepared properly the business planning process helps managers establish checkpoints for key activities and view the big picture. Creating a plan forces the entrepreneur to evaluate every segment of her company (proposed or existing) and to develop a series of strategies for coping with an uncertain environment. In addition to the what-if scenarios the plan forces the entrepreneur to consider, there are other benefits.

1) a systematic, realistic evaluation of the company's chances for success in the market

2) a way to determine the primary risks confronting the business

3) a game plan for managing the business successfully

4) a tool for comparing actual results against targeted performance

5) a primary tool for attracting money in the challenging hunt for capital

This chapter focuses on preparing and using this vital business document; it will build a business plan on the foundation laid in the first ten chapters of this book.

I. The Business Plan

The business plan is a written summary of the entrepreneur's proposed venture, its operational and financial details, its marketing opportunities and strategy, and its managers' skills and abilities. There is no substitute for a well-prepared business plan, and there are no shortcuts to creating it. "Your business plan is like a road map," says one small business consultant. "It describes the direction the company is going in, what its goals are, where it wants to be, and how it's going to get there." Tile plan is written proof that the entrepreneur has performed the necessary research and has studied the business opportunity adequately. In short, it is the entrepreneur's best insurance against launching a business destined to fail or mismanaging a potentially successful company.

The business Plan serves two essential functions. First—and most important—it guides the operation of the company by charting its future course and devising a strategy for following it. It provides a battery of tools—a mission, goals, objectives, budgets, financial forecasts, target markets, strategies, and others—that managers can draw on to lead the company successfully. A business plan gives managers and employees a sense of direction, but only if everyone is involved in creating, updating, or altering it. As more team members become committed to making the plan work, it takes on special meaning. It gives everyone targets to shoot for; and it is an effective tool for measuring actual performance, especially in the startup phase. A chairman of a highly successful family business that is international in scope, relies heavily on business plans to manage his company's diverse holdings. He points to an extraordinary number of computer-generated spreadsheets lining the walls of his bedroom and explains, "This is what is supposed to happen." The sheets are filled with forecasted cash flow statements, income statements, balance sheets, price analyses, and other information. "Below," he says pointing to empty charts waiting to be filled in with actual results "is what will happen." Then, he jokingly adds, "This is the only potential problem in my life." Below are 10 pitfalls that offer advice on how the business owner can put the plan to work for the company.

Ten Planning Pitfalls and How to Avoid Them

It's true: The process of preparing a business plan is itself valuable. But, it doesn't make sense to develop such a comprehensive document and then to forget about it. The following is a list of the ten most common mistakes business owners make in using their plans—and the remedies for them.

1. Single-purpose use. Entrepreneurs typically prepare a plan to raise money and seldom give thought to actually using it.

Remedy: Stress implementation. The plan must include specific objectives for key managers and a plan to accomplish them.

2. One-person commitment. If one person writes the entire plan (e.g., the company president), key managers are unlikely to be committed fully to it.

Remedy: Involve all members of the management team in preparing the plan. Have each member write a section of the plan.

3. Benign neglect. Once completed, the business plan sits on the shelf and collects dust. Out of sight, out of mind.

Remedy: Make following up the plan easy. Schedule regular meetings to discuss the plan and the progress made in accomplishing the goals and objectives established.

4. Unworkable document. Managers create a plan that is so huge and complex that it discourages everyone from actually using it.

Remedy: Give the plan life by developing one-page action summaries for each department. Ask managers to update progress on their responsibilities at periodic meetings.

5. Unbalanced application. Sometimes, managers give a disproportionate amount of attention to one portion of the plan—marketing or finance, for example.

Remedy: Get balanced participation from key managers and employees in all areas of the company. Plus, focus 90 percent of management attention within the next year.

6. Disillusionment. Managers get disillusioned when the scenario laid out in the plan fails to develop.

Remedy: Develop contingency plans—both positive and negative. What happens if.

7. Too action-oriented. Action-oriented managers tend to forget about the plan once it is completed. They want to get back to the real world of business.

Remedy: Use their action-orientation to encourage these managers to develop plans for their areas of responsibility.

8. No performance standard. Too often, managers fail to establish measurable standards in the plan.

Remedy: Encourage managers to establish specific, measurable objectives in their respective areas.

9. Poor progress control. Implementing the plan is without control because progress reports are lost in the jumble of everyday business.

Remedy: Hold regular meetings to discuss progress on the plan and nothing else.

10. Early consumption. The plan becomes outdated because no one bothers to update it.

Remedy: Update the plan every six months. That way you never run out of plans.

The second vital function of the business plan is to attract lenders and investors. Too often small business owners approach potential lenders and investors unprepared to sell themselves and their business concept. Simply scribbling a few rough figures on a note pad to support a loan application is not enough. Applying for loans or attempting to attract investors without a business plan rarely produces the desired results. The best way to secure the necessary capital is to prepare a sound business plan. The entrepreneur must develop it with great attention to detail because it is a key factor in her sales presentation to potential lenders and investors. In most cases, the quality of the firm's business plan will weigh heavily in the decision to lend or to invest funds. The quality of the plan determines the first impression the potential lenders and investors have of the company and its managers. Therefore, the finished product should be highly polished and professional in both form and content.

A plan is a reflection of its creator. It should demonstrate that the entrepreneur has thought seriously about the venture and what will make it succeed. Preparing a solid plan demonstrates that the entrepreneur has taken the time to commit her idea to paper. Susan Garber, a Small Business Development Center (SBDC) director, advises, "To take the step of starting a business without thinking it through is a big mistake." Still, too many entrepreneurs do just that. Garber claims that, of the clients she sees, "only one in a hundred has a reasonable business plan." The main reason is impatience. Another business adviser says, "They want to get on with building the business; they don't have time to write a business plan.'

Building a plan also forces the entrepreneur to consider both the positive and the negative aspects of the business. Explains one venture capital manager, The first thing venture capitalists react to is the business plan because it shows that the individuals have done the necessary spade work to show that they are serious. I want to see that management has had the discipline to put the plan down on paper which means that they have a half-way decent chance of building a business. If they don't do this exercise, they probably won't have the discipline to build a business. "

An entrepreneur cannot allow others to prepare the business plan for him. Outsiders cannot understand the business nor envision the proposed company as well as the entrepreneur can. Also, because he will make the presentation to potential lenders and investors, the owner must understand the details of the entire business plan. If the entrepreneur lacks a complete understanding of the plan, he will receive a negative evaluation, and in most cases, the result will be rejected by the financial institution or investor. Alice Medrich, cofounder of Cocolat, a manufacturer of specialty candies and desserts, recalls her first attempt at raising capital.

First of all, I went to the bank, and I was so ill-prepared and so insecure about what I was asking about. . . I was extremely insecure with a banker. I didn't know how to describe what I was doing with any confidence. I did not know how to present a business plan. And, he was condescending to me. Looking back on it, I can understand why: I wasn't prepared. . . . We didn't get the loan.

Careful, thoughtful preparation can make the difference between success and failure when shopping the capital market. As one successful applicant who used professional assistance stated, "I had never borrowed a lot of money before, hut I felt comfortable talking with bankers because I had a proposition I believed in and had the necessary information."

Although each company's business plan should emphasize the unique personality of the venture, every plan should follow certain guidelines. This section highlights the major elements of an effective business plan.

II. The Elements of a Business Plan

This section outlines the primary components of a solid business plan, but every small business owner must recognize that such a plan should he tailor-made, emphasizing the company's strengths. Many small business managers employ the professional assistance of attorneys and accountants in preparing their business plans. For those owners who are unfamiliar or uncomfortable with business planning, hiring such professionals to organize and polish the plan may be wise. But, the proliferation of standardized planning formats has resulted in a trend toward mass-produced business plans that fail to produce results. The entrepreneur should beware of this cookie-cutter approach because it neglects to sell the unique strengths of a proposed business venture.

Remember: No one can create your plan for you.

Parts of the Business Plan

The Executive Summary. To summarize the presentation to each potential financial institution or investor, the entrepreneur should develop an executive summary. It should be concise—a maximum of two pages—and should summarize all of the relevant points of the proposed deal. The summary should explain the purpose of the financial request, the dollar amount requested, how the funds will be used, and how any loans will be repaid. It is designed to capture the reader's attention. If it misses, the chances of the remainder of the plan being read are minimal. A well-developed, coherent summary introducing the financial proposal will establish a favorable first impression of the owners and the business, and can go a long way toward obtaining financing. Although the executive summary is the first part of the business plan, it should be the last section written.

Company History. The manager of an existing small business should prepare a brief history of tile operation, highlighting the significant financial and operational events in the company's life. This section should focus on the successful accomplishment of past objectives and should indicate the firm's image.

Business Profile. To familiarize lenders and investors with the nature of the business, the owner should incorporate into the business plan a general description of its operation. This section should begin with a statement of the company's general business goals and a narrower definition of its immediate objectives. Together, they define what the business plans to accomplish, how, when, and who will do it. Goals are long-range, broad statements of what the company plans to accomplish in the distant future. They are aspirations that guide the overall direction of the company and express the company's raison d'être. In other words, they answer the question, "Why am I in business?" Answering such a basic question appears to be obvious, but many entrepreneurs cannot define the basic purpose of their businesses. The director of an entrepreneurial boot camp says, It's amazing what a tortuous experience [defining the business' purpose] can be. It's hard for them to distill their ideas . . . Many people don't know what business they are in."

The owner of a small chain of baby products stores has clearly defined his company's mission.

To serve best the needs of customers who are retail stores offering an incomparable combination of selection, quality, and service at competitive prices.

Objectives, on the other hand, are short-term, specific targets that are attainable, measurable, and controllable. Every objective should reflect some general business goal and include a technique for measuring progress toward its accomplishment. To be meaningful, an objective must have a time frame for achievement.

In summarizing the small company's background, the owner should describe the present state of the art in the industry and identify the key factors needed for success in the market segment she will compete in. She should describe the current applications of the product/service in the market and include projections for future applications. For example, a manufacturer of silicon chips could discuss the key role his product plays in computer technology and could project increased demand by robot manufacturers. In addition, the owner should incorporate into the plan general long-term growth trends for the entire industry, including stability for product demand and emerging trends affecting demand. This section also should describe the influence of government regulation and legislation in the business operation.

Business Strategy. An even more important part of the business plan is the owner's view of the strategy needed to meet the competition. It should comment on how the owner plans to achieve business objectives in the face of competition and government regulation. One investment adviser states, "Many business plans give fancy, impressive financial projections, but don't sufficiently tell you how the company is going to reach these projections." The manager also must describe the firm's desired character—the image the business will try to project.

For example, a clothing store could project several images: a high quality, classic merchandise shop; a trendy, high fashion store; or an economy-oriented discount outlet. This segment of the business plan should outline the methods the company can use to meet the key requirements for success identified earlier. If, for example, a strong, well-trained sales force is considered a critical element for success, the owner must develop a plan of action for assembling one. This section should highlight basic strategic elements.

Description of Firm's Product/Service. The business owner should describe the company's overall product line, giving an overview of how the goods/ services are used. Drawings, diagrams, and illustrations may be required if the product is highly technical. It is best to write product and service descriptions so that laypeople can understand them. A statement of the goods' position in the product life cycle might also he helpful. The manager should include a summary of any patents, trademarks, or copyrights protecting the product or service from infringement by competitors. Finally, the owner should provide an honest comparison of the company's product or service with those of competitors, citing specific advantages or improvements that make her goods or services unique and indicating plans for developing next generation goods and services that evolve from the present product line.

Manufacturers should provide a description of the production process employed, strategic raw materials required, and sources of supply used. In addition, they should summarize the method of production and illustrate the plant layout.

Marketing Strategy. One of the most crucial Concerns of potential lenders and investors is whether there is a real market for the proposed good or service. Every small business owner seeking funds must incorporate into the business plan a description of the company's target market and its characteristics. Defining the target market and its potential is one of the most important and most difficult parts of a business plan. It must show how the entrepreneur plans to turn the idea into a product or service customers will want to buy. For example, the owner of a small chain of baby products stores identified his firm's typical customer as an expectant mother 18 to 34 years old (an average of 26.3 years) in the fifth to eighth month of pregnancy, most often shopping with her mother. One venture capitalist claims that the investor "needs to believe that the company has targeted an attractive market and has developed a plan to capture an unfair share of it."

Proving that a profitable market exists involves two steps:

1. Showing Marketplace Interest. The entrepreneur must be able to prove that customers in the marketplace have a need for the good or service and are willing to pay for it. This phase is relatively straightforward for a company with an existing product or service, but can he quite difficult for one with only an idea or a prototype. In this case, the entrepreneur might offer the prototype to several potential customers to get written testimonials and evaluations to show investors. Or, the owner could sell the product to several customers at a significant discount. This would prove that there are potential customers for the product and would allow demonstrations of the product in operation.

2. Documenting market claims. Too many business plans rely on vague generalizations like, "This market is so huge that if we get just 1 percent of it, we will break even in eight months." Such statements are not backed by facts and may not be realistic. Says one venture specialist, "I'm really not interested in having a 2-percent market share of an $8-billion business because I know that you can't get that kind of market share with a new venture."

Claims of market size and growth rates should be supported by facts. Results of market surveys, customer questionnaires, and demographic studies lend credibility to an entrepreneur's frequently optimistic sales projections. Quantitative market data are important because they form the basis for all of the company's financial projections in the business plan.

One entrepreneur set out to prove that there was a sufficient market for his business idea: a convenience food restaurant offering complete take-out meals for professionals who lack the time to cook. He collected volumes of data on customer buying habits and developed a demographic profile of the customer most likely to patronize his restaurant: two-income families and single heads of households. From surveys, he discovered that price is not the primary consideration; quality and convenience outweigh price concerns.

The essential goal of this section of the plan is to identify the basics for the financial forecasts that follow. Sales, profit, and cash forecasts must be founded in more than wishful thinking. An effective market analysis should identify the following.

Target market—Who are the primary customers? What are their characteristics? What do they buy? Why do they buy? What expectations do they have about the product or service?

Market size and trends—How large is the potential market? Is it growing or shrinking? Why? Are customer needs changing? Are sales seasonal? Is demand tied to another product or service?

Pricing—What price tiers exist in the market? How sensitive are customers to price changes? Can the planned price produce a profit?

Advertising—Which media are most effective in reading the target market? How will they be used?

Distribution—How will the product or service he distributed? What is the average sale? How many sales calls does it take to close a sale? What incentives exist for sales people?

This portion of the plan also should describe the channels of distribution the small business will employ (mail, in-house sales force, sales agents, retailers). Also, the owner should summarize the firm's overall pricing policies as well as its promotion policies, including the advertising budget, media used, and publicity efforts. The company's warranties and guarantees for its products and services should be addressed.

This portion of the plan must emphasize the entrepreneur's understanding of her target customers. One private investor advises entrepreneurs writing business plans as follows.

Be market-driven, not product-driven. Show a well-researched understanding of what customers really want. Highlight the benefits to a customer purchasing the product or service. Wherever possible, quantify benefits in terms of cost savings or revenue generation. Show who and where customers are. Quantify the market in terms of units or dollars or both.

Competitor Analysis. The entrepreneur also should describe the competition the company faces. Failure to provide a realistic assessment of competitors makes the owner appear to he poorly prepared, naive, or dishonest. Gathering information on competitors' market shares, products, and strategies usually is not difficult. Trade associations, customers, industry journals, marketing representatives, and sales literature are valuable sources of data. The focus of this section should be to demonstrate how the entrepreneur's company has an advantage over its competitors. What distinguishes her products or service from others already on the market and how will these differences produce a competitive edge? According to one financial expert, "The most successful small companies are those that begin with a marketing approach which determines what the market wants and then invents it"

Officers'/Owners' Resumes. The most important factor in the success of a business venture is its management. Financial officers and investors weigh heavily the ability and experience of the firm's managers in financing decisions. Explains the owner of an executive search firm, "Entrepreneurs must recognize what they do well and what they don't do well, and then create a management team with complementary skills to get the job done. People are the most important part of making a new venture work." The plan should include the resumes of business officers, key directors, and any person with at least 20 percent ownership in the company. Remember: Lenders and investors prefer experienced managers.

A resume should summarize the individual's education, work history emphasizing managerial responsibilities and duties), and relevant business experience. When compiling a personal profile, the owner should review the primary reasons for small business failure and show how the team will use its skills and experience to avoid them. Lenders and investors will look for the experience, talent, and integrity of the people who will breathe life into the plan. This portion of the plan should show that the company has the right people organized in the right fashion for success, One experienced private investor advises entrepreneurs to remember the following.

Ideas and products don't succeed; people do. Show the strength of your management team. A top-notch management team with a variety of proven skills is crucial Show the strength of key employees and how you will retain them. A Board of Directors or advisers consisting of industry experts lends credibility and can enhance the value of the management team.

Plan of Operation. To complete the description of the business, the owner must construct a functional organizational chart which identifies key positions and the personnel occupying them. Assembling a management team with the right stuff is difficult, but keeping it together until the company gets established may be harder. Thus, the entrepreneur should describe briefly the steps taken to encourage key officers to remain with the company. Employment contracts, shares of ownership, and perks are commonly used to keep and motivate key employees.

Finally, a description of the form of ownership (partnership, joint venture, S corporation) and of any leases, contracts, and other relevant agreements pertaining to the operation is also helpful.

Financial Data. One of the most important sections in the business plan is a detailed outline of the loan or investment package—the dollars and cents of the proposed deal, Lenders and investors use past financial statements to judge the health of the small company and its ability to repay loans or generate adequate returns. The owner should supply copies of the firm's major financial statements from the past three years. These statements should be audited by a certified public accountant, because financial institutions prefer that extra reliability. However, a financial review of the statements by an accountant may satisfy some requirements.

The manager must carefully prepare monthly projected (or pro forma) financial statements for the operation for the next two to three years (and possibly for two more years by quarters) using past operating data, published statistics, and judgment to derive three sets of forecasts of the income statement, balance sheet, cash budget, and schedule of planned capital expenditures. She should include forecasts under pessimistic, most likely, and optimistic conditions to reflect the uncertainty of the future. One consultant says that the most common mistake entrepreneurs make when building a business plan is failing to plan for various scenarios. "It's always important to remember what the risks are," she says. It is essential that all three sets of forecasts be realistic. Entrepreneurs must avoid the tendency to fudge the numbers to look really impressive. Financial officers will compare these projections against published industry standards and will detect unreasonable forecasts. In fact, some venture capitalists automatically discount an entrepreneur's financial projections by as much as 50 percent. Once she completes the forecasts, the owner can perform break-even and ratio analysis on the projected figures.

It is also important to include a statement of the assumptions on which these financial projections are based. Potential lenders and investors will want to know how the entrepreneur derived forecasts for sales, cost of goods sold, operating expenses, accounts receivable, collections, inventory, and other key items. Spelling out such assumptions gives a plan more credibility. The table below offers ten ways to enhance the quality of forecasted financial statements.

Ten ways to strengthen internally prepared financial statements.

1. Use a pyramid of reports (i.e., summaries supported by progressive levels of detail).

2. Compare historical statements (actual results) to forecasted statements made in the past. This will help you determine how accurate your forecasting methods have been.

---

3. Include nonfinancial statistics such as units shipped, inventory turnover, etc. Although this information may be contained elsewhere in your business plan, it helps to explain the big picture.

4. Plot trends in key statistics using graphs. A visual interpretation of the information makes it easier to comprehend the course your business is traveling.

5. Isolate all nonrecurring costs and investments that will pay off in the future. This is one of the most important concerns of potential investors/lenders.

6. Show sales detail (e.g., by units vs. replacement parts, by product lines, by distribution channels). Again, the more detail you can provide, the fewer questions that will arise from investors/lenders.

7. Separate discounts using standard selling prices and codes for various types of discounts. Controlling revenue erosion can be just as important as controlling costs.

8. Analyze costs including incremental (variable), programmed (discretionary) and fixed.

9. Separate operational costs by function (e.g., purchasing, marketing). Investors/lenders will want to see where money has been spent in the past, but groups of similar costs are more meaningful than a multiplicity of accounts.

10. Identify total employee costs by grouping fringe benefit costs along with monetary compensation.

The Loan Proposal. This section of the business plan should state the purpose of the loan, the amount requested, and the plans for repayment. When describing the purpose of the loan, the owner must remember to be specific in explaining the planned use of the funds. General requests for funds using terms such as for modernization, working capital, or expansion are unlikely to win approval.

Instead, descriptions such as to modernize production facilities by purchasing five new, more efficient looms that will boost productivity by 12 percent or to rebuild merchandise inventory for fall sales peak, beginning in early summer should be used. The entrepreneur also must specify the precise amount requested and include relevant backup data, such as vendor estimates of costs or past production levels. The owner should not hesitate to request the amount of money needed, hut should not inflate the amount anticipating the financial officer to talk her down. Lenders and investors are familiar with industry cost structures. One experienced investor says, "Indicate the investment expected. Show how much money the enterprise is seeking, the form of investment sought, how the funds will be used, and what portion of the business the investment will purchase [if equity]."

Another key element of the loan or investment proposal is the repayment schedule or exit strategy. A banker's primary consideration in granting a loan is the reassurance that the applicant will repay, while an investor's major concern is earning a satisfactory rate of return. Financial projections must reflect the firm's ability to repay loans and produce adequate yields. Without this proof, a request for additional funds stands little chance of being accepted. It is critical for the owner to produce tangible evidence showing the ability to repay loans or to generate attractive returns. "Plan an exit for the investor, says the owner of a financial consulting company. "Generally, the equity investor's objective with early stage funding is to earn a 30 to 50 percent annual return over the life of the investment. To enhance the investor's interest in your enterprise, show how they can 'cash out,' perhaps through a public offering or acquisition."

Finally, the owner must include a timetable for implementing the proposed plan. He should present a schedule showing the estimated startup date for the project and noting any significant milestones along the way. Entrepreneurs tend to be optimistic, so the owner must be sure his timetable of events is realistic.

Preparing a sound business plan clearly requires time and effort, but the benefits gained greatly exceed the costs of developing a plan. Building the plan forces a potential entrepreneur to look at a business idea in the harsh light of reality. It also requires the owner to assess the venture's chances of success more objectively. Sometimes, the greatest service this exercise provides is the realization that it just won't work. In other cases, it brings to light important problems to overcome before launching a company. As one business consultant states, "If you do a really good job of writing your business plan, it's more than just putting words on paper. You do a lot of research, and you expose a lot of flaws. Each one that you expose and treat, you enhance the chances of your success."

Lenders and investors are favorably impressed by small business owners who are informed and prepared when making a loan or investment request. Failure to collect, to interpret, and to present relevant financial and operational data with a request for debt or equity funds often leads to rejection.

Honesty is also a critical factor in preparing a business plan. It is not wise to try to fool a financial officer by adjusting figures to portray the business more favorably. They know their business and frown on fraudulent attempts to obtain financing.

III. What Does a Banker Look For?

Banks are a common source of debt capital for small businesses. Existing small businesses may need periodic cash infusions, for which they rely on lines of credit from their bankers. To improve the chance of obtaining such loans, the entrepreneur should know what a loan officer looks for in a bankable small business loan. Most bankers consider a loan acceptable if it conforms to the five Cs of credit: capital, capacity, collateral, character, and conditions.

Capital. A small business must have a stable capital base before a bank will grant a loan. Otherwise the bank, in effect, would be making a capital investment in the business. Most banks refuse to make loans that are capital investments because the potential for return on the investment is limited strictly to the interest on the loan, and the potential loss would probably exceed the reward. In fact, the most commonly cited reasons banks give for rejecting small business loan applications are undercapitalization or too much debt. The bank expects the small business to have an equity base of investment by the owner(s) that will help support the venture during times of financial strain.

Capacity. A synonym for capacity is cash flow. The bank must be convinced of the firm's ability to meet its regular financial obligations and to repay the bank loan, and that takes cash. Many small businesses fail from lack of cash than from lack of profit. It is possible for a company to he showing a profit and still have no cash—that is, to be technically bankrupt. Bankers expect the small business loan applicant to pass the test of liquidity, especially for short-term loans. The bank will study closely the small company's cash flow position to decide whether it meets the capacity required.

Collateral. Collateral includes any assets the owner pledges to the bank as security for repayment of the loan. If the company defaults on the loan, the bank has the right to sell the collateral and use the proceeds to satisfy the loan. Typically, banks make very few unsecured loans (those not backed by collateral) to business startups. Bankers view the owner's willingness to pledge collateral (personal or business assets) as an indication of the small business owner's dedication to making the venture a success. But, a sound business plan can improve a banker's attitude toward a venture. One business adviser claims, "A banker will require [less] hard collateral if he sees that he can believe in the business plan."

Character. Before approving a loan to a small business, the banker must be satisfied with the owner's character. The evaluation of character frequently is based on intangible factors like honesty, competence, polish, determination, intelligence, and ability. Although the qualities judged are abstract, this evaluation plays a critical role in the banker's decision. One financier explains, "The most exciting thing to the venture capitalist is talking to management one-on-one. To invest, you have to get caught up in the high-energy level, enthusiasm of people, and their ability to impress you that they know their business."

Loan officers know that most small businesses fail because of incompetent management, and they try to avoid extending loans to high-risk managers. The business plan described in this chapter and a polished presentation by the entrepreneur can go far in convincing the banker of the owner's capability. As one successful loan candidate who painstakingly prepared a business plan and perfected a presentation technique says, "Many applicants shuffle in with their hands in their pockets and their eyes on their shoes. They don't quite know how to make a presentation."

Conditions. The conditions surrounding a loan request also affect the owner's chance of receiving funds. Banks will consider factors relating to the business operation such as potential growth in the market, competition, location, form of ownership, and loan purpose. Again, the owner should provide this relevant information in an organized format in the business plan. Another important condition influencing the banker's decision is the shape of the overall economy, including interest rate levels, inflation rate, and demand for money.

The higher a small business scores on these five Cs, the greater its chance of receiving a loan. The wise entrepreneur will keep this in mind when preparing a business plan and presentation.

IV. Suggested Business Plan Format

Although every company's business plan will be unique, reflecting its individual circumstances, certain elements are universal. The following outline summarizes these components.

I. Executive Summary (not to exceed two typewritten pages)

A. Company name, address and phone number

B. Name(s), addresses, and phone number(s) of all key people

C. Brief description of the business

D. Brief overview of the market for your product

E. Brief overview of the strategic actions you plan to take to make your firm a success

F. Brief description of the managerial and technical experience of your key people

G. Brief statement of what the strategic actions are and what would the money be used for. In addition, income statements and balance sheets for the last three years of operation

II. Detailed Business Plan

A. Background on your business

1. Brief history of the business

2. Current situation

B. Your Business

1. Complete and detailed description of your business

What makes your business unique?

How does it create value for others?

Describe the key factors that will dictate the success of your business (i.e., price competitiveness, quality, durability, dependability, technical features, etc.)

C. Market Analysis

1. Who are the potential buyers for your products? (Please be specific.)

2. What is their motivation to buy?

3. How many customers does the market contain? (How large is the market?)

4. What are their potential annual purchases?

5. What is the nature of the buying cycle?

Is this product a durable good that lasts for years or a product that is repurchased on a regular basis?

Is the product likely to be purchased at only seasonal periods during the year?

6. Specific target market—What do you know about the potential customer you are likely to sell to in your geographic area?

If yours is a consumer product:

a. What are the product features that you feel influence the consumer's buying decision?

b. What, if any, research Supports your feeling?

c. Does the consumer have a preference in where he or she purchases comparable products? How strong is this preference?

7. External market influence. How might each of the following external forces affect the sale or profitability of your product?

Economic factors such as:

a. inflation

b. recession

c. high or low unemployment

Social factors such as:

a. age of customers

b. location demographics

c. income levels

d. size of household

e. specific societal attitudes

D. Competitor Analysis

1. Describe each of the following factors and discuss how these factors will influence your success.

Existing competitors

a. Who are they? Please list major known competitors.

b. Why do you believe the potential customers in your target market buy from them now?

Potential firms who might enter the market

a. Who are they and when and why might they enter the market?

b. What would be the impact in your target market segment if they enter?

What are the strengths and weaknesses of each competitor's business?

E. Strategic Plan for Your Business

1. How do you plan to market your products to the target market you identified above? Please specifically identify your marketing strategy on key factors such as:

pricing

product promotion and advertising

customer services

2. How will your products match up against those presently in the market?

F. Specifics of Your Organization and Management

1. How is your business organized?

legally (corporation, S corporation, partnership, sole proprietorship) functionally

2. Who are the key people (or will be) in your business? What are their backgrounds and what do they bring to the business that will enhance the chance of success?

G. Financial Plans

1. How much money do you need to make this product and your business a long-term success?

Tie the response to this question to your production and marketing plan.

be realistic and specific

2. Create a cash budget. Show the banker or investor what you need in terms of money, when you need it, and how and when you plan to generate revenues from operations and sales.

3. Have a realistic projection of costs of operations

materials

labor

equipment

marketing

overhead

other (i.e., unique startup costs)

4. Present actual and projected balance sheets and income statements

5. Prepare a break-even analysis

H. Strategic Action Plan

1. Clear mission statement for your business

2. Specific performance goals and objectives

3. Restatement of your production and marketing strategies

4. How these strategies will be converted into operating action plans

5. What control procedures you plan to establish to keep the business on track

V. Summary

Attracting capital to launch a new business or to boost an existing one is not an easy task. The entrepreneur must prove to potential lenders that the business is a good credit risk and must show potential investors that an investment in the business offers the potential for an attractive return. To improve the chance of attracting debt or equity capital, the entrepreneur must prepare a well-organized business plan. This document gives lenders and investors an opportunity to evaluate the firm's strengths. Developing a sound business plan also provides the entrepreneur with the foundation for preparing a coherent presentation to lenders and investors. Without these preparations, the small business owner greatly reduces the chances of obtaining financing.

Every business plan should contain a simple break-even anal sis. which shows the level of operations at which total revenues equal total costs. Although just a simple screening device, break-even analysis is a useful planning tool for the entrepreneur, and it allows lenders and investors to evaluate the potential success of a small business.

Too often, entrepreneurs approach potential lenders and investors poorly prepared to prove their need for financing and the worth of their businesses. The result is almost always refusal of the loan request. To avoid being rejected, the well-prepared owner will develop a business plan summarizing the relevant operational details of the proposed venture. Most financial officers weigh heavily the quality of the owner's business plan and its presentation in making a lending or investing decision.

The following should be included in a typical business plan:

1. the cover letter; the owners' and officers' resumes;

2. the company history;

3. the general business summary,

4. defining the organization's primary mission as well as its goals and its objectives;

5. the business strategy;

6. the description of the product or service;

7. the marketing strategy;

8. the plan of operation;

9. the financial plan; and

10. the loan proposal.

Banks are an important source of small business financing. The small business owner seeking additional funds must be aware of the five Cs of credit—capital, capacity, collateral, character, and conditions—and their importance to bankers.

By preparing a thoughtful, coherent business plan and by making a smooth, polished loan request presentation, the entrepreneur can greatly improve the chances of attracting debt and equity funds.

Section 2 – A world class business plan

There are 10 key sections to the classic business plan:

1. The Executive Summary

2. Company History

3. Business Profile

4. Business Strategy

5. Description of Firm's Product/Services

6. Marketing Strategy

7. Competitor Analysis

8. Officers'/Owners' Resumes

9. Plan of Operation

10. Financial Data

It is important that the principle of "less is more" applies to creating a business plan. We have seen a small business plan that exceeded 75 pages and was declined several times. Properly edited the plan was reduced to 30 pages and it received a loan approval on the first submission.

> Please remember you are preparing a dynamic tool to promote your business, not a long, cumbersome document that is put on the shelf and gathers dust.

The Executive Summary

To recap the presentation to each potential financial institution or investor, the dynamic small business owner should prepare an executive summary. It should be concise and should review all of the relevant points of the proposed transaction. (Please also refer to Chapter 10)

Writing an executive summary is not easy, but it is the most important single part of the business plan. It will probably do more to influence whether or not the plan is reviewed in its entirety than anything else you do. It can also make the reader favorably disposed to a venture at the outset—which is not a bad thing.

Ideally one but certainly no longer than two pages, the executive summary should follow immediately after your title page.

These two pages must explain:

> 1. The current state of the company with respect to product/service readiness for market, selling position and past successes if already running, and key staff on board.

> 2. The products or services to be sold and to whom they will be sold, including details on competitive advantage.

> 3. The reasons customers need this product or service, together with some indication of market size and growth.

> 4. The company's aims and objectives in both the short and long term, and an indication of the strategies to be employed in getting there.

> 5. A summary of forecasts, sales, profits, and cash flow.

> 6. How much money is needed, and how and when the investor or lender will benefit from providing the funds.

Summation: A well-developed, coherent executive summary introducing the financial proposal will establish a favorable first impression of the owners and the business, and can go a long way toward obtaining financing.

> Although the executive summary is the first part of the business plan, it should be the last section written.

Example of a firm's executive summary:

Intellectual Movies, Inc. is an alternative video rental store located in Clinton, SC. Go Flicks will rent movies not often available from the larger chains: film festival movies, independent releases, foreign films and other "arts" films. Clinton clearly has the market for these types of films, as evidenced by the general demographics (liberal, educated, college town) and the popularity of the Live Arts Cinema, a first run movie theatre concentrating on this same genre of movies.

This market has been ignored by the dominant stores in Clinton. They may have a few films that fit these descriptions, but in general they are far and few between. It is too difficult for the large corporations to market to this specific segment, particularly with their current business model which is putting a store in all cities that are very similar in feel and library with a concentration on large scale commercial releases.

Through the use of Intellectual Movies' competitive advantage of attention to customers, Intellectual Movies will grow steadily to profitability. This is evident in two ways,

> 1) providing outstanding customer service and knowledgeable help, and
>
> 2) supplying movies that have a demand in Clinton but the demand has yet to be addressed by the other competitors who wrongly assume it is only for the fringe of the general population.

Fortunately, the fringe in Clinton makes up a large part of the local general population. Intellectual Movies begins its 3 year of profitability and projects revenues of almost $265,000 in year four an increase of 14% over year three.

This figure is an example of a highlights chart used for "eye candy" in the executive summary section.

Highlights

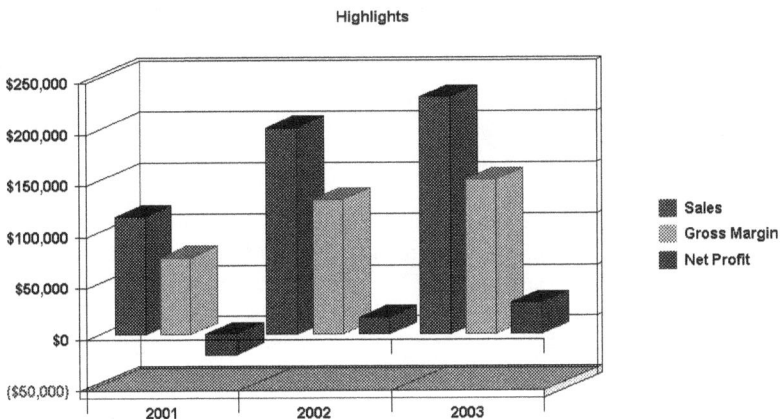

The Table of Contents

A table of contents follows the executive summary. This is the map that will guide the new reader through your business proposal and on to the "inevitable" conclusion that they should put up the funds.

If a map is obscure, muddled, or even missing, then the chances are you will end up with lost or irritated readers unable to find their way around your proposal.

Each of the main sections of the business plan should be listed and the pages within that section indicated.

Company History

The owner of an existing small business should prepare a brief history of its operation, highlighting the significant financial and operational events in the company's life.

This section should focus on the successful accomplishment of past objectives and should indicate the firm's image.

Annual reports and audited financial statements, if voluminous, can be included in an appendix and referred to in this section of your business plan. Otherwise, they can be shown in detail. You should emphasize what you have learned so far that convinces you your strategies are soundly based.

Example of company history:

Cooper Engineering was founded in 1999 by the four partners. In 2000 it was incorporated as a professional corporation. The company was operated as a part time enterprise, building its initial client base. In October 2002, full time operation was started on a progressive schedule, until all of the partners were full time in May 2003.

In keeping with the company philosophy of avoiding the use of large start-up debt, the goal was to start-up as inexpensively as possible. This is in line with industry figures that show that engineering and consulting start-ups are ideal entrepreneurial opportunities with low start-up costs.

Total start-up expense was financed from accounts received from the 1999 through 2002 revenues. No salaries or payments to the partners were made during this initial start-up period.

Full time operation was started with existing revenues and accounts receivable of over $60,000. This was coupled with an initial SBA line of credit loan of $50,000 to cover the day-to-day operation and salary expense. Accounts receivable are billed monthly and usually paid net 60 days.

This figure is an example of a past performance chart in the company history section.

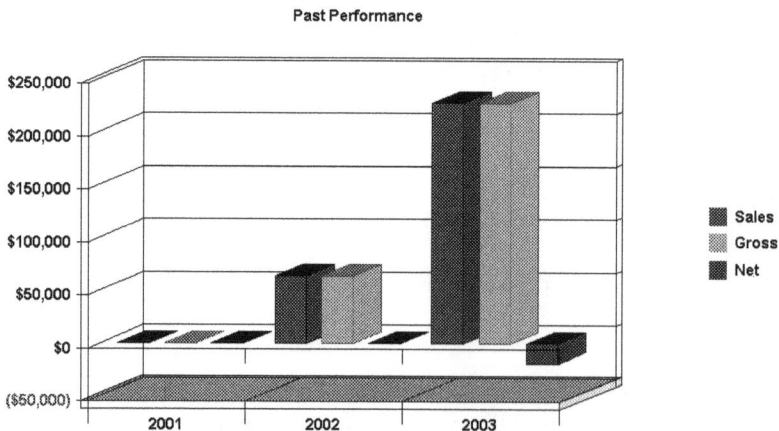

Past Performance

Recession Proofing Your Business

Business Profile

Explain your business concept, why you think people have a need for your product or service, and what your goals and aspirations for the business are. If your business needs financing, you could give some preliminary idea of how much you may need and what you intend to do with those funds. Remember, all these ideas are likely to be significantly modified later on-some more than others-but you need to have some idea at the outset of where you are going if you are to have any chance at all of getting there.

To familiarize lenders and investors with the nature of your business, you should incorporate into the business plan a general description of its operation. This section should begin with a statement of the company's general business goals and a narrower definition of its immediate objectives.

They answer the question, "Why am I in business?" Answering such a basic question appears to be obvious, but many small business owners cannot define the basic purpose of their businesses.

Example of a firm's business profile:

Snobs, Inc. is a retail store offering fine gifts, collectible dolls and doll accessories. The store is located in Atlanta, Georgia, catering to the middle- and upper-class consumers who look beyond the congested retail malls for the special shopping experience. In addition to offering a wide array of unique, quality products, the consumer will enjoy friendly and knowledgeable customer service and a convenient, no congestion location.

Objectives:

> 1. Sell products the customer desires and are of the highest quality.
>
> 2. Provide friendly customer service.
>
> 3. Establish excellent vendor/supplier relations that will facilitate quick shipment of orders.
>
> 4. Continuously review our inventory and sales and adjust our inventory levels based on detailed records.

Business Strategy

An even more important part of the business plan is your view of the strategy needed to meet the competition. It should comment on how you plan to achieve business objectives in the face of competition and government regulation. You also must describe your firm's desired character—the image the business will try to project. This section should highlight basic strategic elements.

Example of a firm's business strategy:

Slide-Rule Engineering will utilize its existing contacts with architects, governmental agencies, commercial developers and local school districts to increase word-of-mouth about our business. We have a standard brochure on our expertise and specialties which will be sent to architectural firms recommended to us by our current contacts.

Our marketing to architects and developers focuses on our thorough engineering expertise across the full range of skills necessary for any project. Examples of previous work and recommendations from former employers are available for the asking. Our individual reputations as reliable, skilled, knowledgeable resources, combined with our range of expertise as a team, will appeal strongly to those looking for subcontractors.

Slide-Rule has focused on the southeastern states initially. We are licensed to practice in most states in the eastern United States, and will continue to expand into additional areas.

Description of Firm's Product/Services

In this section you should describe the company's overall product line, giving an overview of how the goods/ services are used. You should provide an honest comparison of the company's product or service with those of competitor.

To be effective you must explain what it is you are selling. Be specific and avoid unnecessary jargon. The reader should end up with more than just a vague idea about your products and/or services. Obviously, some products and services will require much more explanation than others.

If you have invented a new process for analyzing blood, you will need to provide the reader with many details. On the other hand, if you are selling your services as a bookkeeper, you may need to do little more than list the services you will provide.

A danger of this section is in assuming that the reader can easily understand your products without your providing sufficient detail and description.

Example of a Firm's Product/Services:

On-The-Go, Inc. offers a comprehensive range of services to support the adventure traveler, including pre-and post-vacation briefings, travel insurance, and a Managery of services specific to each destination and activity.

With virtually no marketing effort, On-The-Go has sold some 250 adventure vacations in the past five months, netting $76,900 in commissions.

Sales of insurance policies and other services have added to this total and could potentially add much more.

On-The-Go recently became appointed agents for Omni Travel, one of the largest and most respected tour operators in the market.

Marketing Strategy

One of the most crucial concerns of potential lenders and investors is whether there is a real market for the proposed good or service.

Every small business owner seeking funds must incorporate into the business plan a description of the company's target market and its characteristics.

Defining the target market and its potential is one of the most important and most difficult parts of a business plan.

Example of a Firm's Marketing Strategy:

Backdoor Architecture will provide it's service to home owners who are looking to remodel, as well as developers, contractors and government agencies in the domestic and international markets. Although we are going to cater to a relatively broad scope of customers, the company will decide what the target market is based on sales and trends.

A potential client for Backdoor Architecture's market is broken down into four categories: home owners, developers, government, and contractors. Home owners are the largest group based on shear population and this will be emphasized in all of the firm's marketing and promotional efforts. Targeting the remaining three groups will be dependant upon establishing meaningful relationships, and responding and qualifying for request for proposals.

This figure is an example of a marketing strategy chart depicting market segmentation.

Market Analysis (Pie)

- Home Owners/Remodels
- Developers
- Government
- Contractors

Competitive Analysis

The small business owner also should describe the competition the company faces. Failure to provide a realistic assessment of competitors makes the owner appear to be poorly prepared, naive, or dishonest.

Gathering information on competitors' market shares, products, and strategies usually is not difficult. Trade associations, customers, industry journals, marketing representatives, and sales literature are valuable sources of data. The focus of this section should be to demonstrate how the owner's company has an advantage over its competitors.

Remember that the most successful small companies are those that begin with a marketing approach which determines what the market wants and then invents it.

Example of a Firm's Competitive Strategy:

The architecture business across the country is primarily made up of small- to mid-sized firms specializing in a particular market segment. But there are also a few large firms that have almost dominated the design of large commercial and industrial facilities. Backdoor Architecture's main competitors will be the larger firms. The reason for this is that the larger firms have more capital to work with, which enables them to keep up with technological changes much quicker than a small firm.

Backdoor Architecture will have a competitive edge over both the larger and smaller firms because it will be composed of the new generation of architects which are fluent in the digital world. Many firms today employ an older generation of architects which find the computer a mystery, and those that do use the computer only have the ability to design in 2-D.

Officers'/Owners' Resumes

The most important factor in the success of a business venture is its management. Financial officers and investors weigh heavily the ability and experience of the firm's managers in financing decisions. The plan should include the resumes of business officers, key directors, and any person with at least 20 percent ownership in the company. Remember: Lenders and investors prefer experienced managers.

A resume should summarize the individual's education, work history emphasizing managerial responsibilities and duties), and relevant business experience.

Ideas and products don't succeed; people do. Show the strength of your management team. A top-notch management team with a variety of proven skills is crucial Show the strength of key employees and how you will retain them. A Board of Directors or advisers consisting of industry experts lends credibility and can enhance the value of the management team.

Example of a Firm's Management Resume:

Helen Globe, President and CEO.

Before founding Globe Trots, Ms. Globe owned and operated Globe Clothiers, an outdoor clothing shop in the Joanna area. Prior to that, she managed the Greenwood branch of one of the larger regional chains of general travel agencies operating throughout western North Carolina, where she was responsible for managing the office systems and a staff of eight. She has a degree in travel and tourism from Western State University.

In addition to Ms. Globe, team members John Ticket and Bobby Clampert will be moving into the new venture on a full-time basis, and Marchia Miles has been recently recruited to cover Saturdays and vacations.

John Ticket, Vice President Sales and Marketing.

Prior to joining Globe Trots, Mr. Ticket worked for the maintenance department of a major airline. His current responsibilities include the company's direct marketing campaign and all sales-related issues.

Bobby Clampert, Office Manager.

Twenty years as a travel agent has given Mr. Clampert the ideal background for Globe Trots. A knowledgeable salesperson, Mr. Clampert's expertise in the area of Egyptian travel enables him to entice the adventure traveler.

Machia Miles, Sales Assistant.

After completing her undergraduate degree at the Institute of Global Travel, Ms. Miles spent a year traveling abroad and joined the staff at Globe Trots recently as a sales assistant.

The volunteer members of the Board of Directors provide guidance to the management and staff of Globe Trots. The board meets twice yearly to discuss policy changes, review the mission statement, and update the business plan if needed.

Members include:

> Marla Jones, retail store owner
>
> Arthur Didget, CPA
>
> Sonny Brown, former travel agent
>
> Perry Mason, lawyer
>
> James Cash, retail store owner
>
> Karen Forms, human resource manager
>
> Annette Gorme, caterer

Plan of Operation

To complete the description of the business, you must construct a functional organizational chart which identifies key positions and the personnel occupying them.

The Organization Chart

The Organization Chart is a very important tool and should be displayed for all employees to view.

This figure is an example of an organization chart depicting chain of command.

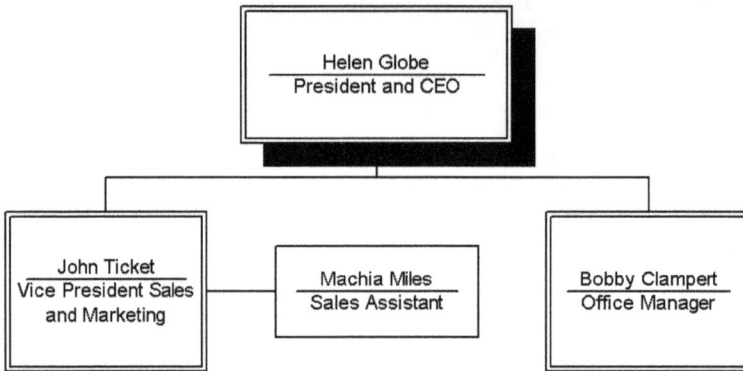

```
                    ┌─────────────────────────┐
                    │      Helen Globe         │
                    │   President and CEO      │
                    └─────────────────────────┘
                                 │
        ┌────────────────────────┼────────────────────────┐
┌───────────────────┐  ┌───────────────────┐  ┌───────────────────┐
│    John Ticket    │  │   Machia Miles    │  │  Bobby Clampert   │
│ Vice President Sales │ │  Sales Assistant  │  │   Office Manager  │
│   and Marketing   │  │                   │  │                   │
└───────────────────┘  └───────────────────┘  └───────────────────┘
```

Assembling a management team with the right stuff is difficult, but keeping it together until the company gets established may be harder. The dynamic small business owner should describe incentives that encourage key officers to remain with the company. Employment contracts, shares of ownership, company car, and other perks are commonly used to keep and motivate key employees.

Finally, a description of the form of ownership (partnership, joint venture, S corporation) is important.

Financial Data

Included in the template folder are several financial templates for this chapter.

1. Balance Sheet

Dynamic small business owners need a method of periodically measuring the growth and development of their venture. The balance sheet is a "snapshot" which shows where the money came from to fund the business and where it was spent at a fixed point in time, usually at yearly intervals.

The "where it came from" will usually include loans received to date (both long and short term), common stock, and the income generated to date.

The "where it went to" will usually include cash in the bank, accounts receivable, inventories, and fixed assets. The parallel in driving would be the odometer, which measures the absolute distance the car has traveled, as opposed to the relative or changing performance measurement offered by the speedometer.

Please open these files from the template folder:

1. Balance Sheet 2 Years (Quarterly).xls

2. Balance Sheet Summary of Years 1 to 5.xls

3. Proforma Balance Sheet.xls

This figure is an example of a two year balance sheet by quarters.

Balance Sheet - Two Years (Quarterly)	Year 1				Year 2			
	Qtr 1	Qtr 2	Qtr 3	Qtr 4	Qtr 1	Qtr 2	Qtr 3	Qtr 4
ASSETS								
Current Assets								
Cash								
Marketable securities								
Accounts receivable, net								
Inventory								
Prepaid expenses								
Other								
Total Current Assets	0	0	0	0	0	0	0	0
Long-Term Assets								
Property, plant, and equipment								
Less accumulated depreciation								
Net property, plant, and equi	0	0	0	0	0	0	0	0
Other long-term assets								
Total Long-Term Assets	0	0	0	0	0	0	0	0
Total Assets	0	0	0	0	0	0	0	0
LIABILITIES AND SHAREHOLDERS' EQUITY								
Current Liabilities								

This is an example of a Balance Sheet Summary of Years 1 to 5.

Balance Sheet - Summary of Years 1 to 5	Opening	Year 1:	Year 2:	Year 3:	Year 4:	Year 5:
ASSETS						
Current Assets						
Cash						
Marketable securities						
Accounts receivable, net						
Inventory						
Prepaid expenses						
Other						
Total Current Assets	0	0	0	0	0	0
Long-Term Assets						
Property, plant, and equipment						
Less accumulated depreciation						
Net property, plant, and equipment	0	0	0	0	0	0
Other long-term assets						
Total Long-Term Assets	0	0	0	0	0	0
Total Assets	0	0	0	0	0	0
LIABILITIES AND SHAREHOLDERS' EQUITY						
Current Liabilities						

This is an example of a Proforma Balance Sheet 4 Years.

Pro Forma Balance Sheet

ASSETS	Year	Year	Year	Year
Current Assets	2001	2002	2003	2004
Total Current Assets	$1,212,200	$1,550,530	$2,187,750	$2,625,710

Fixed Assets	2001	2002	2003	2004
Total Fixed Assets	$2,900,000	$2,487,000	$3,221,800	$3,191,400

	2001	2002	2003	2004
Total Assets	$4,167,200	$4,094,180	$5,467,899	$5,877,126

LIABILITIES AND STOCKHOLDERS' EQUITY

Current Liabilities	2001	2002	2003	2004
Total Current Liabilities	$936,000	$964,080	$993,002	$1,021,363

Non-Current Liabilities	2001	2002	2003	2004
Total Non-Current Liabilities	$781,200	$809,600	$836,592	$864,523

Total Liabilities	$1,717,200	$1,773,680	$1,829,594	$1,885,886

2. Income Statement

This is like a moving picture of how well the business is doing in terms of sales, costs, and profitability, usually prepared on a monthly basis but covering an accounting period of one year. This can be compared to the speedometer in the car, which constantly changes as the car progresses on its journey.

The income statement monitors the day-to-day performance of the business and gives the businessperson the information needed to identify the areas where corrective action should be taken (the equivalent of slowing down and taking notice of the road signs).

Please open these files from the template folder:

1. Income Statement 2 Years (Quarterly).xls

2. Income Statement 12 Months.xls

3. Income Statement Summary of Years 1 to 5.xls

4. Proforma Income Statement.xls

This is an example of an Income Statement 2 Years (Quarterly).

Income Statement - Two Years (Quarterly)					
		Year 1			
	Qtr 1	Qtr 2	Qtr 3	Qtr 4	Q
Sales					
Sales					
Other					
Total Sales	0	0	0	0	
Less **Cost of Goods Sold**					
Materials					
Labor					
Overhead					
Other					
Total Cost of Goods Sold	0	0	0	0	
Gross Profit	0	0	0	0	
Operating Expenses					

This is an example of an Income Statement Summary of Years 1 to 5.

Income Statement - Summary of Years 1 to 5						
	Year 1:	Year 2:	Year 3:	Year 4:	Year 5:	Totals
Sales						
Sales						0
Other						0
Total Sales	0	0	0	0	0	0
Less Cost of Goods Sold						
Materials						0
Labor						0
Overhead						0
Other						0
Total Cost of Goods Sold	0	0	0	0	0	0
Gross Profit	0	0	0	0	0	0
Operating Expenses						

This is an example of an Income Statement 12 Months.

Income Statement - 12 Months					
Period Starting:	Month 1	Month 2	Month 3	Month 4	Month 5
Sales					
Sales					
Other					
Total Sales	0	0	0	0	
Less Cost of Goods Sold					
Materials					
Labor					
Overhead					
Other					
Total Cost of Goods Sold	0	0	0	0	
Gross Profit	0	0	0	0	
Operating Expenses					

This is an example of a Proforma Income Statement.

Pro Forma Income Statement

	Year 2001	Year 2002	Year 2003	Forecasted Year 2004
REVENUE	**2001**	**2002**	**2003**	**2004**
Gross Sales	$2,010,000	$2,560,000	$2,721,800	$3,142,400
Discounts/Allowances	($50,000)	($60,000)	($70,000)	($80,000)
Net Sales	$1,960,000	$2,500,000	$2,651,800	$3,062,400
COST OF SALES	**2001**	**2002**	**2003**	**2004**
Direct Material Cost	$320,000	$427,600	$431,238	$504,184
Direct Labor Cost	$300,000	$315,000	$330,450	$345,600
Other Direct Costs	$125,000	$128,750	$132,613	$136,400
Total Cost of Sales	$745,000	$871,350	$894,301	$986,184
Gross Profit (Loss)	$1,215,000	$1,628,650	$1,757,500	$2,076,216
OPERATING EXPENSES	**2001**	**2002**	**2003**	**2004**
Total expenses	$558,760	$583,787	$647,842	$685,878
Operating income	$656,240	$1,044,863	$1,109,658	$1,390,338
Other income and expenses				
Gain (loss) on sale of assets	$10,000	$10,300	$10,609	$10,912
Other (net)	$20,000	$20,600	$21,218	$21,824
Subtotal	$30,000	$30,900	$31,827	$32,736
Income before tax	$686,240	$1,075,763	$1,141,485	$1,423,074
Income taxes	$205,872	$322,729	$342,445	$426,922
Net income	$480,368	$753,034	$799,039	$996,152

3. Cash Flow Statement

The cash flow statement is another moving picture of how well the business is doing, but this time in terms of cash flow generation. It bears a very close resemblance to the income statement but reflects the effect that credit taken from suppliers and given to customers has on cash flow. Net income does not always equal cash.

Here, the comparison with the car is particularly apt: A car needs fuel to run and the fuel gauge shows how much there is in the tank. A business needs cash to survive and the cash flow statement shows how much there is in the business's "tank."

Please open from the template folder:

> ### 1. Cash Flow Forecast 2 Years (Quarterly).xls
>
> ### 2. Cash Flow Forecast 12 Months.xls
>
> ### 3. Projected Cash Flow.xls
>
> ### 4. Basic Cash Flow.xls

This is an example of a Cash Flow Forecast 2 Years (Quarterly).

Cash Flow Forecast - Two Years (Quarterly)					
	Year 1				
	Qtr 1	Qtr 2	Qtr 3	Qtr 4	Qt
Receipts					
Cash sales					
Collections from credit sales					
New equity inflow					
Loans received					
Other					
Total Receipts	0	0	0	0	
Payments					
Cash purchases					
Payments to creditors					

This is an example of a Cash Flow Forecast 12 Months.

Cash Flow Forecast – 12 Months					
Month:	Pre-Start	1	2	3	4
Receipts					
Cash sales					
Collections from credit sales					
New equity inflow					
Loans received					
Other					
Total Receipts	0	0	0	0	
Payments					
Cash purchases					
Payments to creditors					

This is an example of a Projected Cash Flow statement.

PROJECTED CASH FLOW STATEMENT

	Year 2001	Year 2002	Year 2003	Year 2004	Proje 20(
Cash from operations					
Net cash from operations	$514,118	$787,797	$834,845	$1,198,922	$1,35!
Cash provided (used) by operating activities					
Net cash used by operations	$1,621,000	$1,969,630	$2,619,719	$3,256,237	$3,75!
Investment transactions Increases (decreases)					
Net cash from investments	$0	$0	$0	$0	
Financing transactions Increases (decreases)					
Net cash from financing	$1,831,200	$1,591,100	$2,795,727	$3,443,982	$3,92(
Net increase (decrease) in cash	$724,318	$409,267	$1,010,853	$1,366,667	$1,52!
Cash at beginning of period	$451,000	$464,530	$478,466	$492,820	$50(
Cash at the end of period	$1,175,318	$873,797	$1,489,319	$1,879,487	$2,03(

This is an example of Basic Cash Flow

CASH FLOW STATEMENT

	Week 1	Week 2	Week 3	Week 4
Cash from operations				
Net cash from operations	$514,118	$787,797	$834,845	$1,198,922
Cash provided (used) by operating activities				
Net cash used by operations	$1,621,000	$1,969,630	$2,619,719	$3,256,237
Investment transactions Increases (decreases)				
Net cash from investments	$0	$0	$0	$0
Financing transactions Increases (decreases)				
Net cash from financing	$1,831,200	$1,591,100	$2,795,727	$3,443,982
Net increase (decrease) in cash	$724,318	$409,267	$1,010,853	$1,386,667
Cash at beginning of period	$451,000	$464,530	$478,466	$492,820
Cash at the end of period	$1,175,318	$873,797	$1,489,319	$1,879,487

4. Break-Even Analysis

With the information contained in the preceding financial statements, the businessperson will know if a profit or loss was made in the past but may not know whether the business is still making a profit.

The break-even analysis will show the level of sales required to generate sufficient gross profit to cover the expenses of the business and thereby break even.

The businessperson can now be confident that if the business operates at above this break-even level of sales, it will be operating profitably, barring any changes in the level of gross profit and expenses.

In car terms, the driver knows that in order to arrive at a destination on time he or she has to average so many miles per hour, say 50. If the driver averages less than 50 miles per hour, then the driver will be late, and if the driver exceeds it for any length of time, the driver will arrive early. In business terms arriving early equals making a profit, and arriving late equals taking a loss. The 50 miles per hour is the break-even point.

Please open the template *Break-Even Analysis.xls*

This is an example of a 6-month Break-Even worksheet. Please see the next chapter for more detail in using this very valuable tool.

Johnson Plumbing: 6-Month Financial Projection	
Number of Months	6
CALCULATE YOUR GROSS PROFIT	
Projected Sales	75,000.00
Less **Direct Costs**	
Purchases (material costs)	32,500.00
Labour Costs	20,000.00
Gross Profit	**22,500.00**
Gross Profit Margin	**30%**
CALCULATE YOUR OVERHEADS	
Indirect Costs	
Business Salaries (including your own drawings)	6,000.00
Rent	2,000.00
Rates	500.00
Light/Heating	500.00
Telephone/Postage	500.00
Insurance	500.00
Repairs	2,000.00
Advertising	1,500.00
Bank Interest/Hire Purchase	1,500.00
Other (eg depreciation of fixed assets)	1,500.00
Overheads	**16,500.00**
Break-Even Sales	**55,000.00**
Monthly Break-Even Sales	**9,166.67**
Profit (for 6 months)	**6,000.00**

Section 3 - A concise business plan

Your Business, Inc.

A well-written business plan is a crucial ingredient in preparing for business success. Without a sound business plan, a firm merely drifts along without any real direction. Yet, entrepreneurs, who tend to be people of action, too often jump right into a business venture without taking time to prepare a written plan outlining the essence of the business.

You should begin by writing down the answer to the very basic question, "What business am I in?" This may sound elementary, but answering this question with thought and consideration will help you focus on the major purpose of the business, which leads to establishing goals and objectives. In turn, these serve as aids in creating strategies, policies, and procedures. Every small business should have policies concerning credit, customers, product lines, image, prices, advertising, and so on. It is important to plan in writing; otherwise, the planning function either is ignored altogether or is conducted too informally. This model has all of the ingredients to produce an excellent business plan.

Executive Summary

Key executives:	Mr. James K. Quadrant 978 Lakeside Drive Hamilton, New York 13346 (515) 555-5431	Mr. Isaiah M. Gradient 113 Broughton Road Hamilton, New York 13346 (315) 555-6871
Business:	Quadrant Surveying & Equipment Company 600 Madison Drive Hamilton, New York 13346 (315) 555-4000	
Business size:	$378,000 in billings in latest fiscal year. Qualify under SBA definition of a "small business."	
Form of ownership:	S Corporation	
Loan purpose:	To purchase 1 Zeiss total stage with data storage and transfer capabilities to improve the quantity and the quality of the surveying jobs performed for	

clients.

Amount requested: $25,000

Management

> Mr. James K. Quadrant
> 978 Lakeside Drive
> Hamilton, New York 13346
> (315) 555-5431

Work experience:

1974-present	Quadrant Surveying & Engineering Company, Hamilton, New York. Manager-Partner. Created business and continues to actively manage technical aspects of field operations. Supervised project managers of six field crews.
1970-1974	Boise-Cascade Timber Co., Freeport, Maine. Survey project manager. Supervised field activities of a six-man survey crew. Planned weekly work schedules and monitored work quality.
1965-1970	Hi-Tech Survey Co., Albany, New York Technician. Performed various surveying tasks as a part-time member of a field crew while attending college. Earned 80% of college expenses.
Education: 1969-1970	Rensselaer Polytechnical Institute, Troy, New York Master of Science in Engineering Management. Grades in top 10% of class, GPR of 3.7/4.0.
1965-1969	Rensselaer Polytechnical Institute, Troy, New York Bachelor of Science degree in Civil Engineering Graduated with honors.

References:

Mr. Frank Boland President, Hi-Tech Survey Co. Troy, New York 12180 (315) 555-1890	Mr. Jeff Anderson President, Sound Investment Co. Hamilton, New York 13346 (315) 555-3671

Ms. Sally LeGrand
Account Executive
Merrill, Lynch, Pierce, Fenner, and Smith
Portland, Maine 04111

---

(207) 555-1218

Personal Financial Statement- Mr. James K. Quadrant

Assets		Liabilities	
Cash-Savings account	$12,000	Notes payable	$10,000
Checking account	3,000	Mortgage	41,000
Stocks	22,000	Miscellaneous	6,000
Keogh contributions	31,000	Total liabilities	$57,000
Home	96,000	Net worth	$135,000
Autos	20,000	Total liabilities	
Miscellaneous assets	8,000	& net worth	$192,000
Total assets	$192,000		

Mr. Isaiah M. Gradient
113 Broughton Road
Hamilton, New York 13346
(315) 555-6871

Work experience:

1976-Present	Quadrant Surveying & Engineering Co., Hamilton, New York. Managing partner. Supervises internal managerial operations, including financial, accounting, personnel, and planning duties.
1971-1975	New York Department of Health & Sanitation, Albany, New York. District Maintenance Engineer. Designed water and sewage projects for cities. Supervised staff of twelve.
1966-1970	Hi-tech Survey Co., Albany, New York Technician. Worked part-time as field crew member performed various surveying duties.
Education: 1975-1976	University of Virginia, Charlottesville, Virginia. Master of Business Administration. GPR of 40/4.0.
1966-1970	Clemson University, Clemson, South Carolina. Bachelor of Science degree, in Civil Engineering.
References:	Mr. John Molooney Dr. Fred Target
	Assistant Vice President Professor of Engineering

Con-Edison

New York, New York 10014
(212) 555-2268

Rensselaer Polytechnical
Institute
Troy, New York 12181
(518) 555-3196

Mr. Sam Hough
Certified Public Accountant
Charlottesville, Virginia
22201
(804) 555-3241

Personal Financial Statement- Mr. Isaiah M. Gradient

Assets		Liabilities	
Cash-Savings account	$6,000	Notes payable	$14,000
Checking account	4,000	Mortgage	59,000
Mutual funds	27,000	Miscellaneous	6,000
Stocks	18,000	Total liabilities	$79,000
Keogh contributions	24,000	Net worth	$138,000
Home	94,000	Total liabilities	
Real estate	17,000	& net worth	$217,000
Autos	19,000		
Miscellaneous assets	8,000		
Total assets	$217,000		

Company History

James K. Quadrant created Quadrant Surveying & Engineering Company in 1974 as a part-time business venture designed to serve the surveying needs of the local community. Mr. Quadrant began part-time operation of the business in 1975, and Mr. Gradient joined the firm in 1976 to manage the internal operations of the business, while Mr. Quadrant's major responsibilities remained in the area of surveying operations. The two principals' skills, abilities, and areas of concentration are complementary. Annual sales have increased steadily to a record high of $378,000 in the latest fiscal year, and profits peaked at $48,965.

Industry Trends and State of the Art

Demand for surveying and engineering services should continue to climb during the next decade for three important reasons. First, the rapid escalation of property values during the 1980s has increased the need for these services by several customer groups. Second, greater mobility among the general public has increased the number of land transfers. Third, the trend of larger financial institutions to buy and sell residential and commercial mortgages translates into more work for surveyors, who must provide closing plats showing property boundaries, location of permanent fixtures, encroachments, and easements. There has been an extremely rapid growth in golf course communities in the last two years, with new development announced to begin in the next three years.

The development of "state of the art" equipment in the surveying industry has paralleled the expansion in the service's demand. The surveyor's tools have undergone a major transformation in the last ten years; they are more sophisticated, more accurate, and more refined than ever before. Technological advances have manifested themselves in two important forms: (1) the development of speedy, accurate computational equipment (e.g., microcomputers, programmable calculators, etc.) that allows the surveyor to perform complex calculations on field data, and (2) the introduction of electronic distance meters (EDMs), which yield more accurate survey measurements faster and facilitate data processing.

Key success Factors

The principals see the following factors playing a critical role in the success of the company:

Providing services in a timely fashion.
Accuracy of work.
"Guaranteed satisfaction."
Professional image.
Capable work force.

Market Analysis

Quadrant has been extremely successful in carving out a specialty niche for itself as well as in meeting the surveying needs of the general public. The company has earned a reputation as the expert in surveying and planning golf courses. After completing work on two local courses, Quadrant obtained a contract on a large, "upscale" golf course 125 miles west of Hamilton. The work is progressing on schedule and will be finished on time and within budget.

Target Market

The principals of Quadrant have identified their primary target market (in descending order of importance) as: (1) golf courses; (2) realtors; (3) attorneys; (4) private landowners. The firm's marketing strategy is designed to attain the return customer by providing quality surveying and engineering service with prompt turnaround. The firm has built its reputation by focusing on quality, and its pricing policy reflects this professional image. General strategy is to tailor pricing to the "cream of the crop."

Competitor Analysis

Quadrant Surveying & Engineering Company faces no direct competition in its hometown, Hamilton, New York, but there are three primary competitors conducting similar operations in towns within a fifty-mile diameter of Hamilton.

Geodetic Survey, Inc. A small corporation (three principals) whose primary focus is surveying large land tracts for timber companies. Serves 28% of local markets.

Photogrammetry Engineers, Ltd. A small partnership that performs all types of surveying jobs and specializes in surveying by aerial photography. Controls 22% of local market.

Land Surveyors, Inc. A relatively new, aggressive company that also performs all types of surveying jobs and specializes in surveying for local architectural firms. Controls 18% of the local market.

Plan of Operation

Quadrant employs the S Corporation form of ownership primarily for tax reasons. The organizational chart is attached on a separate form.

Key Personnel

In addition to the principals, whose experience and network of contacts is crucial to the company's success, two long-term field managers play major roles in the firm. As Quadrant grows over the next year, another field manager will be hired,

Financial Data

The following audited financial statements summarize Quadrant's latest operations:

Quadrant Surveying and Engineering Company
Balance Sheet

Assets		Liabilities	
Current assets:		Current liabilities:	
Cash	$5,000	Accounts payable	$2,500
Accounts receivable	4,700		
Total current assets	$9,700	Long term liabilities:	
Fixed assets:		Notes Payable	11,500
20 vehicles	40,500	Mortgages On real	
3 computers	30,000	property	43,000
6 sets EDM equipment	48,000	Total L-T liabilities	$57,000
4 transits	6,000	Total liabilities	57,000
4 levels	4,800	Owner's equity	127,500
Misc. field equipment	20,000	Total liabilities &	
Office fixtures & equip.	18,000	Owners' equity	$184,500
leasehold improvements	7,500		
Total fixed assets	$174,800		
Total assets	$184,500		

Income Statement

Net sales	$378,000
Operating expenses:	
Labor expense	$219,800
Gas expense	29,993
Telephone expense	6,270
Equipment repair expense	5,600
Insurance' expense	9,025
Rent expense	5,400
Depreciation expense	9,200
license expense	1,500
Payroll taxes	11,050
Office supplies expense	7,200
Field supplies expense	10,900
Miscellaneous expenses	4,700
Total operating expenses	$320,638
Net operating profit	57,362
Income taxes	8,397
Net profit	$48,965

Quadrant Surveying & Engineering Company
Break-Even Analysis

$$\text{Break-even sales} = \frac{\text{total fixed expenses}}{1.00 - \text{variable expenses expressed as percentage of sales}}$$

Total expenses	$320,638
Fixed	88,122
Variable	240,913

$$\text{variable expenses as a \% of sales} = \frac{240,913}{378,000}$$

$$= 63.73\%$$

$$\text{Break-even sales} = \frac{88,122}{1.00 - 0.06373}$$

Break-even sales= $242,985

Projected Cash Budget

Cash Receipts			Jan	Feb	Mar	Apr	May	June	July	Aug
SALES COLLECTIONS:			20,000	25,000	28,000	33,000	47,000	54,000	58,000	55,000
20% same month					5,600	6,600	9,400	10,800	11,600	11,000
60% first month after sale					15,000	16,800	19,800	28,200	32,400	34,800
18% second month after sale					3,600	4,500	5,040	5,940	8260	9,720
Other cash receipts					250	50	380	160	400	100
TOTAL CASH RECEIPTS					24,450	27,950	34,620	45,100	52,660	55,620
CASH DISBURSEMENTS:										
Wages					15,680	18,480	26,320	30,240	32,480	31,147
Taxes										
	Payroll				532	628	987	1,011	1,375	1,163
	Property				0	0	400	0	0	0
Transportation					790	840	1,380	1,525	1,780	1,645
Repairs & maintenance					375	450	575	625	700	675
Field supplies					650	800	1,050	1,240	1,500	1,375
Rent					500	500	500	500	500	500
Utilities					100	110	130	140	150	140
Telephone (including yellow					450	575	800	950	1,075	990
Entertainment					200	200	200	200	200	200
Insurance										
	Malpractice				0	9,000	0	0	0	0
	Tenant's				0	0	1,500	0	0	0
	Auto				0	0	0	500	0	0
Licenses					0	0	0	1500	0	0
Miscellaneous					210	340	425	490	510	500
TOTAL CASH DISBURSEMENTS					19,487	31,923	34,267	38,921	40,270	38,335
END OF MONTH BALANCE										
Beginning cash balance					5,000	9,963	5,990	6,343	12,522	25,112
+ cash receipts					24,450	27,950	34,620	45,100	52,660	55,620
- cash disbursements					19,487	31,923	34,267	38,921	40,270	38,335
CASH END OF THE MONTH					9,963	5,990	6,343	12,522	24,912	42,397
	(REPAYMENT)				0	0	0	0	0	0
	or									
	(BORROWING)				0	0	0	0	0	0
CASH END OF THE MONTH					$9,963	$5,990	$6,343	$12,522	$24,912	$42,397

Minimum Cash Balance = $5,000

Pro Forma Income Statement

Net sales	$480,000
Operating expenses:	
Labor expense	$272,000
Gas expense	30,305
Telephone expense	10,650
Equipment repair expense	6,500
Insurance expense	11,000
Rent expense	6,000
Depreciation expense	10,000
License expense	1,500
Payroll expense	12,750
Office supplies expense	7,400
Field supplies expense	11,200
Miscellaneous expenses	5,100
Total operating expenses	**$384,405**
Net operating profit	95,595
Income taxes	13,995
Net profit	**$81,600**

Goals, Objectives, and Strategies

The principals of Quadrant recognize the importance of quality management in successfully meeting their competition. To focus the firm's activities, the principals define its mission: "To meet the spectrum of surveying and engineering needs of private landowners, large tract owners, financial institutions, attorneys, realtors, and timber companies with high-quality service, rapid turnaround, and unparalleled professionalism, at a profit."

The overall mission of Quadrant is more clearly defined by dissecting it into the following objectives:

To boost annual sales to $480,000.

To increase market share from 31 percent to 36 percent of the local market.

To obtain a contract for another golf course.

To increase by 10% the number of engineering jobs performed for local towns and districts (e.g., water and sewage systems design).

To improve profit margin from 13 percent to 17 percent.

To obtain these objectives, Quadrant will employ a business strategy designed to exploit the four key factors for success in the surveying business-to maintain: (1) a prompt turnaround time on jobs; (2) a professional image with the clientele; (3) a continuous relationship with "return customers"; and (4) a healthy customer mix to ensure a steady flow of work. The following key points illustrate this strategy:

To utilize equipment offering the latest technological advances.

To train employees in implementing advanced survey techniques into their work.

To provide the opportunity for clients to consult with project managers (or principals, if desired) on all projects.

To keep the customer informed of the job's progress on a timely basis.

To "crack the engineering market" by obtaining small jobs with cities, districts, and subdivisions.

To increase the number of government contracts bid on.

To acquire and to develop "regional accounts"-clients with large land holdings (e.g., large timber companies).

---

loan purpose: To purchase a Zeiss total station with data storage and transfer capabilities that will facilitate taking angular and distance measurements in the field and performing survey computations.

Amount requested: $25,000 (see attached vendor's estimate)

Terms: One year and no prepayment penalty.

Interest rate: Prime

Collateral: Personal guarantees of principals' title to Zeiss total station.

Repayment: Quadrant's ability to repay is illustrated on the accompanying proforma financial statements. The cash budget projected for the upcoming year shows the company will be able to repay the loan within one year. Benefits accruing from the purchase of this EDM equipment include the ability to:

- Reduce the number of field personnel by one-third.
- Reduce office personnel by the immediate transferring field data to the home office via telephone.
- Minimize the number of return trips to the job site, a significant cost of doing business.
- Improve productivity by performing more jobs in less time.
- Improve the firm's professional image with its clientele by employing the latest, most advanced equipment.
- Obtain golf course that requires a level accuracy attainable only with EDM devices.

INDEX

Payroll Analysis, 38, 102
Payroll Expense, 38
Performance, 18, 19, 21, 22, 23,
  43, 46, 49, 51, 62, 63, 65, 89,
  90, 91, 92, 94, 95, 124, 140,
  159, 169, 173, 175, 179, 202,
  209, 211
Perpetual, 61
Pricing, 23, 24, 145, 147
Privately Held, 73
Productivity, ix, x, 40, 41, 43, 45,
  46, 47, 62, 155, 173, 177
Profit, 20, 21, 22, 23, 24, 25, 31,
  33, 38, 39, 40, 45, 46, 47, 48,
  49, 55, 62, 80, 82, 83, 84, 85,
  86, 88, 98, 110, 112, 115, 116,
  117, 118, 120, 126, 137, 138,
  140, 146, 147, 148, 149, 150,
  152, 153, 154, 157, 158, 159,
  174, 216
Publicly Held, 73, 101
Questionnaire, 42, 45
Quick Ratio, 114, 115
Rating, 45, 53, 60, 62, 64, 65, 112
Recession, 1, 6, 17, 31
Retail, 24, 29, 84, 203, 207
RMA, 53, 54, 62
Salary, 30, 99, 202
Sales, 19, 20, 21, 22, 23, 24, 25,
  28, 30, 31, 32, 34, 38, 39, 48,
  55, 59, 66, 82, 83, 84, 85, 86,
  88, 93, 99, 108, 112, 117, 118,
  120, 121, 124, 127, 131, 132,
  133, 134, 135, 137, 138, 140,
  141, 144, 146, 147, 148, 149,
  150, 154, 155, 156, 157, 158,
  159, 171, 173, 179, 200, 203,
  205, 206, 207, 210, 216
Sales Mix, 140, 154, 156, 158

SIC, 53, 54, 62
Small Business, x, xi, 19, 31, 37,
  38, 40, 46, 49, 54, 56, 58, 59,
  60, 61, 62, 63, 94, 98, 126,
  127, 128, 131, 132, 136, 137,
  160, 169, 170, 171, 173, 177,
  199, 201, 203, 204, 206, 208
Snapshot, 19, 26, 52, 157, 159,
  208
Springate, 68, 69, 81
Strategy, 166, 175, 176, 178, 179,
  203, 205
Strengths, 137, 160, 166, 168,
  169
Summary, 32, 33, 35, 61, 64, 65,
  75, 81, 94, 95, 96, 102, 125,
  159, 161, 162, 164, 166, 168,
  169, 170, 173, 175, 177, 178,
  180, 181, 199, 209, 210, 211,
  212
Terms of Sale, 58
The Dynamic Small Business
  Manager, x, xi, 38, 40, 62
Times interest Earned Ratio, 123
Tracking, 31, 58, 128, 129, 130
Variable Cost, 112, 138, 140, 141,
  142, 143, 144, 145, 147, 148,
  149, 152, 154, 155, 156, 159
Weaknesses, 160, 166, 168, 169,
  175
What-if, 64, 90, 92, 93, 114, 115,
  116, 117, 118, 119, 120, 122,
  123, 124
Wholesale, 85
Working Capital, 61, 66, 111, 113,
  124
Zavgren, 70
Z-Score, 65, 66, 67, 70, 73, 74,
  76, 81

www.ingramcontent.com/pod-product-compliance
Lightning Source LLC
Chambersburg PA
CBHW031808190326

41518CB00006B/245